LEARNING HUMAN BEHAVIORS HOW INFLUENCES

FUTURE SOCIAL CHANGES

JOHN LOK

Contents

Preface

Preface

Human had entered the 21 St century. It means that human will face challenges and we need to solve, if we hope our any dreams or goals can succeed. However, I believe that learning social knowledge , psychological knowledge can help us to achieve any short term goals or long term goals more easily. Because human existence needs to learn any kinds of new knowledge to help us to solve any challenges more easily. It explains that why we need to know psychological science. Although, any science is important to help our social development, e.g. space science, math, engineering, earth science, biology, medical science different subjects etc., but mathematicians will make judgement in error in possible. If math is only learning calculating knowledge, but it does not need and without human's creative and logic mind activities in our learning process. We can not cause including math knowledge system. So, social psychological science can assist any subjects to help human to create any new kinds of knowledge to solve any challenges to achieve any new directions for our social any benefits more easily.

Nowadays, technological development causes there are many businessmen who need to use internet to co-operate their businesses from internet transaction. It will cause employees have chance to use technological methods to steal employers whose cash from whose companies' computer system. So, if whose employers neglect to concern whose employees' behavior. It will have company's loss threats from whose employees' crime behavior in possible. Thus, if employers can permit when those employees' stealing crime behavior will occur or who will be the first one or next one business crime behavior staff or where the business crime place in whose office or store or shop or warehouse anywhere places or locations are. Then, I believe that the businessmen whose loss threats will be reduced from staffs' stealing ensure.

Human development history had been experiencing from fishing and agriculture stage to develop till to technological development stage nowadays. However, there are many kind factors to influence we can develop easily. It means that we must experience difficulties and we must attempt to find the most suitable methods to solve any difficulties if we hope that we can improve our development. What factors will influence our future continue development to be succeed. How can we solve any difficulties if we hope to develop our future to achieve more success.

Nowadays , future global job market competition will be trended serious. Any employers will expert their employees own different skills to know how to do their jobs efficiently and effectively and easily. So, future any organization employees ought considerate how to learn different kinds of skills or knowledges in order to prepare to satisfy their future employers' different new tasks needs. However, if future any new skillful needs or demands will be raised to future employers' demands. It brings these questions: what skills do global any organization employees need own in general? How to improve or raise employees themselves skills more easily and efficiently? What will happen if future employees do not learn new knowledge to improve or raise themselves skills? Why is learning any new skillful knowledge important ? What will be the possible negative and /or positive consequence if future the organizations do not need their employees to learn any new kinds of skillful knowledge?This book explains what factors are the main factors , they may change global human future development in human development history, we are concerning how to create talent human from past till to nowadays. Scientists hope that human needs to be trained to be talent human from foolish human. The question is how to train or create talent human in order to reduce foolish human number in our societies. If one day, our societies can create many talent human, what influences will be brought to our future societies? What are the difficulties that we will encounter when scientists plan to train talent human? In general, human's dream is difficult to achieve because human only believes that dream is difficut to achieve. So, in general, dream is difficult to become goals to common people. Also, it can threaten anyone feels difficult to achieve our dream. In the end, general people's dreams can not implement successfully usually. Hence, usually, general people's dreams can not become any goals to implement in common.

In my this book first part , I shall find what these successful inventors, entreprensurs, country leaders and fiction writers, scientists , their same characteristics own to explain why they can succeed finally. Whether they had ever encountere unhappy or they had felt disappointed in their dream pursue journey. What do factors help them to achieve their dreams to be actual aims to implement successfully. I shall attempt to indicate the different factors to analyze why and how these factors can help them to achieve their dreams successfully finally. I hope my readers can enjoy to read this book and it can provide useful knowledge to help you to achieve your any dreams also.I shall indicate cases to explain whether scientists can achieve to create talent human aim in order to let our societies bring new exciting hope to attribute our societies. I hope that my readers can enjoy to read this book and learn new creative talent human knowledge.

Finally, I shall indicate some actual technologicl skills or soft skills to explain why the organizational employees need to spend time and nervous to learn the kind of new skillful knowledge. I shall also explain the influential consequences are for the organization, if the organization does not need employees to learn any kinds of technological skillful knowledge or soft knowledge.

In my this book, I shall indicate some successful people, how they own these same characteristics to achieve their unsuccessful dreams to become successful aim. I shall indicate these people how they achieve their dreams in their occupations or become business founders.The successful seeking dream people include the micro software founder " Bill Gate" explains how he pursues his computer invention dream to be succeed; the Amazon e-commerce founder , explains how he pursues his electronic commerce to achieve global online consumption leader to influence online shoppers to accept this kind of online shopping model in global; explains what are the same individual characteristics to the successful fiction authors' ; explains how any countries' president individual same characteristics; explains how scientists own same individual characteristics, e.g. internet inventor, sky scientist, they can achieve their scientific research dreams in success.

In my this book second part, I shall research how to change human have comfortable lives. Every one must need comfortable feeling to live in our earth in any country. I write this book aims to give my opinion whether what aspects are our most hope in order we can live more comfortable as well as owning safe feeling. I shall concentrate on researching these several aspects that I feel we need to concern how to improve if we hope
that we can live more comfortable and satisfactory and safe in our future lives.

This book third part explains three stages to our future development: The first stage explains what difficulties we had encountered and how we can solve from agriculties and fishing industry to nowadays technology industry. The second stage explains what we are facing difficulties and how we can solve in nowadays technology stage. The third stage explains what difficulties human shall experience if we hope to continue to develop our future more success. In my this book, I shall attempt to explain whether what factors influence our future development as well as what difficulties that we need to solve in order to continue develop more success. I shall concentrate on discuss these aspects whether how and why their past and present and future development. They include: the timeline of human prehistory, medical development, transport development, technology development, construction development, education development and our society work model changing etc. concerning issues. Readers can predict whether what difficulties we shall encounter and how we can solve if we hope to continue to develop my future to achieve more success. These several aspects that I research my include: How and why can reduce global environmental pollution to bring our advantages ? How and why can improve internet technology development to bring our advantage? How and why can improve medicine health discovery to bring our advantage? How and why can improve living environment to bring our advantage? How and why can improve social welfare to bring our advantage ? Readers can have more clear understanding whether what methods may help us to create talent human development.

In my this book fourth part, I shall indicate how our future transportation tool may be invented in order to improve our qualify of lives or standard of lives to be better. How to improve our future transport tools in order to avoid air pollution more serious? It is my this book discussion about how transport invention or improvement, it will influence public transport passenger service and comfortable need aim. I shall attempt to research how transport improvement question in order to let readers feel how it can influence future public transport tools passenger individual choosing any kinds of pubic transport tools need as well as how is our future actual transport improvement achievement aim in order to keep our standard of lives (quality of lives) can be improved to achieve the best service standard and avoid any kinds of future public transport tools passengers number reduces. Because any public transport needs to be improved in order to satisfy passengers comfortable needs. IN passenger comfortable need psychology view, how to improve public transport service quality. It is my main discussion in this book topic, it concerns bus, ferry and rail public transport passenger psychology.

I shall attempt to indicate cases to explain whether our individual behavior can be influenced to changed by social environment change. Readers can have more understand how and why social change may influence our behavior in possible. Behavioral economy is one useful and fun social subject. Behavioral economists ususally research how and why human behaviors may influence economy growth or recession, or how and why economy environment changing factor may influence human behavior changes.

In my this book final part, I shall attempt to explain how and why ecommerce may be one kind network human job. Also, I shall indicate reasons to explain why human network behavior may bring direct or indirect influences to economy growth or recession in our global societies in macro and micro economy view. Why leisure changing environment may influence human behavior , even economic environment changes. I shall indicate cases to explain any possible human social activities may bring direct or indirect influences to cause our social economic growth or recession in consequency in possible. I hope that my readers can feel more understanding whether what real meaning of behavioral economy is the relationship between our behaviors and our economy.

Prologue

● Why does internet improvement can help any industries services or efficiencies improvment?
● Internet may become any organizational digital assets
● Internet improvement may assist robotic development
● Internet improvement to assist 5G laptop development
● How internet improvement influences AI provides medical service to hospitals ?
● The cyborg generation: Humans will partner more directly with technology when internet is popular to be used in any where
● Everyone agrees that the world will be putting AI to work, when internet is improvement to raise robotic efficiency and performance improvement

Chapter 5 Improving human development history method
    Discovery new health medicine drugs method
    ● Why do we need drug discovery? p.110-117
● Where do new drugs come from? Why does it take so long to get a new drug approved? Why are drugs so expensive?
● The process of new drug experiment success time evaluation

Improving living environment method
    ● Individual and businessmen and governments how to improve living environment p.118-121
● reasons to improve living environment

Improving social welfare
    ● Why do we improve future social welfare ?
    ● Can improve social welfare to influence economy growth?
    World peace method
    ● What does military strategy mean ? p.122-135
● WHAT IS THE TRUE CAUSE OF WAR?
● Avoiding war methods:

Changing human development history method
    ● What is the timeline of human prehistory? p.136-170
● Why do we need to develop and learn human history ?
● past medical development
● past transport development
● past technology developemnt
● past construction development
● past education development
● past work model
    Changing Human present development process method
    ● Human right development history
● Reasons we need to develop human right
● present medical development
● present transport development
● present technology development
● present construction development
● present development
● present work model development
    Prediction Human future development trend method

AIRLINE AND AIRPORT TRANSPORT STRATEGY
● Airline Oil Price Variable Factor strategy
Fuel price rising or decreasing factor
1.1 Positive social change influence to vehicle fuel consumers
1.2 Negative social change influence
1.3 Terrorisms attack influence
● Can airline fuel self-organization avoid fuel price rising cost
● Can tourism industry influence airline profitability
● Is fuel price rising only factor to cause airline risk in short term
● Methods to solve rising air fare prices to decrease travellers'demand
Biofuels energy increases supply
Reducing terrorism occurrence
● Will airline industry's ticket price elasticity be influenced by demand and supply factor
● Boeing 747 manufacturing fuel cost strategy
● How airlines and airports implement successful netwpork strategies
● Performance measurement system strategy
● What factors influence cost-related management quality ?
● Economic Environment Influences Airport
service performance

Economic Environment Influences Airport
service performance

Airline employee positive emotion method
        Emotional labor factor
        Artificial Intelligent In Road Transportation Strategy p.192-220

Chapter 8
How human behavior influences social changes

Human Behavioral network job brings social
economic benefits
        What does human network job mean
        Why human network job behavior may influence economy

Robots take our jobs behavioral and economy influences
        Robot job behavior brings economy influences

Intellectual human economic behaviors
What does intellectual human economic behaviors
mean ?
        The relationship between social change and human
behavior
        How human productive behavior may influence economic development
● New Zealand farmer individual wine productive behavior
● America high technological productive behavior
● China share market investing behavior

Why has any individual country have many people invest share behavior which can influence the country's macro consumption desire?
Can technology influence human shopping behavioral change?
Why and how human behavior may influence the country's economic growth or recession?
Technology how impacts human behavior changing? p.221-240

I

IQ talent human training method

To discuss whether scientists can appy IQ method to create or train talent human. Firstly, we need to know what IQ means. According to the general consensus, the answer is "no." An IQ test measures a person's cognitive ability compared to the population at large. The average IQ is 100, anything above 130 is considered exceptionally smart while a score under 70 is categorized as developmental delays related to intelligence. An IQ test measures a person's cognitive ability compared to the population at large. The average IQ is 100, anything above 130 is considered exceptionally smart while a score under 70 is categorized as developmental delays related to intelligence. Intelligence is defined as general cognitive problem-solving skills.The equation used to calculate a person's IQ score is Mental Age / Chronological Age x 100. On most modern IQ tests, the average score will be 100 and the standard deviation of scores will be 15.

In organizational training working environment, managers across the organization are in touch with the employees you are grooming for their next big role. In larger organizations, talent management requires Human Resources Information Systems (HRIS) that track the career paths of employees and manage available opportunities for talented employees.

● What Is Talent Management? Is talent management be IQ training method to train talent employees in any organizations?

Talent management is just another one of those pesky Human Resources terms, right? Wrong. Talent management is an organization's commitment to recruit, hire, retain, and develop the most talented and superior employees available in the job market. So, talent management is a useful term when it describes an organization's commitment to hire, manage, develop, and retain talented employees. It comprises all of the work processes and systems that are related to retaining and developing a superior workforce.

Is talent Management as a Business Strategy to any organizations ?

Talent management is a business strategy that organizations hope will enable them to retain their topmost talented and skilled employees. Just like employee involvement or employee recognition, it is the stated business strategy that will ensure the attraction of top talent in competition with other employers. When you tell a prospective employee that you are dedicated to a talent management strategy that will ensure that he or she will have the opportunity to develop professionally, you attract the best talent. This is because studies show consistently that the opportunity to continue to grow and develop their professional and personal skills is a major motivator for why employees take and stay at a job.

Differences Depending on Stated Talent Strategy

What appears to differentiate talent management focused practitioners and organizations from organizations that use terminologies such as human capital management or performance management is their focus on the manager's role, as opposed to reliance on Human Resources, for the life cycle of an employee within an organization. For example, practitioners of the other two employee development and retention strategies would argue that, for example, performance management has the same set of best practices.

Talent management does give managers a significant role and responsibility in the recruitment process and in the ongoing development of and retention of superior employees. In some organizations, only top potential employees are included in the talent management system. In other companies, every employee is included in the process. In some companies, the talent management system is accessible via computer programs; in others, informal communication among managers and HR staff is the approach used.

Future manager's Key Role in Talent Management

As stated, the majority of these work systems are squarely in the hands of the employee's manager. HR can provide support, training, and backup, but the day-to-day interactions that ensure the new employee's success comes from the manager. Developing and coaching the employee comes from his or her active, daily interaction with the manager. HR can take the lead in some of the activities you see on this list, especially in recruiting and selecting new employees, and in the case of employment termination. HR is also deeply involved in the performance management system, career planning, and so forth leading the development of the systems. Hence, talent management is a business strategy and you must fully integrate it within all of the employee-related processes of the organization. Attracting and retaining talented employees in a talent management system is the job of every member of the organization, but especially managers who have reporting staff (talent). An effective strategy also involves the sharing of information about talented employees and their potential career paths across the organization. This enables various departments to identify available talent when opportunities are made or arise. On conclusion, An organization that does this kind of effective succession planning makes sure that the best talent is trained and ready to assume the next position in their career path. Succession planning benefits the employees and it benefits the organization. Managers across the organization are in touch with the employees you are grooming for their next big role. Thus, organizational talent mangement strategy may be one kind of IQ training method to raise or improve employee individual work efficiency or productive effort or creating talent skillful abilities for any organizations.

● Is An IQ Test An Accurate Way To Measure Intelligence Or Are Mental Abilities ?

The IQ test is an exam most of us are familiar with, regardless of whether we have taken it or not. The test was originally designed by the French psychologist Alfred Binet in the early 1900s. But in the new millennium, is the IQ test still an effective means of measuring general intelligence? According to the general consensus, the answer is "no." An IQ test measures a person's cognitive ability compared to the population at large. The average IQ is 100, anything above 130 is considered exceptionally smart while a score under 70 is categorized as developmental delays related to intelligence.

However, some scientists believe that intelligence is defined as general cognitive problem-solving skills. Since the days of Binet, psychologists have agreed that intelligence is much more complex than a single number and may be in fact divided into many subcategories. This is where the IQ test falls short. A Canadian study published online in the journal Neuron concluded that the IQ test is "fundamentally flawed," seeing that its questions "grossly oversimplify the abilities of the human brain." The report identified three indications of human intelligence: short term memory, reasoning skills, and verbal ability. None of these skills are at all accurately measured in the traditional IQ test. So what does the IQ test accurately measure? While the IQ test may give an indication of general intelligence, it can't measure the entire complexity of the human thought process. Creativity, emotional sensitivity, social understanding, and various acquired skills such as music or art, are excluded from test's measurements of intelligence. If you'd like to get an idea of your IQ take this test, but just remember that whatever your score be, it doesn't necessarily define how smart you really are. So, it seems that IQ test training can not guarantee to raise or improve any foolish person to be talent person in possible. So, IQ test training may not be the most suitable talent human creative method to any one. It depends on whether the suitation how to provide IQ training , e.g. organizations may attempt to apply IQ skill test method to raise or improve employee efficiency or skill to serve their organizations effectively. But, schools will be difficult to apply IQ test training method to raise student learning effort effectively.

However, I believe that IQ test training can create these kinds of talent human as below:

Your answer to that question probably depends pretty heavily on your grades in school or, if you've ever taken one, the results of an IQ test. But are those a fair basis to assess a person's mental capabilities? Everyday language suggests maybe not. We speak of street smarts and EQ, for instance. Both terms suggest that there are abilities that deserve to be considered as forms of intelligence but that fall well beyond the scope of traditional academic measures. Does science go along with common sense in seeing that intelligence and IQ are far from the same thing? More than you probably imagine. According to Harvard's Howard Gardner, intelligence actually comes in an incredible eight flavors. I shall indiate these most popular six kinds of IQ test training talent human as below:

1. Musical intelligence.

"People say, well, music is a talent. It's not an intelligence. And I say why, if you're good with words, is that an intelligence, but if you're good with tones and rhythms and timbres, it's not. And nobody's ever given me a good answer, which is why it makes sense to talk about musical intelligence.

2. Spatial intelligence.

This is the easy grasp of how things lay in space that allows a chess master to win or a surgeon to perform near miracles. It's also "what an airplane pilot or a sea captain would have. How do you find your way around large territory and large space," Gardner notes.

3. Bodily kinesthetic Intelligence.

Forget the cliché of the dumb jock. Coordinating your body actually takes a great deal of intelligence -- just not the kind measured by IQ tests. This type of smarts "comes in two flavors. One flavor is the ability to use your whole body to solve problems or to make things, and athletes and dancers would have that kind of bodily kinesthetic intelligence. But another variety is being able to use your hands or other parts of your body to solve problems or make things. A craftsperson would have bodily kinesthetic intelligence" too, according to Gardner.

4. Interpersonal intelligence.

This one seems a bit similar to the popular concept of EQ. "Interpersonal intelligence is how you understand other people, how you motivate them, how you lead them, how you work with them, how you cooperate with them," says Gardner, who adds that it's a particularly important type of intelligence for leaders to have.

5. Intrapersonal intelligence.

Intrapersonal intelligence, or self-knowledge, is both very hard to assess and very important, Gardner says, particularly in today's fast-changing world. "Nowadays, especially in developed society, people lead their own lives. We follow our own careers. We often switch careers. We don't necessarily live at home as we get older. And if you don't have a good understanding of yourself, you are in big trouble," he explains.

6. Naturalist intelligence.

This one is "the capacity to make important, relevant discriminations in the world of nature between one plant and another, between one animal and another. It's the intelligence of the naturalist, the intelligence of Charles Darwin," Gardner says. And before you argue that you live in Detroit or Manhattan and so have no need for this type of smarts, he adds that "everything we do in the commercial world uses our naturalist intelligence. Why do I buy this jacket rather than another one? This sweater rather than another one?" Those fine distinctions are made by the part of the brain that used to discern a tasty small animal from a poisonous one. "When an old use of a brain center no longer is relevant, it gets hijacked for something new. So we're all using our naturalist intelligence even if we never walk out into the woods," Gardner concludes.

The bottom line? If you've been thinking of your mental horsepower solely in terms of high school report cards or a single number from an IQ test, you're probably selling yourself short. And if you're focusing your energies only on boosting your book learning, you may be wasting efforts that could be better focused on other strengths. Hence, above six kinds of talent human ought be trained to raise skill effort on music, calculation, interpersonal communication , athletes and dancers etc. sport skill aspects. IQ test training method may be one kind of effective talent human training method choice.

● Can IQ test train talent human ?

What does science say? Is innate talent a myth? This question is the focus of the new book Peak: Secrets from the New Science of Expertise by Florida State University psychologist Anders Ericsson and science writer Robert Pool. Ericsson and Pool argue that, with the exception of height and body size, the idea that we are limited by genetic factors—innate talent—is a pernicious myth. "The belief that one's abilities are limited by one's genetically prescribed characteristics....manifests itself in all sorts of 'I can't' or 'I'm not' statements," Ericsson and Pool write. The key to extraordinary performance, they argue, is "thousands and thousands of hours of hard, focused work."

To make their case, Ericsson and Pool review evidence from a wide range of studies demonstrating the effects of training on performance. In one study, Ericsson and his late colleague William Chase found that, through over 230 hours of practice, a college student was able to increase his digit span—the number of random digits he could recall—from a normal 7 to nearly 80. In another study, the Japanese psychologist Ayako Sakakibara enrolled 24 children from a private Tokyo music school in a training program designed to train "perfect pitch"—the ability to name the pitch of a tone without hearing another tone for reference. With a trainer playing a piano, the children learned to identify chords using colored flags—for example, a red flag for CEG and a green flag for DGH. Then, the children were tested on their ability to identify the pitches of individual notes until they reached a criterion level of proficiency. By the end of the study, the children had seemed to acquire perfect pitch. Based on these findings, Ericsson and Pool conclude that the "clear implication is that perfect pitch, far from being a gift bestowed upon only a lucky few, is an ability that pretty much anyone can develop with the right exposure and training." This sort of evidence makes a compelling case for the importance of training in becoming an expert. No one becomes an expert overnight, and the effects of extended training on performance can be larger than might seem possible. But does the fact that training leads to improvements—even massive improvements—in skill level mean that innate talent is a myth? This is a much harder scientific argument to make, and is where Peak runs into trouble. Ericsson and Pool gloss over or omit critical details of research they review that undermine the anti-talent argument. As one example, although they claim that the results of Sakakibara's training study imply that "pretty much anyone" can acquire perfect pitch, the sample in that study did not include pretty much anyone. It included children who had been enrolled in a private music school from a very young age (the average age at which training began was 4). It does not seem likely that this non-random sample was representative of the general population in music aptitude or interest—factors that are known to be influenced by genetic factors. It's also not clear whether the children had acquired true perfect pitch, because there was no comparison of the children after training to people who possess this rare ability—for example, in terms of speed of identifying notes or neural correlates of performance.

As another example, describing the results of a study of ballet dancers by Ericsson and colleagues, Ericsson and Pool claim that "the only significant factor determining an individual ballet dancer's ultimate skill level was the total number of hours devoted to practice" and that there was "no sign of anyone born with the sort of talent that would make it possible to reach the upper levels of ballet without working as hard or harder than anyone else." Not mentioned is the exact magnitude of the correlation—a value of .42, where 1.0 is perfect. The fact that the correlation was modest in magnitude means that factors not measured in the study—including heritable aptitudes—could have actually accounted for more of the differences in ballet skill than deliberate practice did. As it always is in scientific debates, the devil is in the details in the debate over the origins of expertise.

Ericsson and Pool also leave out a good deal of evidence that runs counter to the anti-talent argument. For example, they claim that professional baseball players have "no better eyesight than an average person," but there is evidence to suggest otherwise. In a study published in the American Journal of Ophthalmology, Daniel Laby and colleagues assessed the vision of major and minor league baseball players in the Los Angeles Dodgers organization over the course of four spring training seasons. As David Epstein recounts in his book The Sports Gene, in the first year of the study the researchers used a standard test of visual acuity, and it turned out to be too easy. Over 80% of the players got a perfect score of 20/15, meaning that they could see at 20 feet what an average person can see at 15 feet. In the following seasons, using a custom test, Laby and colleagues found that 77% of the 600 eyes tested had visual acuity of 20/15 or better, with a median of about 20/13. Even for young adults, this is excellent vision. Overall, Laby and colleagues concluded that "professional baseball players have excellent visual skills. Mean visual acuity, distance stereoacuity, and contrast sensitivity are significantly better than those of the general population."

Based on scientists own evaluation of the evidence, we argue in a recent Psychological Bulletin article that training is necessary to become an expert, but that genetic factors may play an important role at all levels of expertise, from beginner to elite. In other words, some people take much more training than other people to acquire a given level of skill. As it happens, Sakakibara's pitch training study provides some of the most compelling evidence of this type. There was a large amount of variability in how long it took the children to pass the test for perfect pitch—from around 2 years to 8 years. As Sakakibara notes in her article, this evidence implies that factors other than training may be involved in acquiring perfect pitch, including genetic factors. This finding is consistent with the results of recent reviews of the relationship between deliberate practice and skill, which include numerous studies Ericsson and colleagues have used to argue for the importance of deliberate practice. Regardless of domain, deliberate practice leaves a large amount of individual differences in skill unexplained, indicating that other factors contribute to expertise.

The more direct evidence for the multifactorial view of expertise comes from "genetically informative" research on skill—studies that estimate the contribution of genetic factors to variation across people in factors that may influence expert performance. In a study of over 10,000 twins, two of us found that music aptitude was substantially heritable, with genes accounting for around half of the differences across people on a test of music aptitude. As another example, in a pioneering series of studies, the Australian geneticist Kathryn North and her colleagues found a significant association between a variant of a gene (called ACTN3) expressed in fast-twitch muscle fibers and elite performance in sprinting events such as the 100 meter dash. There is no denying the importance of training for becoming an elite athlete, but this evidence (which is not discussed in Peak) provides compelling evidence that genetic factors matter, too.

On conclusion, based on this sort of evidence, many human behavioral scientists have argued that the experts are "born versus made" debate is over—or at least that it should be. There is no doubt that training is required to become an expert. Notwithstanding a report by North Korea's state-run news agency that Kim Jong-il made five holes-in-one his first time playing golf and rolled a perfect 300 his first time bowling, no one is literally born an expert. Expertise is acquired gradually, often over many years. However, as science is making increasingly clear, there is more to becoming an expert than training. Moving ahead, the goal for scientific research on expertise is to identify all of the remaining factors that matter. Hence, it seems that human behavioral scientists feel that IQ test may be one good skills to create talent skill to some kinds of humans if IQ test may prove the person has the kind of talent skill, e.g. music, sport, reading, writing, draw picture etc. art creative skills for future new creative art talent human method.

II

Educational learning training talent human method

What are the difference between TRAINING, EDUCATION, DEVELOPMENT AND LEARNING: WHAT IS THE DIFFERENCE? Employee training may be one kind of organizational training method example to any organizations, in particular, is associated with on-thejob skills acquired for a particular role, while education is seen as relating to a more formal academic background. In increasingly complex organisations, it may be argued that aspects of each are necessary to ensure full employee potential. Hence, it implies that educational learning training is not only focus to implement to school organizations . It can be applied to any organizations to train talent employees.

However, the terms training, education, development and learning may often be used interchangeably, but they can have very different, if overlapping, meanings in different contexts. In terms of human resource development, it is often necessary to define and delineate these in a bid to clarify the associated activities and desired outcomes within an organisation. Employee training, in particular, is associated with on-the-job skills acquired for a particular role, while education is seen as relating to a more formal academic background. However, in increasingly complex organisations, it may be argued that aspects of each are necessary to ensure full employee potential. For example, for human resource development, and demonstrate how they are best viewed as interconnected. So, human resource department may apply educational method to educate or training new employee individual skill in order to raise efficiency or improve performance before he/she begins to do her/his tasks for his / her department in the organization. So, education and training and development have close or interchangable relationship to be applied to improve or upgrade any new employee individual from low skill to high skill to be talent or excellent skill new employee in order to serve his/her organization efficiently.

● The best types of employee training methods for your workforce may include:

1. Instructor-led training

Instructor-led training is the traditional type of employee training that occurs in a classroom, with a teacher presenting the material. This can be a highly effective method of employee training, especially for complex topics. Instructors can answer specific employee questions or direct them to further resources. They also allow for highly-skilled instructors to match the training level and style to the employees in the room.

However, instructor-led training does have some drawbacks, including cost and time to implement. It can also be unnecessary for concise topics. We discuss more about this in our post, "Instructor-Led Training Vs. eLearning.".

2. eLearning

eLearning, on the other hand, relies on online videos, tests, and courses to deliver employee training. Employees can do their training right in the palm of their hand with a smartphone or on their company computers.

It's one of the easiest types of employee training to roll out to larger populations, especially for employees who are remote or have high-turnover rates. With interactive games, tests, videos, activities, or even gamified components, it can also go a long way towards keeping your employees engaged with the training. Of course, eLearning also has its own challenges. Without a solid instructional design strategy behind it, the graphics and visuals that make eLearning fun can also make it gimmicky or quickly outdated. Keeping it up-to-date is also a necessary best practice. We cover the major advantages, and disadvantages, of eLearning here.

3. Simulation employee training

Simulation training is most often provided through a computer, augmented, or virtual reality device. Despite the initial costs for producing that software or technology, however, simulation training can be a necessary option for employees in riskier or high-stakes fields. You'll often see simulation training for pilots or doctors, but it can be useful for other employees too. This type of employee training is also highly-effective and reliable, allowing employees to progress consistently and at their own pace.

4. Hands-on training

Hands-on training includes any experiential training that's focused on the individual needs of the employee. It's conducted directly on the job. Hands-on training can help employees fit perfectly into their upcoming or current role, while enhancing their current skills.

A LinkedIn post notes:

"One advantage of hands-on training is that they are applicable immediately to the employees' jobs. They are also effective for training when it comes to new business equipment and procedures."

This is a time-intensive method of employee training, however, that's best used when there are enough resources available to support employees during the program. Learn more about experiential learning here.

5. Coaching or mentoring

Coaching or mentoring can share similar qualities to hands-on training, but in this type of employee training, the focus is on the relationship between an employee and a more experienced professional, such as their supervisor, a coach, or a veteran employee. The one-on-one mentoring style creates a relationship between employees that carries far beyond training. It also allows the employee to ask questions they may not feel comfortable asking in a classroom, instructor-led training. This training method can be done in person or virtually, through online coaching sessions. For all its benefits, mentoring is costly in terms of employee hours and should be used appropriately to reduce those associated costs. Coaching—bringing in a trained professional—can sometimes provide a more time-efficient alternative, but without the relationship building that's so valuable in mentoring.

6. Lecture-style training

Important for getting big chunks of information to a large employee population, lecture-style training can be an invaluable resource for communicating required information quickly. However, use this type of employee training sparingly. HR.com writes: "It has been said to be the least effective of all training methods. In many cases, lectures contain no form of interaction from the trainer to the trainee and can be quite boring. Studies show that people only retain 20 percent of what they are taught in a lecture."

7. Group discussions and activities

For the right group of employees, group discussions and activities can provide the perfect training option. It allows multiple employees to train at once, in an environment that better fits their current departments or groups. These discussions and activities can be instructor-led or facilitated by online prompts that are later reviewed by a supervisor. This type of employee training is best used for challenges that require a collaborative approach to complex issues. Find ideas for training activities here.

8. Role-playing

Similar to group discussions, role-playing specifically asks employees to work through one aspect of their jobs in a controlled scenario. They'll be asked to consider different points-of-view and think on their feet as they work through the role-playing activity. Like other group activities, role-playing is highly effective but may be unnecessary for simple, straightforward topics. It also requires more employee time, potentially taking time away from an entire department while they're going through the training.

9. Management-specific activities

Management-specific activities are just that—employee training that's focused on the needs of managers. They may include simulations, brainstorming activities, team-building exercises, role-playing, or focused eLearning on management best practices. While management training can include many different types of training, it's important to consider the additional needs of your managers separately from the rest of your employee population. This ensures they have the foundation they need to support the rest of their staff.

10. Case studies or other required reading

Finally, some employee training topics are readily accessible through required readings. Case studies, in particular, can provide a quick way for employees to learn about real workplace issues. Employees can read through these at their own pace, or while working in a team-building session with other employees. Case studies are a great option for focused topics, but more complex topics will likely require more advanced types of employee training.

All of above these education or training methods may be any schools or organizations may choose to apply in order to teach their employees or students to learn effectively.

● What is Talent oriented education to human development?

One lesson is that talent-oriented education builds a strong sense of self-efficacy, effective goal setting, and a personal commitment that can enhance students' specific achievements and lead them to higher-level career accomplishments. Others favoring the establishing of a talent development group in their organizations believe the term will help promote training. As one participant noted, "It helps with the marketing of 'training' itself. Everyone needs the basic training when they enter an organization, but they need to continue learning. To continue the training, through the concept of developing an employee's talent, goes a long way toward reception and retention." Still others favoring the establishment of a talent development group see the primary value as motivational. For Role Of Education In Human Development example, education gives the ability to think with reason, pursue dreams and aspirations in life and live a respectable life in the society. Education gives us a definite path to follow, to lead our lives by principles and gives us the freedom of expression. It frees our minds from the prejudices and motivates it to think with logic and reason. It is essential for the overall development of the human mind and brain. The literacy rate of a country determines its prosperity and economic health.The benefits of education are numerous, but a few points are highlighted below, which shows how education helps in human development from different aspects – personal, social, economic and spiritual.

In fact, every human has dreams and aspirations. So, education is a medium to pursue and fulfill them. It increases the knowledge of a person in different fields of studies. It helps to determine a path to follow and express your talent to the world. Enhance creativity and imagination: Education opens up new ways and ideas to ponder. It cultivates a young mind to think out-of-the-box and explore different things in life. Education also helps to know about things and stay healthy, fit and follow a productive lifestyle.

Education is a way of academic excellence and paves the path for economic growth of the country. Research and development in sectors like technology, medicine, and others, breakthrough innovation and progressive mindset – all of this are fruits of education, which takes a nation and its people forward. Educated people contribute towards advancement in every sector. Education opens up every channel of knowledge and wisdom. It exposes us to a whole new world of information, invent new things and know how we can make our surroundings a better place to live and out our lives to a greater, and better use. Education can train any poor knowledge students to learn new knowledge or poor skillful staffs learn new job knowledge for organizations. So, education is one kind of new learning method to train poor or foolish knowledge student to be clever or poor performance staff to be clever or talent staff both in schools or business organizations.

● Raising knowledge and skills in educator method

Future educators need to be raised knowledge and skills in their major subject aspect, they need to prepare to programs of research and evaluation of 21 ST century education, educator preparation programs will be recognized as sources of leadership in developing 21ST century education and learning strategies. Each educator preparation program will develop a 21 ST century blueprint for transforming itself into a 21 ST century program, higher education leaders will work with leaders in local communities to inform the redesign of education preparation programs to more effectively meet the needs of 21 ST century learners, new teachers will be prepared to become change knowledge and skills in all subjects in accordance with national standards. If they expect to raise students' learning effort in short term successfully. Future teachers are asked to achieve significant academic growth to all students at the same time, but they instruct students with even more diverse needs. Teaching has never been more difficult, it has never been more important, and the desperate need for more student success has been raised need.

On the one hand, I shall indicate many successful engage in strategies to assist teachers to raise teaching knowledge level, such as : Providing high quality alternative routes to teaching , building on private and public partnerships that share common sets of ideas in advancing education reforms, e.g. effectively partnering with urban schools to prepare teacher canadidates to teach in urban environments with large numbers of urban school learners' raising learning effort needs, playing a greater role with charter and other experimental / alternative schools, effectively recruiting career changes to build the teacher workforce , creating a robust clinical experience for teacher candidates, including year long teaching of learning how to raise students' learning effort programs, growing a network of over 1,000 raising students' learning effort research development schools to attempt to helpt to find any methods which can raise students' learning effort effectively.

On the other hand, in order to meet the challenges and demands of the poor learning effort of students. I suggest that as below: schools ought provide evidence that the teachers prepared at the raising students' learning effort and member institutions will have a positive effect on their students' learning, going beyond providing content knowledge and prepare teachers to differentiate their institution to reach all poor learning effort students especially.

The most at risk for school failure: Low income homes' students, poor english language learners, poor learning effort of students with disabilities, ensuring that teacher candidates receive extensive , in-depth how to raise students' learning effort experiences with mentoring support that requires teaching to poor learning effor of students' performance evaluation tied to the teacher licensure process and high standards for beginning practice, creating fast, track, yet high teaching quality , raising students; learning effort of teacher preparation programs in close partnership with school districts to meet specific teacher shortages in order to train future many teachers who have efforts to assist to raise student's learning effort to pursue top-performing student number to be raised successfully.

On the one hand, how to raise teacher's teaching effort in order to raise student learning ability? The important themes will include: Global awareness, e.g. understanding global issues, other nations and other culture, financial , economic, business and entrepreneurial literacy, e.g. knowing how to make economic choices, understanding the role of the economy in society, civic literacy, e.g. learning how to participate effectively in civic life, exercising the rights and obligations of citizenship, high literacy, e.g. obtaining interpreting and understanding basic methods how to raise student' learning effort in short term.

On the other hand, future teachers also need have learning and innovation skills, e.g. critical thinking and problem solving, effectively analyze and evaluate evidence, argument, cliams and beliefs, solve different kinds of non-familiar problems in both conventional and innovative ways: Effective communication skill, e.g. articulate thoughts and ideas effectively using oral and writtn communication skills iin a variety of forms and contexts; effective collaboration skill, e.g. demonstrate ability to work effective and respectfully with diverse teams; creativity and innovation ability , e.g. use a wide range of idea creation techniques to create new and worthwhile ideas. They also need to learn information, media and technology skills, e.g. access and evaluate information critically and competently; manage the flow of information from a wide variety of sources; understanding both how and why media messages are constructed; creating media products by understanding and utilizing the most appropriate media creation tools; characteristics and conventions; learning how to use technology as a tool to research ; organize and evaluate and communicate information.

Finally, they need to know life and career skills, e.g. flexibility and adaptability, initiative and self-direction, social and cross cultural skills productivity and accountability, leadership and responsibility. Consequently, when future teachers can be trained to own these skills. Then, they will have ability to prepare how to raise students' learning efforts in future global education industry development more easily.

Teaching to use data in school improvement efforts

What are teaching to use data in school improvement efforts? Why and how can teaching to use data in school improve students' learnings efforts? How to integrate data to raise school improvement process? Why has the need for data instead of intuition, tradition and convenience to guide administrative and educational decisions become increasingly important?

I shall indicate why educators need to learn how to use data in their schools to improve planning process in order to raise students' learning efforts more easily. I shall also indicate some foundational information on types of data, strategies for analyzing and understanding data and methods for determining how these efforts can influence goals and planning.

The types of data that educators can use to define their problems and needs, select improvement strategies and goals, change and monitor progress. These data includes achievement data, demographic data, program data and perception data. They will be useful to be applied to raise students' learning efforts by teachers (educators). For this situation example, a school leader needs to meeting to discuss how to solve one problem solving issue, pooling their knowledge, talent and ideas. The leader and his/her other school department leaders need to join teachers, support and parents in teams to explore students' learning improvement issues. How to say that gathering data to prepare to discuss this issue which can raise their leadership skills in creating numerous and diverse partnerships, sustaining a vision, focusing on group problem-solving, using conflicts resolution in order to conclude the most useful ideas or methods to raise the school's students learning efforts. Because every school's environment situation, learning environment, school and teachers' qualities , teaching experiences, students' learning efforts, kinds of courses are different. So, they need time to gather data to prepare every different meeting discussion topics to already discuss any challenges about teaching, the time will be long or short to gather data to prepare every meeting discussion to cause time preparation challenge. For example, the process enquires time, time during the day and the week , even on month or more to involve teachers always cause a time meeting preparation and meeting discussion time challenge. If the meeting discussion topic is experienced and difficult to gather data , then it will need to arrange longer time to prepare the meeting and the meeting time. Otherwise, if the meeting discussion topic is not experienced and simple to gather data, then will need to arrange shorter time to prepare the meeting and the meeting time. If one week , the school only has one meeting , then it is not a time arrangement problem to prepare the meeting. But, supposing the schools has ten departments and if one week the school's every department has at least one meeting , even more than one meeting to prepare time to discuss different kinds of teaching challenges and the school's resource and rooms are not enough, So, the school must need have good time arrangement to be organized to gather data and pre-booking rooms for the ten meetings at least or more. Hence, every school is committed to use data to guide its work allocate time for teachers to meet, discuss, reflect upon data and make informed instructional decisions. Schools identify the need for this time, then find it through a combination of creative scheduling (e.g. having all good grader teachers share student data , when students attend a interesting course, e.g. art and music , sport and priority setting, e.g. using one to three maximum weekly faculty meetings to analyze student data). Thus, data can help to build a district and school culture that values the use of reliable, complete information to guide their every meeting decisions and solve problems more effectively. Although, for many school meeting members, they will have idea to feel difficult of working with data is unfamiliar and perhaps uncomfortable. But the fact is, whether teachers need to realize data or not, they use data every data to help make any decisions, data will help them to make decisions about school improvement more accurately.

How to apply data gathering method to improve every student learning effort challenge? If schools are to provide learning environments that are meaningful and engaging, educators must continually reflect on the quality of school systems and focus their efforts to make them better.

Firstly, the school needs have an effective learning improvement cycle. The school improvement cycle includes four major activities: plan (developing a plan for improvement) implement the plan, (study) ,evaluate the impact according to specific criteria action (adjust strategies to better meet criteria).

How to apply data gathering for this school improvement plan? Data are the key to continuous improvement. When the school plans, it must for its goals. Data patterns reveal strengths and weaknesses in the school plan system and provide excellent direction. When the school does (acts) the school collect, data that will tell the teachers what the impact of their strategies are between the school and teachers. Through collaborative reflection, the school leaders " studies" the feedback offered by its teachers data and begins to understand when to stay the course and then to make changes. Then, the school can act to refine what are the best raising students learning efforts strategies.

Eventually, the whole cycle begins again. The data throughout the school improvement cycle can be applied to help teachers to gather to make decision making regarding student learning as below:

The data gathering driven decision making based on intuition, tradition or convenience includes focused staff development programs, as an improvement strategy to solve documented problems needs, budget allocations to programs based on data-informed need, staff assignments based on skills needed as indicated by the data, organized factual reports to the community about the learning progress of students, goal-setting based on data about problems and possible explanations, staff meeting that focus on strategies and issues raised by the local school's data, regular parent communication record regarding the progress of their children learning effort record, grading systems based on common student performance criteria that report progress on the standards as well as work skills and past administrative team meeting that focus on measured progress toward data-based improvement goals. Hence, an effective and efficient data in school improvement efforts record system can help teachers to gather data regarding every different challenge to let them to uses actual data to further discuss data analysis to assist school leaders in the creation of research-based strategies data –based goals and make an evaluation plan to measure results in order to achieve the most effective methods to solve students learning effort raising challenge.

Consequently, I recommend that every school needs to understand what it is building knowledge around different aspects of school improvement processes, it can get started learning about how to use data in above those areas in order to achieve how to implement the most effective methods to solve students learning efforts raising challenge. For example, they include that how to record data to develop a leadership team, how to collect various types of data , how to analyze data patterns, how to generate hypotheses, how to develop goal-setting guideline, how to design specific raising students' learning effort strategies, how to define evaluation criteria and how to make the commitment to let students who feel that their learning efforts are raised by their teachers. Hence, efficient and systematic data gathering record system tool can assist any schools to give opinions to make decisions to achieve strategies to raise students' learning effort more accurate, due to past all data is the school's actual record, it can reflect all past every student learning performance in order to let teachers to make more accurate judgement to decide whether to choose the method(S) is (are) the most suitable and effective solution(S) to raise student learning effort.

Teaching and classroom learning method

School leaders and teachers both have responsibilities to attempt to find what methods can raise student learning effort in their schools in education industry. Which aspects of consideration are needed to think about what they wish to assess. I shall access as below:

On teachers' consideration aspect, the qualities of teachers who wish to access include: How to organize subject matter and courses, how to communicate between students and students' parents, how much knowledge of the subject matter, who is familiar to teach, how much enthusiasm for the subject and for teaching, how the teacher's attitude toward students, how fairness in testing and grading, how flexibility in approaches to teaching, how appropriateness of student learning outcomes. All of above factors will influence every students' learning efforts in the school.

So, every teacher needs to find or choose which aspects can influence his/her teaching qualities to be poor and how he/she wishes to assess it in order to improve / raise his/her teaching performance to satisfy students' learning needs. They can collect data in many ways in order to assess which aspects of teaching methods need to be improved. They ways include: structured interviews with students, instructional rating surveys, tests and exams, content analysis of instructional materials and review of classroom records.

When, he/she had chosen methods to assess the effectiveness of his/her teaching. He/she needs to follow these guidelines: avoiding technologies that don't appeal to his/her intuition and judgement as a teacher, not allowing and self- assessment to become a burden, choosing techniques that will benefit m/herself and his/her students, planning how to introduce the techniques to students, estimating and planning for how much class time it will take, not using these techniques for often, if the students find them predictable, the information won't be as useful , needing brief written exercises are good for encouraging shy students to express their thoughts, encouraging students to be frank without the possibility of penalty, remembering that assessment and analysis probably take twice as long as he/she thinks and allowing enough time to plan for teaching method change.

What will students be influenced from the teacher's teaching method change after he/she assessed which aspects are needed to influence his/her teaching performance to be poor? Usually, qualities students want in an instructor to willingness to take extra time to answer questions and solve problems, well organized presentations and lessons , real world experts respect for students and sense. All of these requirements are students whose expectation to every teacher's teaching attitude and quality or performance.

Teachers have responsibilities to do these behaviors in classroom. They include: students attendance record, student participation in classroom activities and her/his own feelings record three aspects. For example, one student attendance record aspect, the class of student attendance records. Do students miss a particular class or activity? It aims to find what the seasons to influence the student often absent, e.g. he/she has less interest in this topic of activity and this attitude is being communicated to the student or perhaps the student doesn't understand why certain content is important or may be the way the teacher delivers his/her lectures needs to be more lively or interactive or personal issues cause absent, e.g. medical problems, religious and cultural activities can affect student attendance and learning performance.

On student participation in classroom activities aspect, teachers need to know whether students are more involved at certain times than at others. Do they often or sometimes ask questions? Why do they not like to ask questions? Do they request extra resource material? What is their need? Hence, teachers ought be often observant note their reactions to something they do or say. If students, are not sure the teachers perception is right, try something similar again and see if the student reaction repeats.

On teachers' own feeling aspect, every teacher needs to know themselves feeling. Does the teacher aware of whose own feeling as he/she teaches? His /her feeling may be sad, angry, enjoyable, excited, depressed, worried. When the teacher recognize his/her feeling, he/she can examine the actions (his/her own and the students) that led to these feeling. Their mood and feeling will affect whose students, and their mood will also affect the teacher's teaching actions. Hence, teacher's mood will influence every class student's learning effort in the classroom, if the teacher has enjoyable mood to teach his /her students, then his her teaching mood and behavior will influence his /her efforts to raise more nervous to teach whose students to learn in the classroom.

Another discussion issue concerns how to access classroom learning. Classroom assessment will make a strong contribution to the improvement of learning . In classroom, how students; feedback to the teacher's teaching contents. It is one important factor to raise student's effort to learn because feedback is more reflective theoretical, presenting, grounded in evidence of the nature of feedback , a concept , which is central to formative assessment. Hence, when the teacher may receive either positive or negative feedback form his/her students immediately in the classroom. Then, his / her can know whether his/her teaching what weaknesses are for her/her teaching method or skill. Then, he/she can concentrate on revise the weaknesses to avoid next occurrence to let students to feel her /his teaching performance is poor or unsatisfactory due to whose teaching weaknesses cause as well as he /she can know how to revise whose teaching weaknesses and improve whose teaching skill or method more clearly.

Another considerable aspect is that learning or teaching system aspect , schools need to consider that the grading function is whether over-emphasized and/or the learning function under-emphasized. There is a tendency to use a normative rather than a criterion approach, which emphasizes competition between pupils rather than personal improvement of each.

The evidence is that with such practices the effect of feedback is to teach the whether pupils that they lack ability. So, that they are de-motivated and lose confidence in their own capability to learn strategies for " slow learners" to raise learning. In general, it is difficult to discover (find) who are the slow learners, slow learners in the regular classroom are neither rare nor unique. Slow learner is one who can't learn at an average rate form the instructional resources, text, workbooks, and learning materials that are designed for the majority of students in the classroom.

These students need special instructional frequent feedback, corrective institution and/or modified materials, all administered under conditions sufficiently flexible for learning to occur.

I shall recommend that slow leaders are usually taught in one of two possible instructional arrangements: The first is that a class composed mostly of average students , in which case up to 20% may be slow learners or the second is that a class specially designed for slow learner. The most obvious characteristics is a limited attention to compare to more able students.

However, I believe these teaching methods can be used to attempt to raise slow learners' attention during they need to listen teachers' speaking in any class time. The first kind is compensatory teaching method, it is an instructional approach that alters the presentation of content to a student's fundamental weakness or deficiency. This teaching method recognizes contents, transmits through alternate modalities (pictures versus words, and supplements it with additional learning resources and activities) learning centers and group discussion, and co-operative learning. It aims to give pictures, films, visual representation of contents what the teacher's teaching speaking is. Another kind is remedial teaching. This is an alternate approach for the regular classroom teacher in instructing the slow learner . It is the use of activities, techniques and practices to eliminate weaknesses or deficiency that the slow learner is known to have. For example, deficiencies in basic math calculation skills learning effort are reduced or eliminated by re-teaching the content that was not learned earlier. The instructional environment does not change, as in the compensatory approach. Conventional instructional techniques such as practice might be used.

In conclusion, every teacher needs to learn which kind of teaching and classroom learning method or technique is the most suitable skill in order to raise whose students' learning effort to learn easily. So, learning which kind of teaching method is important to influence the teacher's performance to be improved to influence each student's learning mood in classroom ad he/she needs to spend time to find which are whose teaching challenges to need to be improved.

Educational training tools for raising student learning effort development

Improving students' learning with effective learning techniques, knowing which kinds of educational training tools which can raise students' learning effort that is very important. Because every school has different educational method(s), so , it causes every school ought choose the most suitable kind(s) of educational training tool(S) to raise its students learning effort. I shall indicate some kinds of educational training tools to raise students learning effort as below:

Firstly, it is direction from cognitive educational psychological method. The techniques include elaborative interrogation, self exploration, summarization, highlighting, the keyword mnemonic, imagery use for text learning, re-reading , practice testing , distributed practice and interleaved practice. When every student learns, who needs to read the book , how to raise his/her reading effort to know all main contents (main points) of any books' chapter(s). What mean of the chapter is? It is very important to let the student really remembers or knows the chapter contents or what the author's writing mean of the books' chapter/ So, in educational psychological view point, summarization , highlighting, the key word mnemonic , imagery use for text , learning and re-reading technique can help every student to rise effort to remember the chapter's contents. For example, summarization and imagery use for text learning have been shown to help some students on some criterion tasks, but yet the conditions under which these techniques produce benefits are limited, and much research is still needed to fully explore their overall effectiveness. The keyword mnemonic is difficult to implement in some contexts, and it appears to benefit students for a limited number of materials and for short retention intervals. However, more students report re-reading and highlighting, yet these techniques do not consistently boost students' performance. So many students like to use practice testing instead of re-reading techniques when they are reading any books.

About above those reading techniques, I bring some questions: If simple techniques were available that teachers and students could use to improve student learning and achievement, whether every student's learning performance will be poor if the teacher was not being told about those techniques and if many students were not using them? What if students were instead adopting ineffective learning techniques that undermined their achievement or at least did not improve their prior ineffective learning techniques?

To assess above questions. We need to know whether what different learning benefits to the student. I shall explain every kinds of learning technique benefits to students as below:

Flaborative interrogation means generating an explanation for why a stated fact or concept is true. Self explanation means explaining how new information is related to known information is related to known information , or explaining steps taken during problem solving, summaries means writing , summaries of various lengths of to be learned texts, highlighting means making potentially important portions of to be learned materials when reading, keyword mnemonic means using keywords and mental imagery to associate verbal materials, imagery for text means attempting to form mental images of text materials when reading or listening, re-reading means restudying text material again after an initial reading, practice testing means self-testing or taking practice tests over –to-be-learned, distributed practice means implementing a schedule of practice that spreads out study activities over time, interleaved practice means implementing a schedule of practice that mixes different kinds of material within a single study session. So, every kind of learning technique will have different reading or learning benefits to adapt to every student's different reading habit or personal reading need. If the student expected to raise whose learning effort in short time. He/she must need to know whether which kind of learning technique(s) can be the most useful or suitable to him/her to use in whose learning or reading practice.

I shall indicate what the suitable learning materials and learning condition are for the different kind of student characteristics to be adapted in order to raise whose learning effort need as below:

Materials remember words cards is suitable to be used in amount of reading remember practices learning condition and age is student characteristics , material translation equivalents is suitable to be used in open vs closed book practice learning condition and prior domain knowledge is student characteristics, lecture content materials is suitable to be used in reading vs listening learning condition and working memory capacity is student characteristics, science definition materials is suitable to be used in incidental vs intentional learning condition and verbal ability is student characteristics, narrative texts can be used on direct instruction learning condition and interests is student characteristics, expository texts can be used on discovery learning condition and intelligence is studied characteristics, mathematical concepts can be used on rereading lags learning condition and motivation is students characteristics, maps can be used on kind of prior achievement is student characteristics , diagrams can be used on group vs individual learning condition and self efficacy is student characteristics.

Hence, every school needs to know very student's learning characteristics and what the learning techniques in order to achieve to raise every individual student's learning effort effectively.

Instead of learning techniques can be attempted to use to raise training activities and teachers' teaching abilities, it will also be one important factor to raise students' learning efforts. There are five key areas of student assessment as below:

Firstly, the school needs to know how inclusive education is the school current student assessment system. This activity takes readers through a series of tasks linking student assessment to the inclusive education. Secondly, the school needs to know how to make student assessment contribute to better quality and more inclusive education. The school will need introduce interesting practices and models that promote greater inclusivity in education, including the development of formative assessment, the use of summative assessment, for inclusive progress and the design and use of quality educational methods for student assessment. Thirdly, the school needs to know what basic competencies are needed to make student assessment more inclusive. The basic competencies (knowledge, skills , values , attitudes, etc.) that are required to access the student learning in inclusive education. Fourthly, the school needs to know what the relationship between student assessment at different levels, such as intentional, regional, national and school levels, as well as various countries' approaches to these assessments. Finally, the school needs to know how to adopt an approach to student assessment. It needs to introduce a series of tools and models for student assessment education system and society . Thus, the purpose of training activities to the school that lets the school teachers who can analyze or apply assessment practices in response to specific student learning challenges or issues that the schools' teachers may encounter during the educational process. The school teachers may be required to do this individual as a raising student learning effort topic meeting of the school.

Consequently, student educational techniques and teaching improvement effort activities techniques will be one good method to raise student learning effort method.

Reference

Buyees, V., Sparkman, K. L. & Wesley, P. W. (2003). communities of practice; connecting what we know with what we do, exceptional children, 69(3), 263-277.

Cook-Sather, A. (2002). Authorizing students; perspectives: Toward trust, Dialogue and change in education, education researcher, 31(4), 3-14.

Cook-Sather, A. (2009) from traditional accountability to shared responsibility: The benefits and challenges of student consultants gathering midcourse feedback in college classrooms assessment evaluation in higher education 34(2), 231-241.

Fielding, M. (2006) leadership radical student engagement and the necessity of person- centered education. International Journal of leadership in education , 9 (4) , 299-313.

Good, T. F. & Brophy, J, (1986). School effects. In M. Wittrock 9 ed.) handbook of research on teaching (pp. 570-602). New York : Macmillan.

Lewis, K.G. (2001). Using midsemester student feedback and responding to it. New directions for teaching and learning 87(3) 33.44.

Seale, J. (2010). Doing student voice work in higher education: An exploration of the value of participatory methods. British educational research journal, 36(6) , 995-1015.

Warren , M. (2005), communities and schools: A new view of urban school reform. Harvard educational review, 75(2), 133-173.

Raising learning interest

Behavioral economic solves classroom

management discipline

How to apply behavioral economic method to help teachers to solve classroom management discipline in order to raise student indiviudal learning interest in classrooms? Students need to know what classroom management means. It means effective discipline, it is being prepared to motivate students to raise interesting to learn in classrooms. It is providing a safe, comfortable learning environment, it can build the teacher individual student's sale esteem and creative and imaginative in daily lessons.

Why has classroom management relationship to student individual behavior as well as why behavioral economic method can be applied to solve classroom management discipline in possible? It is simple because every teacher teaching styles, personality attitudes and every teacher managment strategies are different and are not effective. It is possible that due to teaching experiences. Student population to every lesson, low or high salary level, every teacher individual time preparation and time management factors. Then all issues concern whether every teacher to do choice to arrange whose time to prepare before he/she will teach which lesson on that day. For example, if the teacher feels tried to teach more than fine lessons on that day, because he/she is sick. But the school has no enough teachers number to replace the student to teach his/her students on that day. So, he/her teaching performance can not b better , satisfaction and enjoyment in teaching are dependent upon how he/she leads students to cooperate.

Hence, he/she can not permit to so personal rest behavioral choice, and he/she feels that salary can not be raised to double payment or more to get overtime allowance on that teaching day. It will bring any unsatisfactory and unenjoyable teaching attitude or poor teaching behavior or performance and teacher won't deal with discruptive behaviors. Buy, also manage to minimize off task, non-disruptive teaching behavior to teach students and manage their own behavior to learn in classroom effectively and efficiently. Their poor classroom management behavior will bring poor teaching performance. Hence, students won't feel the school teachers are good teachers and students' families will lose confidence to let the school teachers to teach their students.

In Behavioral economic teaching method view point, the school needs to review whether its teachers number is enough to prepare some teachers need to rest at home suddenly. So, other teachers can replace them to teach any his/ her lessons on that day immediately. If the school neglected to employ extra enough part time teachers number to prepare to replace any full time teachers who have need to rest on any days. Due to salary expenditure increasing reason, it is not good choice to reduce to employ extra part time teachers number to avoid the sudden full time teachers numbe shortage need. It will bring classroom management changes poor, due to unsatisfactory teachers' teaching need to go to classroom to teach their students in classrooms when they are sicknessess on that teaching day suddenly. Therefore, poor teaching performance or poor classroom management behaviors to the teacher which will bring poor economic loss, e.g. student enrollment number reduces, students absent number to every lesson increases school teaching subjects number decreases too the school in long time.

Therefore, all these poor influences will cause the school's economic loss, it is due to the school teachers' teaching behaviors are poor , due to many teachers do not enjoy and feel satisfactory to teach these students and manage classes disciplines effectively. It seems that whether the school has enough teachers number, it can infuence how teacher individual teaching and class management behavior to be better or worse and then which will have relationship to influence the school's economic gain or loss in long term consequently.

Therefore, in teacher individual behavioral psychological view point, every one ought have effective time allocation method to prepare how to teach whose students in every lesson. I shall recommend how the teacher individual behavioral economic choice to solve discipline challenges in classrooms as below:

1. Transitions vs. allocated time method

The school teachers can allocate time periods they intend for their students to be engaged in learning activities as well as they can arrange transition time allocated for learning activities. For example, getting students assembled and attentive, assigning reading and directing to begin, getting students' attention away from reading and preparing for class discussion in their schools.

The transition is allocated time to teacher individual behavioral goal is to increase the variety of learning activities , but to decrease transition time, student engagement and non-task behaviors are dependent on how smoothly and efficiently to teachers more from one learning activity to another.

Therefore, teacher has withitness if when classroom discipline problems occue, the teache consistently takes action to solve the misbehavior of exactly those students who do in classrooms, when two discipline problems arise as the same time, the teacher can deal with the more serious first. The teacher can decisively handle instances of off- task behavior before the behaviors either set out of hand or are modeled by others. When handling misbehavior makes sure all students learn what is unacceptable about that behavior, deal with misbehavior without disrupting the learning activity.

2. Classroom rules for student individual behavioral conduct. Formalized statements that provide students with general guidelines for the types of behaviors that are require and the types that are prohibited a few rules are easier to remember than many rules, each rule in a small set of rules is more important than each rule in a large set of rules. Why do need necessary classroom rules of conduct? It aims to maximize on -task behaviors and minimize off-task (esp, discuptive) behaviors, secures the safety and comfort of the learning environment, prevents the activities of the class from disturbing other classes, establish an learning environment in which achieving specified learning goals takes priority over other concerns in classrooms, be particularly prepared and organized to minimize transition time and utilizes a communication style that establishing non-threatening, comfortable environment to let students to learn in classrooms. Other components of disclosure statement include: basis course outline, grading procedures, include procedures for making up missed work, extra credit homework expected etc., attendance policies should be consistent with school policy, other class rules, policies procedures, safety considerations as necessary , accommodation for disabilities statement, signature of student and parent / guardian. Therefore, classroom rules can influence how student individual chooses to do whose learning conduct or behavior , even improving their learning attidude in classrooms. Classroom rules are the best method fo influence every student how to choose to do whose learning behaviors in classroom in order to earn the most effective learning benefits for themselves.

Finally, I shall discuss how to apply behavioral economic mehod to raise student learning interest at classrooms? As I explained that when teacher feels that individual satisfactory or enjoyable teaching feeling to do his/her teaching job,which will influence whose teaching performance in classrooms. Thus, how to improve every teacher individual teaching performance or method or teaching quality which will be important factor to influence whose student individual learning interest to be raised in classrooms indirectly.

I recommend that teachers need to concern how to arrange classroom teaching environment to be attractive or safe or enjoyable to influence every student individual learning attitude to increase more attention or concentate to hear whose teacher's teaching to his/her any lessons in the classroom more considerately. Arrangement is determined by learning activity (lecture, class discussion, small group work etc. learning activities in classrooms). Thinking thorugh class procedure and learning activities and arrangement the classroom in the best possible way.

Teachers need to know why the student chooses to do his/her behavior in classroom. Usually, every behavior has a function , three primary reasons for disputive behavior in the classroom include power, attention, wnat to be left alone (i.e. disinterest or feelings of inadequacy). Many misbehavior are exhibited by students are responses to a behavior needs exhibited by the teacher to understand why a person exhibits behavior is no reason to tolerate it, teacher needs to understand the function of a behavior will help in knowing how to deal with that behavior. When, the teacher can understand why the student chooses to do his/her behavior to find the solutions to persuade or dissuade the student does not choose to do the harmful behavior or change the harmful behavior to do right behavior in order to influence other students can not concentrate on learning considerately.

Consequently, if th school expected to raise every student individual learning interest in classrooms. The school needs to find methods to let its teachers feel satisfactory to teach their students in the school as well as the school's teachers need to learn how to understand why the student chooses to do harmful behavior to influence other students concentrate on easier learning in an enjoyable learning classroom environment.

When the school can let its teachers to enjoy to do their teaching jobs and they can feel more satisfactory when they are teaching every time in classroom as well as its teachers can understand some students why they choose to do harmful learning behavior to influence the other students to concentrate on learning in classrooms and they can find the solvable methods to dissuade they do not choose to do harmful learning behavior ro influence other students can not conentrate on learning in clssrooms again. Then, between the school's teachers and students both can build positive teaching attitudes and learning attitudes in order to cause they can choose to do enjoyable and satisfactory teaching behaviors or performances to teacher and concentration on learning behavior or attitues to students in classrooms.

Consequently, when the school can build a good classroom learning environment to let teachers consider to teach their students in order to bring whose students can concentrate on learning in classrooms. Then, a good classroom learning environment will bring good learning economic and non-economic benefit , such as student number increases , school income increases and teachers salaries increase, student individual attention will raise, student will enjoy to go to school and absence number will reduce. Consequently, any schools' teacher individual teaching behvior and student individual learning behavior both in classrooms which must have positive or negative relationship to bring the school itself and the teachers themselves long term economic and non-economic benefits in learning behavioral economic view point. Also, the importance is that learning behavioral economic analysis, can explain why the teacher individual good or bad emotion can influence his/her every lesson student individual learning emotion to be good or bad to do learning behavior in clasroom. So, schools need to concern every teacher individual emotion whether he/she feels enjoyable or satisfactory to teach his/her students in classrooms in order to avoid every classroom students' learning emotion will be influenced to be poor to bring long time economic loss to the school. It is one importnat factor to influence any school's teaching performance to be succeed.

Successful persuasive teaching method can raise student individual learning behavior

Can teachers apply behavioral economic method to raise student individual learning behavior? Behavioral economic method is explained by psychology and other disciplines to create models of limits on rationality, willpower and self-interest. Although, economic professionals believe it can be applied to predict consumer behavior. But, how any why can it be applied to raise student personal interest to learn new knowledg in education industry aspect? This is one valuable research question. If it can be appled to eduational psychology aspect to raise student individual learning interesting influentially, educators ought need to learn to how to do in order to persuade student indivudal has more interest to learn in anywhere schools or homes or libraries in habitually persuasively. I shall explain some possible educational psychological methods as below:

When one student discovered that learning will bring much tangible and intangible benefits to infulence his/her career development in the future. For example, he/she can find good jobs, earn more salaries, raise the high class social positon, build personal successgul image or raise satisfactory feeling, raise social competitive effort in job market etc. different economic related benefits or non economic related benefits both. Then,the teacher or the school will have possible to persuade whose students to raise learning interest when they choose to learn in the school.

How to let the student to feel the school can give good economic related or non-economic related benefits to satisfy the student future career plan successful development need persuasively and attractively? It will need to include psychological factor to influence its students to raise learning interest when they are studying in the school in whose whose learning expereince stage. I assume that every student will learn hardly when the school can persuade its students can believe that they must earn good career benefit when they can follow the school's discipline to learn hardly in whose whole learning stage in the school.

Therefore, one successful persuasive teaching method can influence or persuade the students choose to learn hardly . Usually, in general students need not expect to waste learning time and money to chose one poor teaching quality of school to study. If they can not achieve good examination resultes or they need increase long time to extend their graduation time, then they will feel waste money and time loss to choose the wrong or unsuitable school to study. It is one rational either positive or negative learning feeling when one student gain good or bad examination result consequently.

Hence, one successful school must let students to have confidence , it can raise good quality teaching method to let them to study as well as it can provide good learning environment to let them to feel safe, enjoyable , attractive , persuasive learning attitude when they go to school to enter the classroom to learn every day. So, the school must need to let all students to feel they won't waste money and time economic or non-economic related losses when they choose the school to learn, if the school expected to persuade its students to choose to learn easily.

Therefore, learning behavioral economic theory explains that student individual learning interest whether whose interest is raised or not which has been related to influence whether he/she feels his/her learing attitude or learning behavior will bring either waste learning time and money loss or not in whole learning career in the school consequently. Usually, every student won't expect to waste his/her learning time and money if he/she can not earn economic or non-economic related benefits to his/her future job career.

It implies that non-wasted time and money psychological factor brings to the student feeling to learn that will be one man economic factor to influence the student chooses to do hard learning behavior. For example, when a young age student does not choose to go to the school, because he/she does not conern whether he/she will earn a better life in the future. He/she must be persuaded to feel the school is fun now or is given no better opinion to compare the school. Hence, the school needs to let the young age student to feel there are not other schools opinions are better to compare to the school as well as the school can provide attractive teaching method to let the student to feel more fun to lern when he/she chooses the school to learn.

Therefore, providing fun learning environment and fun teaching method both factors will be one important to encourage the stdent to learn hardly. The particular educational outcomes worth encouragement, such as attainment, attendance, and homework issues of these educational components will must be achieved fun learning feeling to let the student to whose learning interest encouragingly or persuasively. So, fun learning environment can bring the student individual learning interest in possible. It means that if the student does not feel fun to learn when he/she goes to the school to learn every day. Then, he/her poor fun learning feeling will discourage he/she feels why he/she needs to go to school to attend every lesson to learn in classrooms hardly. So, fun learning environment. fun teaching method, hun homework, fun learning content etc. teaching related components factor will encourage every student likes to go to school to listen every lesson hardly every day in possible.

Present-biased learning behavior has important implications in education. Doing fun homeowrks, studying for fun exams, researching fun colleges or potential opportunities for financial aid and completing applications all involve educational cost which will let any students choose to weigh the future learning cost to evaluate which school will be possible to bring educational loss spending cost to evaluate whether he/she ought to choose which school to study in preference. Hence, it explains that the student will consider whether the school can prvide fun learning environment and fun learning subjects or courses to let them to choose to study and whether he/she can feel fun teaching method to satisfy whose learning need. Then, the school will be possibe increased successfuly chance to let the student to choose it to enrol to study in preference. Moreover, attractive courses choices, providing fun learning environment, providing good and fun teaching method quality , fun teaching book contents choices to let students to study etc. thesefactors will encourage students to raise learning interect successfully.

However, any schools need focue only on salient factors , it implies that even simple optimizing decisions may not always be made. So, with a better understanding of student individual fun learning environment and fun teaching method learning need and fun courses teaching learning contents , subjects choices etc. these factors will possible bring knowledg to design more effective learning policies and improve student individual learning outcomes.

Moreover, improving student learning attitude factor is also important to raise whose learning interest. For example, by reading motivational passages or watching tagic movies which can encourage students to focus on positive identifies related to learning and intellectual curiosity may be one approach a growing evidence suggests that many students and parents are not fully informed about education costs , future economic and non-economic related benefits and options. It is possible related to whose low-income family backgrounds and poor learning attitude both factors. So, if the family was one high income family, it will have possible to influence whose sons or daughts to build good learning attitude. When they have good learning attitude and good family growing relatonship . Theb, they will raise learning interest , due to they had built from good learning attitude when they are living in one good family relationship environment. In special, when the family is one low income family and low educational level background, parents will beed to work, so they will neglect to teach whose sons or daughters to know whether they ought how to learn easily, which wil be one correct or right learning attitude to learn by themselves successfully. They will neglect and lack useful educational recommendation to compare education cost, future economic and non-economic eduational benefits and learning attitude and opinion methods and the suitable courses and teaching books contents opinions to let whose their sons and/or daughters to know how to learn effectively by themselves, instead of school teaching method. So, these students' parents' lacking useful learning recommendation or negligent education learning recommendaton behaviors which will also cause the low income family students to build " discouraged hard learning attitude" to let them to raise interest to learn any more new knowledge persuasively. Even, due to the non-educational behavioral opinion of pre-school decision making opinion, if the parents discovered that the school is one suitable school to let their sons and/or daughters to learn persuasively or attratively in order to let they can earn good examination resultsor pass subjects more easily. Then, these disappointed parents and low grade examination result of students will feel need to learn more hardly if they are still not improving theire grade when they feel that they had been studying hardly in the school. Consequently, it will bring more negative learning emotion to the students and families. Hence, disappointing or poor or negative learning attidude or emotion to the student's feeling , this factor must not raise the student individual interest to learn in the school. Otherwise, positive or good learning emotion or attitude will influcence the student to raise learning interest to continue to learn in the school consequently. hence, schools ought not neglect to improve students to build positive learning emotion or attitude habitually in order to raise whose interest to learn in the school more easily.

Can effective school management behavior method raise student learning interest

How and why effective school management behavior can influence the school's student individual to raise learning interest. What is the relationship to bring student individual learning interest to be raised between the student and the school? An effective school mangement behavior can make the function bring that teaching and learning take place in the most effective way. In managing school's systems have to operate so that a whole range of social, intellectual and emotional activites can evolve and develop (pay foot et , 1989). It seems that an effective school management system can change student individual to do a range of positive social, intellectual and emotion activities in order to raise whose learning interest.

Therefore, innovating the traditional education system, changing many aspects of school structures, systems and organization as well as recognizing that the more teachers at all levels in a school's hierarchy who had management training of some kind, the better is needed to some traditional educational organzations. Any educational organizations need have good management functions ,which include: setting the right aims and objectives, planning how a goal will be achieved, organizing available educational resources (how teaching time arrangement, how to select teachers and clerical staffs, homework, how revision time allocation, how educational material opinions, e.g. computers facilities, classrooms number and design method and teaching environment, lecture hall seats number, tables and chairs number, library teaching book lending supplies number etc. resources arrangement). Therefore, the school can be economically achieved in a planned way, controlling the teaching process (i.e. ensuring that the goal is schieved, e.g. raising learning interest to every individual student when he/she is learning at classrooms, reducing the students fail exam and/or test result number.

In fact, if the school expects it can be one real teaching organization, if the school can arrange internal and external structures effectively. Then, the school let students to have more confidence to choose the school to study. Internal structures include: class organizing, sibject choice organizinf, departments organizing, responsibility arranging. Otherwise , external structures include: admission numbers, numbers on raising salary scales, schol budget, leaving ages, staturory length of the school day, arragement methods of appraisal etc. Hence effective school management system can bring more confidence to the student to choose to the school to study and it can encourage him/hse to raise learning interest effectively.

So, it seems that student learning interest has close relationship to concern how the school manages its organization. Because good school management can influence its internal and external teaching reasources how to allocate to use and manage effectively. For example, good classroom teaching environment can influence students to feel easily, an teaching book library can have enough different topic teaching book to let students to borrow to read, or it has enough comouter facilities to let students to find any reading data from internet conveniently. Then , they will be influenced to raise learning interest more easily, because the school has one attractive and fun learning environment to let its students to learn.

Therefore, an effective school management system can influence its students to raise more interest to learn in order to influence they choose to do learning behavior to study more harder in homes or schools. How to bring one effective school management system to infuence students to feel? I shall indicate the main factors as below:

The first factor is one effective school management system needs have an effective hierarchy of headteachers, deputy heads, heads of department different effective organizing systems. It aims to achieve more directing, controlling and commanding to any department leaders to manage themselves departments more easily.

One educational organization's hierarchical pyramid can indicate such as: a headteacher manage or leads one deputy or more than one deputys on the top level, the middle level will include one deputy or more than one deputy manager(s) or lead(s) in one department head or more than one department heads. Next, the middle level will include one department head or leads more than one teacher at the low level. However, any school organization expects to manage or lead themselves schools effectively. They need to organize in such a way that they will try to achieve effective reaults and make every effort to maintain good relationships between those who work in these departments. Consequently, when the school can have effective hierarchical structure to manage all different teaching staffs to do whose individual teaching behavior effectively. Then, it will bring positive emotion influence to every teacher to teach whose students more effectively. Hence, every classroom students' learning attitude will enjoy to bring more learning feeling when they are real raised learning interest from their teachers' teaching method influence persuasively.

The second factor is that each staff group participation. It will be the school's staff group participation behavioral factor, how it influences every classroom overall students' learning behaviors to be positive learning emotion or attitude when they (every classroom overall students) are listening their every teacher indiviual teaching in every lession in every the classroom. It is important to find out who participates a lot and why, as well as why someone, e.g. teacher contributes every little to the classroom students. For example, it is because of fear, disagreement or disinterest, the group of teachers may under have useful point to make. So, a group should ideally encourage all its participates to contribute to any discussions and decison making. This issue of participation is one that group leaders have to consider very carefully.

In fact, influence and participation to every teaching group are not always the same. Some teaching staffs who tell a lot may not always be listen to . Others who are quiet and speak very little can, when they do speak, capture, the attention of everyone. If this is the case then whoever participates may alter and change depending on who has influence at a specific time and who needs certain individuals to speak and support his or her particular cause.

The final factor is that the school needs to know how the stykes to be influenced to every teaching group. Influence can take may forms, it can be both positive and negative. It can either to support or co-operation of others or refuse or nor support or co-operation of others. How this happen with a teaching group can be autocratic teaching colleagues who will attempt to impose their will on the teaching group by movement towards directions in which they eagerly support everyone and everything and try to avoid conflict at any cost and those who is influenced by distancing themselves from the whose procedings influence others to do the same. Hence, in a effective teaching group , the teacher's header, e.g. deputy or headteacher ,the middle level staffs or the top level staffs will need to manage themselves every teaching group, e.g. each classroom teacher individual teaching behavior is more easily and effectively. When the classroom teacher can have good teaching performance to teach his/her students in the lesson. Then, he/she can raise every lesson's student individual learning interest more easily or persuasively.

The final school management factor is that, what is the most suitable or right school ethos and whose school aims to the school. If the school chose the most right school aims, then it can able to develop attitudes which won't only help pupils to learn more effectively or raise their interet to learn only, even , it can shoe them the technique of learning and how to continue to want to learn. I shall recommendation that these characteristics of the most suitable or right school aims in order to achieve effectiveness and a positive ethos the following characteristics will help as below:

An effective and powerful leadership, the deputy head needs to be involved in all major decisions, all teachers need to feel that they own those decisons that directly affect them, there to be consistency and continuity throughout the school organization, e.g. in terms of discipline, patterns, homework number and course content test or examination questions contents allocation policies, resource management, subject courses timetable structures etc. teaching sessions need to be structures, matched to pupils' needs, the actual teaching should be intellectually challenging for all pupils, the learning environment of the school whether it will be task -and -work orientated, i.e. every pupil will recognize learning is the norm rather than the exception, there will be lots of communication between teachers and pupils both inside and outside the classroom, record-keeping and assessment are sensible and thorough and are communicated to parents when necessary in a way that they can understand, whether there is a positive learning climate where emphasis is placed on praise rather then criticism control in classrooms is firm , but fair, with children being treated as individuals, any teaching or resource allocation , teaching time allocation activities whether are organized to take place outside the classroom and away from the school. This is a means of offering pupils wider experiencs and a way of putting. The academic content of the curriculum into a different content.

Consequently, how to organize the school in effective way factor which will be one main influential factor to influence teachers to do positive or negative teaching behavior to persuade whose students can raise more learning interest in classrooms. So, it seems that teacher indivivudal positive or negative teaching emotion or attitude will influence their teaching performance or teaching behavior to improve to be better in order to raise the school's students' learning interest more easily or persuasively.

Improving financial education effectiveness through behavioral economic to raise student individual learning interest

How any why does improve financial education effective behavior which can raise student individual learning interest? How to innovate application of lessons from psychology to a financial education programme which can raise student individual learning interest effectively? I shall apply student learning behavioral economic methods to explain why and how improving financil education can be effective to raise student individual learning interest.

The standard economic approach to financial education argues that financial consumers will behave in their own best interests of the financial market is perfectly competitive. In fact, in educaton industry, education consumers, e.g. student parents do not have enough all the knowledge and information concerns what where their sons and/or daughts ought need to choose which subject(s) to study which are(is) the most suitable their interest and effort to learn, whether what the school fee budget level is the most reasonable, what the course contents are the most effective to let their sons or/and daughts to learn easily etc. different related educational institutes information questions to have enough time to prepare to gather these information in order to compare which school is the best or the most suitable school choce for their son and/or daught to study more easily. Thus, of the student consumer's parents can have enough fully information concerns to education institutions how to assist them to make the most reasonable school choice making decision more accurate.

III

Skill training talent human method

Skill is an ability or effort that you need to put time to develop. Talent refers to an inborn and special ability you own it. So, when one person can attempt to learn ths kind of skill. It is possible that he can be trained to be talent person. How to Create Effective Skills Training with Career Pathing ? Your company's ability to address the skills gap is going to be the most significant issue facing HR in the next decade. Relying on the recruitment of new hires will no longer be a viable solution. Digital transformation of the workplace means that AI and automation are continually rendering skills obsolete while creating new jobs in the process. As those new roles emerge, the existing talent pool will be insufficient to meet demand. Employers will no longer be able to fall back on their default strategy of hiring new workers.

● How to improve staff skill to be talent labour ?

As the 'future of work' begins to assume a more defined shape, the majority of employers are placing more emphasis on training of their existing talent, but skills development is not moving fast enough to keep up with demand. Ongoing upskilling and reskilling can help to offset the impact on your workforce from these fundamental changes.

Creating personalized development opportunities

When it comes to developing your talent, there is no 'one size fits all' approach. To succeed in today's workplace the following steps are recommended. Your approach must become more personal, placing development at the center of your overall business strategy.

Personalized development opportunities should be offered to enhance skills acquisition. This approach enables you to provide your employees with the tools they need to acquire new skills.

As well as being targeted to the individual, employees should be able to learn in their own time. Technology can help to support this. A further, critical point to note is that learning and development is not exclusively for the C Suite but should be offered to all of your employees.

● Career pathing strategy improve employee individual skill ?

Career pathing provides a clear route into all of these options, enables you to create individual learning programs for all of your employees and offers the following benefits.

Employees create their own career paths, which are aligned with your organization's business goals. All employees are guided to understand their own strengths and weaknesses and are empowered to identify key areas for development. They are inspired to work towards vertical or lateral moves within your organization, for example, through job rotation (ie, where employees assume new tasks in a different role for a specified period before they 'rotate' back to their original post). Career pathing enables HR and management to understand and analyze employee aspirations through internal mobility programs and aligns well with your succession planning program. So, career pathing strategy is one kind of good skill to raise staff efficiency or improve performance.

● Strategies learning new skills

Are you a visual learner? Or is your learning style kinesthetic or auditory? I'll tell you a secret: you're none of these. As much as we'd like to believe that we learn better in a certain style, the truth is, these have little impact on our ability to learn.

In an intriguing talk at TEDxUWLaCrosse, Dr. Tesia Marshik shares a startling fact: 40 years of research on learning styles has found that matching teaching styles to learning styles makes no difference at all. In her own experiments, Dr. Marshik found that students learned the same way, regardless of the way material was presented to them.

Another study was a little more blunt in its judgments:

1. Learning from technological channel

The contrast between the enormous popularity of the learning-styles approach within education and the lack of credible evidence for its utility is, in our opinion, striking and disturbing. For example, if you're trying to learn a new language, don't just read the textbook. Watch TV shows, listen to music, and converse with a native speaker through a language exchange app. Learners can apply internet to learn any kinds of new kowledge easily.

One main reason why "learning styles" don't work is that we learn things in terms of meaning. Finding meaning in our learning is the key. A 1973 study by Chase and Simon illustrates this well. In the first part of the test, amateur and expert chess players were shown a chessboard arrangement from a game in progress and asked to recall the position of the pieces. While amateurs players could barely recall any of positions, the experts were able to recall most of them. The experts see the strategy, the meaning behind why the pieces are where they are.

In the second part, experts and amateurs were shown boards with the chess pieces arranged at random and asked to recall them. Both groups performed about equally. This time, the experts couldn't find any real connection or meaning in the way the pieces are arranged.

2. Learning from life experience

The same goes for learning. We all learned various facts and figures in school but how many of those do we actually remember? Only the information that was meaningful to us, that we've been able to connect to our own life and experiences. If you try to force yourself to just memorize random facts, you're likely to forget them. Remember all those times you tried to memorize formulae without understanding their relevance? In order to make your learning stick, it's important to make real life connections and see how it fits in the larger scheme of things.

3. learning by attempting doing.

Humans are natural learners—and we learn best when we perform the tasks we're trying to learn. No matter how good your grades were at college, most of your learning takes place once you enter the workplace and start applying what you've learned. Let's say you're trying to learn SEO. Don't invest all your time in learning the jargon and theory—dive in as soon as you can to master the skill through trial and error. Start a blog. Write a few posts. Find out for yourself what works and what doesn't. The more you do it, the more you learn.

Better yet, build new habits to enforce your new skills. Start small and reward yourself to start building a pattern of behavior that will reinforce what you're learning.

4. Learning by study

Aspiring writers hear over and over that the best way to write better is to read a lot of books, especially the classics. Why? Because they'll learn a lot more by studying the writing styles of great writers, than they would by taking a course on writing. Let's take this advice a step further. While studying the greats is essential, it is more of a passive exercise. In order to gain from it, you need to apply that learning to your own work as well. One way to do this is to mimic experts until you eventually develop your own style and technique. Benjamin Franklin taught himself to write this way, as he shares in his autobiography:

I took some of the papers (from The Spectator magazine), and, making short hints of the sentiment in each sentence, laid them by a few days, and then, without looking at the book, try'd to compleat the papers again, by expressing each hinted sentiment at length, and as fully as it had been expressed before, in any suitable words that should come to hand. On comparing his work with the originals, he found where he was lacking, and started turning the tales into poems and then back again. This is how he learned to express himself better. This form of learning can be applied to any skill, be it writing, speaking another language, or even sports. Compare your work with that of experts in your field and you will notice areas that need improvement. Then, refer back to step 3 and keep practicing your skills. You will notice the difference.

5. Learning from past what your teacher tought

One of the more surprising ways you can learn a new skill is to teach it to someone else. Much research has been done on this phenomenon, but one study illustrates it particularly well. In the study, two sets of participants study the same passage, with different expectations. One group was expected to teach it later, the other one expected a test on it. At the end, both groups were eventually tested on the material. Guess which group did better? Yep—the one that expected to teach it.

Why is this such an effective way to learn? Because when we learn with the intention to teach, we break the material down into simple, understandable chunks for ourselves. It also forces us to examine the topic more critically and thoroughly, helping us to understand it better. You don't have to be an education major to use this trick. Try explaining what you're learning to friends or coworkers. If you're learning a new business software or skill, ask your boss if you can make a presentation to your team about it. See if you can field all their questions. Write regular blog posts or make vlogs while you're learning. See if you're able to express what you learn in simple words. The results might surprise you.

6. Learning from spend more time to practise things you feel difficulties

Practice in itself is great, but if you're practicing things you know well, you're doing it wrong. In order to excel at any skill, you need to push yourself out of your comfort zone and practice things you aren't good at. This is known as deliberate practice, and was popularized by Anders Ericsson. Ericsson and his team studied expert athletes, violinists, and memory champions and found that they spent a lot of time improving areas they were weak. Additionally, they consulted their teachers to find out where exactly they were lacking. Along with spending more time on your weaknesses, Ericsson also emphasizes the importance of concentration while practicing. If you're practicing while your mind is all over the place, you're not getting much out of it. So the next time you sit to practice a new skill, step out of your comfort zone and challenge yourself. Concentrate on whatever is most difficult for you, and with time you'll find you achieve a higher level of overall efficiency.

7. Learning takes frequent breaks

The brain has two modes—focused and diffused. For learning to happen, both modes are equally important. While in focused mode, you're able to learn the nitty-gritties of a problem. In diffused mode, you're better able to see the big picture and bring it all together. You might have noticed this happening in the shower, when you're not focusing on anything in particular, then you suddenly remember a fact that was eluding you, or the solution to a problem. It's important to let your brain relax for a while after a particularly intense session of study or practice, to give it time to connect the dots. One good way to practice this is using the Pomodoro technique, which has you work on a project for 25 minutes, and then give yourself a 5 minute break. After four such sessions (that is, 100 minutes of work, with 15 minutes of break) you take another break for 15-30 minutes. This technique helps to keep your mind invigorated, and ensures you don't suffer mental fatigue. Equally important is learning how to procrastinate productively, so your brain has time to truly recharge itself.

8. Learning from test yourself skill again

We all loved to hate tests in school, but do you know just how effective they are in helping you learn? Turns out testing is one of the best ways to boost learning—even if you're simply practicing on your own, and not taking a high-stakes exam. Testing even beats out methods such as re-reading and reviewing notes when it comes to making sure your learning sticks. An examination of the study techniques of top students by Elevate Education found that while most students re-read notes before exams, top students spend their time solving problems and taking practice exams. Why is testing so effective? Because it takes recall a step further. Recall shows how much of the material you remember. Testing shows you how well you can use what you've learnt. After all, that is the ultimate goal of learning, isn't it?

9. Finding a mentor help

Mentorship is perhaps the quickest way to take your skills to the next level. A mentor helps you navigate your field by offering invaluable perspective and experience. Initially, look to friends, family, and coworkers for an expert in the skill you're trying to learn. If you come up with no one, start branching out your search to your larger community and industry. When reaching out to experts, describe what you have to offer, rather than what you will gain. For example, maybe you could manage their social media accounts or help write their website content. Whatever services you can offer, be sure to let them know.

All of aboves are skill learning method to help foolish person to be clever or talent person. So, it seems that learning skill may be one kind of good method to become talent person.Becoming talent human encountering difficulties What are the difficulties to the person who hopes to be talent person ? I shall indicate as below:

● How to solve talent management challenges and difficulties?

Firstly, we need to know what talent management means and what difficulties we shall encounter in talent managment process. What is Talent Management? Talent management is defined as the methodically organized, strategic process of getting the right talent onboard and helping them grow to their optimal capabilities keeping organizational objectives in mind. The process thus involves identifying talent gaps and vacant positions, sourcing for and onboarding the suitable candidates, growing them within the system and developing needed skills, training for expertise with a future-focus and effectively engaging, retaining and motivating them to achieve long-term business goals. The definition brings to light the overarching nature of talent management – how it permeates all aspects pertaining to the human resources at work while ensuring that the organization attains its objectives. It is thus the process of getting the right people onboard and enabling them to enable the business at large.Under the umbrella of talent management, there are a string of elements and sub-processes that need to work in unison to ensure the success of the organization. For example, analyzing the right talent gaps for the present and the future, identifying the right talent pools and best-fit candidates, getting them to join and then optimizing their existing skills and strengths while helping them grow are touch-points that are all equally important.

Talent Management Model

Over the years, there have been multiple models made for talent management that have been created b organization who have felt that they have finally cracked the code on the perfect model. The thing with talent management, however, is that it needs to morph to suit the latest talent trends, digital disruptions, and employee expectations.

● Talent Management Strategy

Talent management is not a mere checklist of requirements that need to be sufficed – it is a strategy that needs careful implementation, regular checks, and continual improvement. The following are the six primary talent management strategies that serve as the pillars of people functions.

Person-organization fit

An employee that does not fit into the organizational culture can neither be the happiest employee nor the most sustainably productive one. While the culture can be difficult to define in words, it is prevalent in actions and quite easy to understand whether a candidate would be a good fit or not. Personal and organizational values need to have a certain degree of overlap for any employee to feel at home within the organization. Without a comfortable person-organization fit, the most amount of time, effort and energy would go into attempts at adjustment. Hiring candidate with the right P-O fit (or PE fit) thus greatly improves the chances of better employee engagement, higher employee satisfaction, and usually better performance.

Collaborate-coach-evolve

An important strategy to make talent management more effective involves creating a culture of coaching, mentoring (even reverse mentoring) and collaboration. Constructive feedback goes a long way when it comes to helping employees evolve and develop their skills and expertise. Managing talent is thus also about preparing them for the future of the organization – to be ready for changes down the path and to be able to rely on each other.

Reward and recognize right

The process of rewards and recognition forms an important part of the strategy to motivate, engage and manage employees better. This goes beyond financial rewards and bonus packages. Studies point towards the fact that employees often want R&R schemes that motivate them with "prizes" that are most relevant to them as individuals. This is a great opportunity for organizations to show their employees how much they care for them as persons and as integral aspects of the organizational machinery.

Opportunities for continuous improvement

Managing talent needs to be put in the context of the future that the organization has envisioned for itself. Thus, employees need to be equipped with the right tools to be able to maximize their own potential. For the continuous improvement of the organization, there needs to be the scope and opportunities for the continuous development of its employees. Moreover, this ensures that the cumulative skills within the organization is updated, upgraded and upscaled.

Talent management involves strategically planning career paths that make sense for every employee. We all tend to work better we know where we are headed and what the next stop is for our careers. This does not entail making empty promises of promotions but rather creating a career map in discussion with the employee, making sure that they relate to it and feel that it is realistic while also providing them with all the necessary tools to make the map a reality. Having a map to follow also improves retention scores since employees then know what they have to look forward to and work towards and can then collaborate effectively to achieve it. So, any organizations may attempt to apply talent management strategy to solve any difficulties when they hope to train talent employees in their organizations more easily.

Skills shortages on developing country market

Future developing countries need to develop their economy, so they need to employ many employees who own technical skills and /or soft skills. What kind of technical skills and/or soft skills , the developing countries' employees who will need to order to raise competiton in local job market ? I shall indicate the developing country China example. China is one developing country, employers will need different kinds of skillful labors to assist them to develop their businesses. However, China employers will face skillful labour shortage challenge. Although Chinese young age population is high, but many of them do not to be encouraged to learn enough skillful knowledge to fill future new skillful positions. So, the fast speed of training will be important to influence China supply and demand labour market to be more accurately as well as future China's the quality of labour demand number will be influenced to be raised after they have enough training to learn new skills.

How to solve future China skillful shortage of labour? Firstly, nowadays, China employers need to teach their employees to learn how to use and how to operate robotic skills in China's factories. AI robotic has been early developing, so they need to prepare to learn robotic management and operating technical and soft skills in order to satisfy future China factory automation industry development.

China is one world's factory for low-end products to high quality information products, high end technology and services. So, China will need many high skilled workers to assist manufacturers to manufacture many different kinds of products to export or local sale. Moreover, robotic manufacturing skillful workers will also need because robotic will be accepted to assist manual workers to work in China's any factories. This has led to greater demand for labour wirh upgraded skills and competence. So, it seems that China's orkers need to lern any high technological manufacturing knowledge, e.g. learning how to co-operate with robotics to raise productive efficiencies, which will be future many China's manufacturers' skills need intention.

So, when any one of China manufacturer invests robotics to work in its factory . Then, the China manufacturer's labours ought need to know how to co-operate with th robotics to raise productivities and efficiencies. Moreover, these China service industries, e.g. IT, software, accounting, finance, marketing and customer service management, e.g. waiter, property security, shopping center customer service etc. service occupations. In the future, robotics can also used to participate any one of these service industries' part of tasks in order to raise service performance. So, any one of these service industries' employees need to learn how to operate with robotics in order to achieve the most excellent servvice performances to satisfy consumers' needs. So, China service industries labours ought need to learn how to co-operate or manage service natural robotics to work together more efficiently because future China manufacturers will prefer to employ the labours who know how to co-operate and manage and control any service natural robotics more easily and efficiently in order to achieve the most excellent service performance to satisfy customers needs.

Hence, it seems that China manufacturing and service workers need to spend time and effort to learn how to co-operate with manufacturing natural robotics to manufacture any products in factories efficiently or deliver any cargos in warehouses more efficiently or serve customers to let them to feel excellent service performance in restaurants or shopping centers or properties or offices reception counters. Then, when their China employers apply robotics to participate to work in factories, restaurants, shopping centers, cinemas, offices or properties reception etc. different working places . These low skillful labours will be dismissed easily, due to robotics can replace them to manufacture any products or provide services to satisfy clients' needs in order to let them to fell robotics' performances are more excellent to compare human service labours or their productive efficiencies are more effort to compare workers. So, future China workers need to learn how to cooperate or manage or contol with robotics to work more efficiently, if they do not expect to be dismissed easily.

In the future several occupations have been identified as the most frequent movers between all labour market states. The elementary occupations include: waiters, bar staffs, clearners, catering assistants, construction and security service workers, care workers, sales assistants and general clerks etc. So, the low educational level workers can learn these soft wkills to raise whose professional workering level to prepare to do these above positions in global elementary occupation job market.

The changes of employer were most frequent for IT programmers, doctors, electricians, carpenters, skilled workers in global labour market. These skilled occupations will have manpower shortage supply challenge, due to either people feel the educatonal level is under low. So, there has no many people have interest to know these knowledg to prepare their elementary careers. So, these kinds of low skilled occupations will have not enough human power supply to global labour job market also, the high skilled or educational job support.

Moreover, the high skilled occupations also encounter labour shortage issue. The skills in short supply related to experienced canadidates e.g. five years or more. For example, pharmaceutical , biogharma and food innovation industries. The occupational shortage roles include: Chemists, analytical scientists, product formulation, analytical development for roles in biopharma, quality control analyst includes pharmaco-vigilance, i.e. drug safety roles. The demand for engineering industry aspect which will aos increase the labour shortage includes process and design (research and development, quality control, automation, lean processes) are skillful labours need to help employers to achieve these intentions. They may include raising competitiveness, boosting productivity and skills availability. So, if future these above any one of occupation labours can not achieve these benefits to satisfy their employers' needs. Then, his/her average weekly or hourly wages will be reduced. It means that the unskilled labour under skilled labour wage can not increased more easily, even they own many year working experiences in any one of above these occupations. If the employer feels the labour is unskilled or below skilled level for any one of these occupations in these any one industry aspect, e.g. wholesale and retal , human health, education, accomodaton and food , construction, professional activities, financial service , public administration, and defence, transportation etc. occupations. Then, these industries' unskilled or below skilled level workers' salaries will be lower level to compare the higher skilled workers who work in any one of these industries.

The reason why future employers need to employ skilled labours. One explanation for slow recovery in demand in negative impact on investment is a prolonged period of high unemployment. This is led to job weekers left labour market or became unemployable due. So, future low skillful level will be one important factor to cause unemployment in society as well as nowadays labours ought need consider whether their skills are needed to improve in order to avoid future competition in job market.

2.1 Why do future labours need to learn worldwide readiness skills

Future employers need employees own worldwide readiness skills, such as reading , writing and arithmatic. Why do employees need worldwide readiness skills? In the future, high economic growth countries need high wage positions, high opportunity jobs which need a large number of skills required of job candidates of these positions " job readinss" and not " job training" , which support developments of these importance and widely desired skills won't only support the success to high-opportunity positions, but also be developed for future success in the competitive global economy. Because real-time business intelligence is needed for the talent marketplace to employ talent employees. So, it explains that it will have many future employers hope to employ owning readiness skillful employees to help them to develop their businesse intelligently. Hence, present employees ought need to hard to train readiness skills to prepare whose future employers' job requirements in the future competitive global job market.

2.2 Why these occupations need readiness skills

In the future these occupations will need to raise readiness skills. For example, mathematical science, teachers (post-secondary), management analysts, computer and information systems, managers, first-line supervisors of construction traders, solar photovoltaic installers. All of these occupations , employers need staffs to own good readiness analytic ability to help them to do more accurate real-time business intelligent decisions. The representative occupations include oral and written communication skills, project management, teamwork, marketing and creativity . Moreover, they need to own specific technology skill, deep science and math or even most business skills as well as these skills are "soft" skills more than hard skills. These kinds of occupation employees need own cooperative effort, creativity, problem solving, detail orientation and integrity personal characteristics, which are relevant across all knowledge and domains.

Therefore, in the future, science, technology,engineering and mathematics relevant occupations need to own more readniness and analytic skills more than othe kinds of occupations. Because these organizations need those professionals on knowledge acquisition, literacy analysis, synthesis and critical thinking skills that will impact their organizations to bring more critical thinking beneficial team culture. These occupational top skills will include oral and written communication skills, project management skill, team oriented skill, marketing and creativity skills, problem solving skill, detail oriented skill, self-motivated skills, management and analytical skills, coaching skill, business process modeling skills, work independent skill, strong leadership skills, management experience and business requirements gathering. All of these skills which will be future employers who need to employ these kinds employees who own these skills in preference. Also, all of these skills concentrate on soft skills more than hard skills. It seems that when above occupational applicants who own any one of thes skills, evn more than one skills. Then, he/ she will have more chance to be selected to employ. Also occupation specific skills requirements are more needed to compare cross-functional skills for above of any one occupation. Because the high concentraton of cross-functional skills require " job readiness" and not " job training" for success, e.g. communicaton, integraton and presentation skills, entrepreneurialism and related skills, microsoft office software skills.

Of particular interest is communication, integration and presentation skills. These skills include ability to seek, evaluate and examine information and data create a reasoned position, present findings and make a case for or advocate for position. So, these skills are very important and they can help future applicants who expect to win any kinds of these positions easily. However, the hard skills can help these applicants to be more successful to win any kinds of these positions when they own these hard skills, e.g. microsoft offic, powerpoint, excel , word, microsoft project etc. softwares.

In conclusion, the global economy is dynamic and many of the skills required for positons in the future will need good technologies and work practices to be developed. The number of skills required t be successful in the jobs forecast to be most in demand in the future is growing. So, it explains that why future any one of these occupations which will need soft skills more than hard skills, due to organizations like to employ the employees who own managerial and analytical effort more than hard skills productive effort to assist their organizations to develop more easily.

2.3 Data -analysis skill needs

In the future, most organizations will have a number of jobs that include data analysis. Economists and labor market forecasters predict occupations need data analytical skill will need much. In addition, fast technological development means th types of technologies and applications workers in this field will need to be familiar with data analytical skill rapidly. It seems that data analytical jobs will have new job opportunity to employees with in-demand skills in future global labor market.

Why and how do employers demand for data analysis skills? Data analysis skills mean the ability to gather, analyze and draw practical conclusions from data as well as communicate data findings to others. The occupations include: data analyst, data scientist, statistician, market research analyst, financial analyst,research manager. In business career, many employers expect to employ statisticans, operations researh analysts, market research analysts and marketing specialists to assist their organizations to gather useful data from market in order to analyze and draw practical conclusions and finding the best solutions or methods to win their competitors.

Therefore, these data analysis jobs will have much need. Large size organizations with 500 or more employees were more likely than small or medium size organizations with 25 to 499 employees to plan hired data analysis positons in the future. For example, human source department will use big data to help make strategic decisions. How HR uses big data . HR will use big data for sourcing, recruitment, or selection, identifying causes of turnover and/or employee retention strategies or trends, managing talent and performance. Why organizations do not use big data. It is possible that they lack of knowledg expertise, the majority of organizatons will have data analysis positions within accounting and finance department, human resources department, business and administration department, information technology department, marketing, advertising and sales department, supply chain and operations department, research and development department, customer service department and other departments. So, future data analysis skill will need to used in different organizational departments.

However, publicly and privately owned for-profit organizations were more likely than government organizations to have data analysis positions in the marketing, advertising and sales function. Also, data analysis skills are required to different levels in any organizations , such as entry level, non-management / individual contributor level, mid-level management level, seniot management or executive level. The analyst, research analyst, market research analyst, scientist-based titles include: data scientists , research scientist, scientist, other descriptive titles include researcher, statistician, mathematician and other . So, data analysis positions will have many different skills to be selected to any one data analysis professional. For example, the data analysis professional can select either to learn the ability to interpret and communicate data analysis results skill or to learn how gathering or analyzing data skill. So, data analysis skill is not onlyone skill, it is more than one skill to let any one employee to select to learn.

Why do organizations need data analysis professionals? On workforce planning aspect, organizatons expect to let strategic direction and content of workforce needed for future business objectives easier, analyzing workforce: supply analysis, demand analsis and gap analysis more earier, developing action plan : recruiting and training plans to deal with gaps more easier, implementing action plan, monitoring, evaluating and revising plan more easier. So, organizations expect the data analysis professionsla can help them to solve these challenges, such as using of advanced technology solutons to integrate disparate planning sources; data availability and format; accessing to and understanding of the organization's data and analytics, developing business case to gain support from senior management and collaboration among HR staff, managers and executive easier. Future industries need data analysis professionals may include manufacturing health care and social assistance, scientific and technical service, finance and insurance, educational services , government agencies, retail trade, transportation and warehousing, construction, utilities, accomodation, and food services, waste management and remediation services, entetainment, and creation, real estate and rental and leasing , repair and maintenance, agriculture, forestry, fishing and hunting, personal and laundry services etc.

In conclusion, data analysis job need explains why future readiness and data analytical skills will be popular needed in globl labour market , due to these both skills are labour shortage and employers will need employees own big data readiness and data analytical both skills in order to win whose competitors more easier.

2.4 What are regional dynamic skills
of global labour market demand

Businessmen expect to improve better economic environment, they will prefer to recruit the most sought after skills of intelligent employees to bring positive beneficial impact to organizations. However, technology and digisation has had a significant influence on workers. Future globalization will trend digital economic development. Hence, it will influence workers' skills to be changed also. In fact, not all changes are positive because some workers will possible lose jobs, either due to new technology replaces their jobs or they lack enough effort to improve their skills in global digital economic labour market environment.

It brings this question: What are regional dynamic skills need whn digital busines environment is growing. In fact, organizations will continue to deal with skills shortages, labour markets across the global are continually changing. so, more employers and workers will need to adopt innovate working pattern, e.g. on call jobs, freelance jobs will grow popularly. The greater flexibility afforded to employ regardly.

Finally, digitalisation includes artificial intelligence, big data , online platforms. All these new technology will influence future employees how to worker. For example, they can apply online platform to work at home conveniently. So, they do not need to go to offices. They can finish their jobs and send to their employers by email easily. This kinds of job pattern can raise efficiencies and employers do not need go to offices often.

An important implication of innovating working which needs the employees who own digital skills in order to serve organizations more efficiently. So, employers are increasingly able to access demographics that were hitherto less active in labour markets. For example, future more women are joining the labour market because part time and self employment opportunities make it easier. This kinds of job pattern can raise efficiencies and employees do not need go to offices often.

An important implication of innovating working which needs the employees who own digital skills in order to serve organizations more efficiently. So, employers are increasingly able to access demographic that were hitherto less active in labour markets. For example, future more women are joining the labour market because part time and self employment opportunities make it easier to manage family with work life. So, digital skilling needs will cause many women lose jobs in possible. If the women lack digital job skills. Because high digital skill occupations need, like those requiring research, medical treatment and architectural design occupational digital skills are more common in the services sector, more women who own digital skill who can compete to win.

High digital skill occupations more easier than men because employers usually select female to do high skill occupations easier than make. However, if those professional service female employees can not learn how to apply digital skills to do these researchs medical treatmentm architectural design professional service jobs. Then, it is also different for these professional service femal employees to raise competition in global labour professional service market. So, these professional service female employees need to learn how to apply digital to do themselves jobs in future global professional service labour market. Otherwise, if the male professional service employees can attempt to learn how to apply digital skill to do themselves jobs in order to improve efficiencies and service performance to satisfy patients, such as medical service needs, school search service needs, construction firms' building needs. Then, the owning high digital technology skillful female employees will be more easier to find the professional service jobs which need digital skill more easier than the lacking digital skill female service professionals in future global digital service professional labour market.

On the other robotic communication skill need aspect, future employers expect workers to know how to communicate with robots to work efficiently in any working environment if the employers need robotc to serve their organizations. For example, communication between the robots on factory floors, and between people and robots could allow robots to start and stopr processes based on real-time conditions around them and alert people when there is a problem, so robots could increase their own efficiency if the workers could monitor themselves and determine when they needed maintenance; efficiency would also be improved if machines and robots could make production decisions on their own by. For example, ordering new suppliers when existing inputs into a production process run low. The increase in productivity of industrial robots will likely reduce the number of manual jobs on the shop floor.

At the same time, the increased output made possible by such robots will mean that manufacturers need more people in accounting, finance, sales, advertising and other roles. The increase in putput may also drive increased employment on manufacturers' supply chains. Hence, future employers expect to employ the workers who can know how to communicate with robots to work efficiently in order to raise productivity in any working environment. It means that it the worker can know how to control and communicate with the robots to work together in the team. Then, his/her communication and controlling robotic skill will help the organization's team to work efficiently and raise productivity in order to reduce time waste and human waste and resource waste considerately. So, future shortage of communication and controlling robotic skillful workers number will increase. It has much beneficial to workers who choose to attempt to learn how to communicate and control robots to work together in any working environment team efficiently. Because future employers will like to use robots to assist manual workers to attempt to raise productive efficiency in any working environment. So, the need of employees who know how to cooperate or communicate with robots whose talent skills will be useful to any future employers.

Future global business leaders will need human machine cooperation skill. This technological skill includes artificial intelligence (AI and internet of things (IOT), will reshape our working change. These machines will participate to our daily working environment. For instance, many business leaders agree that automated systems will free-up their time as well as they also believe they'll have more job satisfaction by offloading the tasks that they don't want to do to intelligent machines.

Therefore, future leaders will expect humans and machines can work as integrated teams within their organizaton in order to their workforce and machines are already successfully working this way. So, they need to expect future employees can know or learn how to work with automated systems more easily, because many jobs will be participated by automated systems, e..g simple accounting tasks, legal administration tasks etc. clerical tasks. They will be participated with (AI) technology, it learns how to cooperate with (AI) technology to finish simplt clerical tasks efficiently.

Future workers will need have autrmated system operational skills: They include that how to operate automated systems to free -up workers' time. Workers will need to learn how to operate automated system to better with healthcare tracking devices workers will need to learn how to operate automated systems to absord and manage information in completely different ways. Workers will need to learn how to operate automated systems of smart machines to work as admin. in any orking environments. Workers need be needed to learn how to operate (AI) automated machines to mak more accurate clerical tasks or efficiencies. So, the automated system (robotic) operational skillful workers' demand and number will increase.

In the future, employers need automated machine manufacturing and service with workers cooperation reasons include that clear protocols, will need to be established if autonomous machines fail. So, they need their workers to learn how to control and manage and communicate with autonomous machines skillfully. They believe move they depend upon technology, the more they'll have to lose in the event of a cyber attack. So, skillful workers are real required to let them to know how to cooperate with autonomous machines more efficiently and easily. Computers will need to be able to decipher between good and bad commands, so future employers have much chance to need the owning automated machines operating workers to assist any robots to make more accurate good or bad decision when robots and workers have need to make immediate judgement in their any related job responsibilites aspect.

Therefore, future owning automated machines operating workers' skillful level will be high. It bases on automated machine manufacturing environment trend factor. Finally, future technology will connect the right employee to the high task at the right time. It implies that when future global employers began to accept to apply robots to help them to raise any productivities efficiently. It will influence many manufacturing positions which need to employ any proficient skillful workers who own automated machines operational skills to know how to communicate or manage or control , even supervise any robots to work in teams in any organizational manufacturing environment efficiently.

In the future, employers also expect employees to own sufficient digital vision and strategic skills, manifest among other things. They can know how to apply data to demonstrate any senior support and sponsorship digital technological skill. They expect to reduce a skill gap and avoid a lack of employee buying and a workforce culture to change in their digital technologicl manufacturing organizations. Future employers also believe outdated technology that can't work fast enough, data overload, privary and security concerns. So, it explains why it is possible that future employers also need digital working environment and automated robots machines to attempt to achieve raising productive efficient aim.

Moreover, it also explains why digital transformation need will be raised. The reasons include: They feel digital technology can gain employees' buying in , making customer experience a boardroom concern, achieving fair compensation , training and goals and strategy achievement more easily, tasking senior leaders with digital working environment change putting policies and technology to support a fully remote, flexible workforce , empowering lines of team work more efficient, teaching all employees how to code/understanding how to adopt to work with automatic machines or rots in any team efficiently. So, automate machine can raise efficiency in manufacturing society.

In conclusion, in the future business society, employees need to be stronger human machine partnerships. So , future manufacturing or service industries will have digital technology and automated machine robotic technology to assist workers to work in any working environment efficiently. They expect digital technology and automated machine robotic technology anticipation to workers' daily jobs in order to bring positive impacting to the customer experience from business owners to decision makers in marketing, customer service, research and developmnt and finance etc. They also expect technological productivity can bring positive relationship between technology and workers emerging technologies' impact on business and the way workers and automated machine work together.

In the future whether in general organizations need what kinds of employees' skills, they expect employee individual own. It is one interesting question. The common skills that employees need to own in order to any duties to any organizational departments efficiently, e.g. human resource, marketing, administrative, logistic etc. different departments. For hospital, school, business, professional occupations etc. different organizations. Whether future school ought implement one system educational method to teach different common skills to students in order to let them to leave schools to jobs more easier.

Future employers need to create new technologies including automation and algorithms, in order to create new high quality jobs and improve the job quality and productivity of the existing work of human employees in any organizations, e.g. accounting department will need intelligence (AI) to assist account clerks to do simple repeating accounting job tasks in order to share their work load and raise performance efficiency or legal organizations will need (AI) to assist law clerks to do simple repeating legal draft or legal document revising job tasks . All future general clerical jobs will apply (AI) technological tools to assist human to job, it will produce a comprehensive platform for managing workforce change.

Hence, human manual(employees) need to learn how to adopt (AI) job participation to assist them to do different kinds of simple clerical jobs in any organizational administrative departments . They , clerical employees or white color workers need to learn how manage or dominate (AI) tool to improve job performance to be better. However, (AI) administrative workforce change, it is not only one kind of job automation change role in any physical offices. It influences future administrative clerks need change a more flexible manner, utilizing remote staffing beyond physical offices and decentralization of operations organizational workforce change.

Instead of (AI) participation to administrative job aspect, (AI) will also participate to manufacturing industry environment aspect, a new human-machine manufacturing workforce change will exist to any factories, warehouses working environment. Scientists predict that in present an average of 71% of total task hours across the industries are performed by humans, compared a 29% by machines. In this average is expected to have shifted to 58% task hours performed by humans and 42% by machines. In fact, nowadays, in terms of total working hours, no work task was yet estimated to be predominantly performed by a machine or an algorithm (AI). But, this picture is predicted to have somewhat changed with machines and algorithms (AI) on average increasing their contribution to specific tasks by 57% . For example, in the future, 62% of organization's information and data processing and information search and transmission tasks will be performed by machines compared to 46% today.

Therefore, these high technological skillful job change will bring negative influence to some demotive-skillful or low skillful labors to be dismissed, if they can not upgrade or raise or reskillgul their skill level to improve their analytical thinking , technology design and programming skills to cooperate with (AI) tools to work efficiently together in any organizational manufacturing or offie work environment. Because it will have many employers apply (AI) automation tools to participate with blue -color or whiate -color workers' tasks in order to raise efficiencies or improve performance in any working environment. So, it is right time to young or mid age employees need to upskill and/or reskill their rihgt type of skills to prepare future technology risch work environment changeing needs.

Future technological advances will permit an increasing number of tasks traditionally performed by humans to become automated. It seems that , such automation focused primarily on routine tasks, e.g. clerical work, bookkeeping, basic paralegal work and reporting etc. However, with the advent of big data, artificial intelligence (AI), the internet of things and ever-increasing computing power , i.e. the digital revolutions, non-routine tasks are also increasingly likely to become automated. For example, the recent development in robotics and 3D printing allow firms in advanced economies to locate production closer to domestic markets in fully aumomated factories. As a result, the future strongest incentive to automate because of their relatively higher labour costs will be reduced, when production automated will bring the negative influence to dismiss some foolish or low produtive or low skill workers , the owning high automated productive skillful workers will replace the low productive skillful workers in any factories' manufacturing environments. So, technological progress participates to raise quantity of jobs will cause result in significant job losses to low skillful workers. Because future employers will need many high automated productive employees to help them to cooperate with (AI) automated machine to work together efficiently. For example, many proportion of occupations at high risk is greatest in Germany and lowest in Korea, these countries organizations will accept to spend technology investments and education of workers to prepare future automatability manufacturing development successfully.

However, future automatability manufacturing development will bring technological unemployment in possible, due to workers need to adjust to the challenge of automation by switching tasks. Thus, preventing technological unemployment, also technological change does not just destroy jobs, but also generates new roles through its effect on productivity and the demand for new technologies. For example, it has been estimated that, for each high tech-job created in the industries , such as computing equipment or electrical machinery, some 4.9 % additional jobs are created for lawyers, taxi, drivers and waites in the local economy (Moretti, 2011).

Therefore, automated will also influence service industries' job nature change, e.g. taxi drivers need to apply (AI) automated machines to assist them to drive their taxis. When the passenger tells the taxi driver where he/she wants to go. Then, the (AI automated machine will follow the GPS road direction map to be indicated how to drive the taxi to go to the destination automatically . So, future taxi driver is one assistance role to assist the (AI) automated driving tool to dominate the (AI) tool to drive the taxi to catch the passenger to arrive the destination safety in the short time in possible. For another example, future restaurant waiters will need (AI) automated machines's assistance to help them to deliver or dispatch any foods and soft drinks to send to the identified eater's table carefully in accurate and efficient service performance way from the kitchen, in especially in the busy time and many people are sitting in the large size restaurant environment. So, future, waiter roles will be the leader , they need to manage or control or supervise the (AI) robotics how to make decisions to arrange to dispatch which foods or soft drinks to the different tables in preference immediately. Also, future law clerks need to supervise or manage the law robotics how to help them to make decisions to do revision or draft or filing legal tasks in preference in order to avoid any typing words are mistaken to type on computers or revised draft in wrong way to assist manual legal clerks' mistaken words are appearanced on any legal documents. So, the law clerk future role will be the trainer role , he/she eeds to teacher the robots how to check any words, e.g. grammers to correct them to be right grammers, or giving the accurate revision legal documents' instruction to let the legal robots to know how to revise each legal draft to prove whether which part of the legal draft will have wrong to be needed to revise.

In conclusion, future many manual workers' service or manfacturing job natures will become automated assistance to robotics. So, employees need to upgrade their skills in order to adopt new technological work nature change.

Reference
Moretti, E. (2011) local labor market in O, Ashentelter and D. Card (eds.) handbook of labor economics, Elsevier, North Halland.

IV

Social environment changing factor create talent human

Nowadays we tend to think about social and digital technology more from a personal or consumer perspective than their business or professional applications, but as the Digital Era continues to progress, many of technology's most profound impacts are likely to be in the world of work. In addition to changes in product and business development, knowledge management, data analysis, and other operational processes, transforming talent management will be a key priority for organizations striving to be employers of choice.

● Digital technology encourages to create talent human

Why does digitial technology encourage to create talent human or excite human to learn new things ? The human capital implications of social and digital technologies impact virtually everyone, regardless of the type of organization they work for, their profession, their functional area, or their career stage. That means that the talent management functions in all organizations, as well as the professionals who staff and lead them, have a critical role to play in ensuring the efficient and effective transition and transformation from Industrial Era models and processes to their Digital Era upgrades.

It's no surprise that talent management has already become more "high tech." Many employment related activities have been digitized, and there has been a corresponding increase in employee self-service. It's important to remember, however, that digitization is not the same thing as digital engagement, and that the rise of "high tech" solutions doesn't necessitate the loss of a "high touch" approach to managing an organization's human assets. Transforming talent management requires digitization, to be sure, but it also involves leveraging social and digital technologies in ways that promote and enhance communication, collaboration, and engagement - not just between an employee and the organization, but between and among employees themselves.

Talent Acquisition

The logical place to start when talking about the impact of social and digital technologies on talent management is talent acquisition, where the greatest advances have been made. Anyone who has searched and applied for jobs in the past 10 years is very familiar with how technology has transformed the application process, which in most organizations (and virtually all large ones) is now almost completely digitized and automated. However, there are other ways in which social and digital technologies are impacting talent acquisition that may not be as well-known or commonly understood. Social media sites in particular (such as Facebook, YouTube, and Pinterest) are a great way to promote an employer's brand and offer realistic previews of work life, people and culture in organizations. Online games and simulations can also be used to get a sense of what working for an organization would be like, and give organizations themselves an opportunity to determine if a prospective candidate would be a good cultural fit and potentially successful.

On organizational working environment aspect, some employers are recognizing the value of digital alumni networks or communities to maintain strong relationships with former employees. One of the primary motivations for doing this is that the employees may return one day and/or make referrals to or from their personal and professional networks. Similarly, talent networks enable organizations to establish and maintain relationships with professionals in key areas like IT and engineering, even when there isn't a current opportunity to have those folks be a part of the organization. Moreover, social media can bring positive influence to impact organizations to encourge employees to attempt or feel needs to learning new things for their tasks needs. Due to social media has actually transformed every stage of the recruiting process in significant ways - so much so that the traditional recruiting funnel can be recast in "social" terms. At the top of the funnel are activities like social advertising (i.e., placing job ads on social networks like Facebook), social sourcing (i.e., searching for candidates who meet certain criteria on networks like LinkedIn), and social referrals (i.e., having current employees share position openings with their online personal and professional networks). And at the bottom of the funnel is social screening (i.e., reviewing a candidate's public activity in social networks to identify potential hiring risks).

● Learning management is needed to feel needs to any organizations

Learning management is probably the another most advanced area when it comes to adopting and adapting to new technologies. As with recruiting and other processes, the initial advances are in the area of digitization, with social software applications evolving next. One of the obvious digital impacts is the increased use of elearning and online learning platforms with self-paced study. There are also countless instructional videos on the web, both free and fee-based, that address a virtually unlimited range of topics. And we can't forget MOOCs - massive, open, online courses - which have proliferated in the past couple of years. Finally, many organizations have also started to leverage tablets and other mobile devices for learning, as well as using simulations and games to help employees develop specific skills. In addition to offering training through a variety of multimedia channels, organizations are increasingly using a range of digital tools for assessing employees' skills. They're also allowing employees to play an enhanced role in identifying their key skill sets and training needs, and can even have them create their own learning and development plans. Allowing employees to take a more active role in their own learning and skills management enables organizations to develop and maintain a more complete and accurate knowledge and skills database, which in turn enables them to maximize the value of the workforce in which they've already invested.

1. Formal learning management systems and platforms are also beginning to incorporate social technologies in a variety of ways. Promoting connections and interactions among participants, as well as with the instructor, can enhance the learning experience both during and after a course. Creating course-based cohorts that allow people to continue to interact with each other via a digital community - even when their shared learning experience is face-to-face - can promote both knowledge transfer and retention, in addition to increasing commitment and engagement through interpersonal connections.

2. Informal learning - which is now also referred to as social learning - is greatly enhanced by social technologies as well. In fact, this is probably the greatest opportunity and area of growth for organizations of all types and sizes. Through private social networks, intranets and other internal platforms that have incorporated social technology elements, organizations are better able to facilitate employee learning as they perform their job duties and complete work activities. Along with the networks themselves, features like advanced search, identified subject matter experts, digital communities of practice, wikis and more enable employees to access and learn from colleagues who are not just next door or down the hall, but even in another city, state or country!

As organizations move forward with leveraging technology to enhance learning initiatives, it will become increasingly important for them to address issues related to digital literacy and digital competencies. For the past several decades we've generally taken what I refer to as an LIY, or Learn It Yourself, approach to digital knowledge and skills. Although organizations may invest in teaching someone how to use a specific application related to their job, they make virtually no investment in helping individuals learn how to use general digital tools like Microsoft Office and even email. Left to their own devices, most people - and I include myself in this group- are much less efficient and effective at using these tools than they could or should be. As our tools get even more sophisticated, we need the foundational knowledge and skills to be able to use them well - and this foundation should probably be provided via more formal training. In other words, many people need to be "taught how to learn" in the Digital Era. If organizations aren't going to provide the formal training workers need to do that, it's probably in an individual's best interests to pursue those kinds of development opportunities on their own.

● What are social influences on human behavior when talent human number increases?

Social Influences on Human Behavior Because human beings are social and learn from observation rather than depending entirely on instinct, almost all aspects of human psychology and behavior are socially influenced. Languages, modes of dress, gender roles and avoided taboos are all agreed upon at a group level and form the basis of culture. What are the characteristics of social change? Small-scale and short-term changes are characteristic of human societies, because customs and norms change, new techniques and technologies are invented, environmental changes spur new adaptations, and conflicts result in redistributions of power. This universal human potential for social change has a biological basis.

This universal human potential for social change has a biological basis. It is rooted in the flexibility and adaptability of the human species—the near absence of biologically fixed action patterns (instincts) on the one hand and the enormous capacity for learning, symbolizing, and creating on the other hand. Because human beings are social and learn from observation rather than depending entirely on instinct, almost all aspects of human psychology and behavior are socially influenced. Languages, modes of dress, gender roles and avoided taboos are all agreed upon at a group level and form the basis of culture.

On conclusion, when one country can create many talent human, e.g. students, workers. Then they can bring more positive attribution to help or assist themselve country to develop rapidly. Consequently, the country's economic growth speed will be rapid. So, I believe that it has close relationship between economy growth and talent human number to any countries in nowadays societies.

IBM founder successful factor

When "IBM" Micro soft firm is building its computer business in US in the beginning. It must encounter much problems, e.g. introducing and persuading computer users to accept and feel what the IBM software products can bring advantages to them to compare other kinds of similar computer software or desktop products when they turn on their computers to use at homes or offices or libraries or anywhere. So, IBM must need to spend much time to let them to accept to use its software products and computers in computer market. Why do they must need to buy IBM micro soft to use? It is one influential question to need to solve their psychological problem.

IN the beginning, because it is a kind of new software product invention in the beginning. Desktop computer is not very popular to be used in global. So, it brings the competition is serious between IBM and Big Apple both computer brands. When Big Apple computer is the main competitor to threaten Micro Soft exists in this computer market. How can Bill Gates IBM founder attract many Big Apple computer users to choose to buy its any software and desktops to use in the beginning.. Because Big Apple brand was popular to be accepted to use its computers and software products by computer users in the beginning. So, Micro soft IBM must need to spend much time to let Big Apple computer clients to accept to use its any software or desktop computers products when laptops did not been invented before 2000 yr. So, Big Apple is one monopoly computer firm in computer market in the 1980 year. I shall indicate these important factors to explain how IBM can develop its computer market in success as below:

Bill Gates , IBM founder is one computer university student, although he did not graduate, because he felt his software invention can bring high technology to help humans to apply computer " word" software to replace hand writing conveniently. So, any office administrative staffs won't need to spend long time to write any documents or apply typewriters to type. Hence, Micro soft, IBM " word" software invention can help office jobs raise efficiency and documents productivities as well as reduced staffs number in office because computer typing speed is rapid to compare handwriting or typing machines. Employers can pay less salary to employ less office workers when they had learnt how to apply " word" software to do any clerical tasks. So, it seems that Big Gates can tough computer users' hopeful needs in offices or homes. So, global offices start to apply computers and Micro soft " word" software to do their administrative tasks and students and teachers can apply this kind of clerical software to do their homework and teaching tasks in schools and homes or libraries. It seems customers number will increase and Micro soft, IBM can attract many Big Apple computer clients for long time.

Intellectual means that to students with exceptional abilities in one or more of the learning areas(i.e. English, the arts, health and physical education, learning languages, mathematics, and statics , science and technology). Creativity means to students with general creative abilities as evidences in their abilities to problem –find and problem –solve , and their innovative thinking and productivity as well as social or leadership means that students with interpersonal and intra-personal abilities and qualities, which enable them to act in leadership roles. However, these are not the important personal characteristics factors to influence Bill Gates personal success. I assume that he can not achieve his software and computer invention in success if he lacks hard working attitude and learning any new technological knowledge attitude, even he own talent, creative and leadership abilities because one successful scientist must need to spend long time research tasks and he also needs to pursue any new technological knowledge to help him to solve any research problems. Otherwise, he must forget his scientific research when he feel difficulties and disappointment when he encounters any problems in his researching process. Hence, I feel that hard working and pursuing learning is the important factors to influence Bill Gates success. In fact, Bill Gates individual success. It is not only his talent and creative factor. I believe his hard work attitude and learning any new technological knowledge mind factor is more important to compare his personal characteristics. His hard working behavior on computer software research aspect, it can bring more influential to his final invention in success more than his talent and creative natural ability. So, I feel his non-natural effort, such as his hardworking and learning new technological knowledge and research attitude is his important factor to influence his software invention and laptop and desktop invention in success.

How did Bill Gates grow up? His father is one lawyer. So, it proved that he can not learn any scientific knowledge from his father teaching, he has only technological teacher can teach him some computer science basic concept knowledge in school. Hence, Bill Gates family is not a scientific background family. He may own creative and talent abilities to bring his success. When he left his university. Then he attempts to find or discover any new computer knowledge when he does any computer scientific investigation at homes or lab. However, he must encountered any several scientific research fails before he achieved the Micro software " word" software invention and then different types of desktops, even nowadays, laptops , smart phones technological communication products invention royalties in global computer market. So, Bill Gates is not only one successful inventor, he is also one successful businessman. He can have good leadership ability to lead his whole different departments to work efficiently and improve the best sale service performance and the most satisfactory products productive qualities to let his clients to feel habitually. So, his hard working factor can influence his whole IBM success till today.

However, Bill Gates is as a diligent learner. His early age became a diligent learner. He read the Word Book. Encyclopedia series start to finish. His parents also encouraged his appetite for reading by paying for any book, he wanted. Knowledge can help or hinder creativity. One needs to know enough about a field to move forward into more creative ways of thinking. So, none any ones can control or threaten Bill to stop to learn any new knowledge easily. His unique charters can influence his success, such as he is not limited to a willingness to overcome obstacles, willingness to take risks , willingness to tolerate ambiguity and self-efficacy. For example, he left his university to learn computer science, his reason ensures not due to his lazy or feeling failure to graduate. I ensure that he feel he has responsibility to invent one kind of computer software to attribute global office or home computer users to use and to let them feel this kind of software can raise office efficiency and productivity and it can bring rapid typing speed to let students or white color workers to finish their home work or office tasks in short time. The important factor is his confidence , he believed that he is the only inventor to invent this kind of unique software to attribute to any computer users to use in success. In fact, his confidence can help him to achieve his dream and earn much money and successful feeling and social high class position in our societies.

He also own unique personal characteristics, such as he have confidence to change accustomed or conventional thinking to unconventional thinking to bring human's new hope when one day any computer users buy his software or desktops or laptops to use. So, in the right place , at the right time with the right set of skill, all of these natural environment advantages can help him to create invention success. In the 1980 year, computer industry is needed to research any creative software products or desktops products from any one inventor.

By the late 1970s, the computing giant IBM had plans for marketing a personal computer for home use. They approached Microsoft to develop the standard operating system for their home computer models. Gates and Allen then went out and purchased for $50,000 an operating system called Q-Dos, which had been developed by Seattle Computer. Q-Dos Was compatible with the Intel processor that IBM intended to use. The two then adapted Q-Dos system and presented it to IBM. Money magazine quoted Gates as recalling. (July 1986).

It can give one good business environment to help Bill to build his computer software and computer products sale business in success at the moment. So, it is one right time to let Bill have chance to be one computer software and desktop inventor, and US is the only one country to provide any scientific resource to let him, Bill, American to research as well as there is lack any computer scientists at the time. So, the right time and right place and right skill environments can help Bill to be one successful inventor. All of these factors are external environment factors to assist him to carry on his computer scientific research tasks in success. If he born in one developing country, such as India or China. I believe that he can not be one successful inventor in possible because these both countries can not provide good technological resources to support him to carry on his computer science research at the moment. So, external environment factor will influence him to be one successful inventor in success in the past.

Conclusion, IBM success is due to the founder, Bill Gates whose hard work and acceptable to attempt to learn any new technological knowledge personal attitude more than creative, talent factors. Moreover, the right time, right place and right skillful external environment factors can assist or help him to become the first technological inventor easily. If he born in one low technological resources and skills supplying country, his country lacks enough money and computer technological professor to teach his computer basic knowledge and research expenses. I believe that his invention will have encounter fail in possible. So, external resource supplying environment factor as well as his personal abilities and invention attitude factor will influence his final invention in success.

Amazon ecommerce founder successful factors

Nowadays, we are encountering digital age period. Many customers choose to apply websites and mobile apps to buy their products. So,many merchants also choose online e-commerce channel to build online purchase platform to raise its competitive ability in online e-commerce market.

So, customers can apply mobile apps or merchants themselves websites to buy any products in any time and any places conveniently.

However, in electronic (ecommerce) industry, Amazon is the global largest online retail delivery provider. It sells different kinds of products from internet, e.g. books, electronic products, music, movie Cd, DVD, magazine, garden and homw useful tools, children toys, computer,

software, even, cars from online channel to global online shoppers. So, there ate many online buyers choose to buy any products from Amazon web services middle channel. In fact, its products prices can be low, a wide selection, ease website use and convenience to meet all of its customers' needs in one virtual store. So, it can still own the high share market in online retail delivery service industry. I shall indicate that Amazon successful factors as below:

It has a clear aim or mission. It's mission is to be Earth's most customer-centric company , where people can find and discover anything , they want to buy online. So, it will gather data ro analyze whether why and how customers will select to buy the kinds of products from internet. Why do its customers forget to choose to buy any products from shops and they choose Amazon to buy their preferable products from online? I believe that it has these characteristics to attract them such as:

It can provide return after sale services within the reasonable time when the customer feels that he does not need to use the product or feels unsatisfactory to the product, then he can return the product to Amazon and Amazon must refund money to him as well as it can provide free charge of grocery delivery service to every customer home. Instead of these attractive service, it also began to enter publishing market. In July 2002, Amazon started offering services to website developers, marketings its kindle

product, aimed at capturing the publishing market for digital books, then it can sell paper books from online channel. It aims to let readers can choose to either download to read ebooks from its website or borrow ebooks to read from its electronic library or paid visa to print paper books to deliver their paper books to their homes conveniently. So, readers feel that they can enter Amazon publish website to choose any interesting books to buy or borrow to read , they do not need to go to book stores or libraries.It is Amazon's competitive and attractive and unique strengths to build its customers on this online retail market.

On its organization mamagement aspect, it has one effective and efficient management strategy. It has a good CEO manages his e-commerce business. Bezos has been chairman of the board of Amazon , since he founded the compnay in 1994. Amazon has a limitless stock on hand at all time, it enables Amazon to collect high margins when providing low prices, and lets customers to feel consideration every second. So, when the customers feel any enquiries, his customer service team members can apply its intra website email message channel to send email to answer his enquiries when they enter Amazon intra-website email message channel to send email to ask them any enquiries and they can reponse their enquiries immediately in any time or they can phone to Amazon customer service hotline to enquiry them directly. So, its customer service staffs can answer their enquiries either by phone or email communication in short time rapidly. They
won't delay to response their enquiries to avoid they feel worry or unhappy or complain. So, efficient customer service performance can help it to satisy its customer service needs and build good customer service relationship and repeat purchase chance will increase also.

However, global online retail marketplace is expanding rapidly. So, Amazon will have many new or potential online retail competitors, if it neglected to improve its strategy to adapt every online customer individual need or purchase taste, due to customers' purchase need will often change, such as price demand, product delivery time demand, customer service demand etc. spects. So, Amazon needs have different market strategies in different time in order to attract customers' choices in different economic environment, if it hoped to keep online retail leader position.
For example, how to encourage or raise customers' online purchase desires when economy is poor environment. When many people loss jobs, due to many businesses liquidate and loss many clients. So, they need to dismiss many staffs. Then, in society, many families will reduce their consumption desires because their parents loss jobs. So, Amazon needs improve its strategies on above different aspects in order to attract or persuade them to spend much time on internet shopping activities.

Instead of organization management aspect and customer service aspect, the other critical success factors for developing an e-business strategy to Amazon, they may include: How to apply network technology to keep long term close relationship between Amazon its e-commerce organization, online customers, partners, stakeholders and product suppliers. It is very important to influence Amazon's success, because Amazon , such as the e-business delivery service provider will loss the kinds of product sale chance, if the product providers dislike its sale delivery service or feel satisfactory to
its sale strategy or promotion methods or when its online sale delivery service can not let its customers feel its online sale delivery to be satisfactory. Hence, online sale delivery service performance is very important to influence Amazon's success.

Moreover, in its business model, Amazon.com also needs have these key succes factors. They may include: Building strong brand name location, because when online shoppers can remember its brand or loyalty easily when it is famous. Then they won't choose any online retail delivery providers to replace its delivery service easily. So, building one famous and confident online retail delivery service provider loyalty or brand , it can help Amazon to influence many online shoppers have confidence to choose its online retail delivery service in the first time. When they can often remember Amazon and feel it is only one online retail delivery serivce provider, the repeat online purchase chance will also increase, due to they only choose to click on its website to choose any kinds of products to buy more easily.

So, Amazon.com's marketing strategy is needed to design to strengthen the Amazon brand name, increases customer traffic to the Amazon.com web sites, builds customer loyalty, encourages repeat purchases or attracts them to clicks on its websites again to develop incremental products and retail delivery service revenue opportunities. Also, how to design its efficient products delivery value to let product buyers to feel. This factor is important to influence Amazon's products delviery service in success in online
retail delivery service market. Moreover, Amazon publish service also needs to build attractive reading feeling to let readers to satisfy its reading provision needs to replace book stores or libraries.

On conclusion, Amazon ought need to continue to change its marketing strategies in order to adapt to its online retail product delivery service changes as well as lets they believe that it is one online customer care product delviery service provider to comapre other online retail delivery service providers, if it hopes to keep its online retail relviery provider top leader position in this e-commece market.

Successful president personal characteristics

Every country must have one president, he/she needs to manage his/her country to keep the crime ratio reduces to let its citizen feel to live safely and build good economic environment to let buisnessmen have any kinds of business chance to do their import and export business, provides enough education resource to let young people have chance to learn etc. different aspects social responsibilities. So, one successful president must also be one successful leader, he/she is such as one CEO , he/she needs to know how to organize his/her organization to achieve the most efficient and the most effective performance. It brings this question: What are the president personal characteristics, he/she must need to own in order to achieve above

any one responsibilites successfully. I shall indicate these similar personal characteristics to every president, he/she ough own as below:

What is a great leader or CEO or president their similar personal characteristics? What is a popular leader, president, CEO reasonable performance? Are they the either same or some difference? Are they the result of the same or different factors? I feel that their same personal characteristics have these similar characteristics, such as they can create

themselves own greatness, has long been challengedby scholars from diverse disciplines who analyze leadership appeal and performance into broad impersonal forces and social -structural factors. Such as president case, if he/she hopes that his/her citizen feels he/she has enough abilities to solve any social problems. He/she must have abilities to know or evaluate

whether which kind(s) of social problem(s), he/she must need to solve in order to avoid this social problem continues grow to cause more difficulties. For example, if the country has many young people feel housing supplying number is not enough or young people feel difficulty to find jobs to do. Then the president needs to find what the factors cause these both social problems to young people. It is due to many young people are low education level, but there are many employers need high education level workers more than the low education level workers. Then, the factor ought be due to their low education level causes they feel difficulty to find jobs in job market. Then, the president ought concentrate on providing more skillful education to let these young people to learn different kinds of skills, e.g. computer, building, accounting etc. skills in order to them to apply their skills to find any jobs more easily. They feel housing supplying number is shortage, the solutions may seek new lands, or refill sea to increase land on sea, or rebuilding the old building etc. different methods to increase more lands to build more houses. So, one successful president could analyze whether these two social problems , which one is more important and young people hope to solve in the short time as well as he/she ought attempt to find the effective solution(s) to solve these both social problems within one to three years.

Because long time solution, it will cause young people feel satisfactory and complaint government. Because one succcessful president needs have good analytical abilites to judge whether next steps , he she needs to do in order to achieve the best solution.

Can these phenomena of greatness and appeal among political leaders or president be analyzed in psychological terms? They ought have these personal characteristics as below:

Leader characteristics means that the leader's personal appeal and performancewhen structural and traditional factors are held constant.He is set apart from ordinaryof personality to posses a certain quality of personality from ordinary men and treated as owed with supermatural , superhuman, or least specifically exceptional powers or qualities. Because president's

responsibility is different to CEO. One CEO only needs to manage his firm, it concerns to solve any firm's internal strategic challenges.Otherwise one president needs to manage whole country. It concerns to solve any social problems. So, I believe that one president's responsiblity must have more than one CEO's responsibility. He needs to concern how to let citizen feels satisfactory to live in this country. Otherwise, they will feel satisfactory to complain their government, even they can perform anti-threat government behaviors, e.g. many Hong Kong, France, US,UK people are walking on the road, or young people damage any roads or shops facilities. Their behaviors can perform their unsatisfactory emotion to let HK government to know. So, one president must need to supervise his government departments, e.g. education, transport, house and building and land, police force, administrative, leisure, environment protection etc.

How they can implement the most effective strategies to let the country's citizen feel satisfactory to live in the country. It seems that the successful factor is that how to avoid young or old
citizen feels unsatisfactory to complain or do anti-social damage behaviors. If one country have one long time anti-social damage behaviors, then it will bring long time unsatisfactory feeling or negative emotions to itself citizen and they will feel that the president's performance is poor and even he/she needs to be dismissed in possible.

So, one successful president needs to know whether what the social suitation or what social needs to its citizen are. In fact, any country's young people must consider education, jobs, living needs as well as old people must consider retirement, leisure needs both aspects. So, these departments' responsibilities are ususally much to compare other departments in government organization , such as education, house and land and building, labor departments because these are every people's basic living needs. For example, living and jobs must be needed to eveyr young people. They must need money and house. Otherwise, old people do not want to work, they must need have good retirement welfare to compare young people when they are facing old age. So, one successful president needs have abilities to solve these social problems if he /she hopes that his/her country has many young and old people like him or her to be their president.

Every country needs one effective election to elect themselves president. So, one president needs have good influential ability to persuade his/her citizen to elect him/her in order to he/she can do this president position. During this election process, he/she must need have good leadership abilities to lead his/her election team to know how to use what
methods to advertise and build good image or loyalty to let his/her citizen believes and have confidence that he/she can do this president position to satisfy their any needs in society. So, how to lead his/her team in order to achieve the high vote number to support his/her president election, this leadership ability factor will influence him/her to be succeeded in the time of selection. If he/she can not lead his/her selection team how to persuade citizen to believe he/she has ability to manage their country, then he/she will have high chance to let many citizen to vote him/her and then he/she can not do this president position. So, the president election participant personal leadership ability will influence whether he/she can succeed to do this president position in the president election process. So, leadership ability is very important to cause anyone to be president in success in the
election process.

Successful fiction author personal characteristics

In publishing industry, there are many different kinds of topics to let authors to write. However, in author career, it has two both topics choices, either ficition or non-fiction. So, fiction authors must need have more creative mind to write any horror, science, sad, happy, fun etc. stories. Otherwise, non-fiction authors, e.g. teaching writers , they must not need more creative mind , because they only need to apply theories, e.g. economy, accounting, law, science, engineering etc. different subjects to support their conclusion
to write any teaching books. Mostly technical writing does have something to teach writers, particularly in the areas of organizational behaviors and research skills, it has little relationship to the ability to write a novel , such as creative mind ability. So, one fiction author must need have good creative mind to compare one non-fiction author. It is the personal characteristics between fiction and non-fiction author.

Every writer has his or her own experience, and every writer has his or her own ideas about writing, so what any one writer may think
can only go so far.But there are some basic principles that seem to hold in vast majority of cases to every fiction author, they have these same characteristics. However, to be one successful ficition author, he also needs have these personal characteristics, instead of creative ability as below:

In english novel, it must need have a theory, a conviction, a consciousness of itself to let readers themselves to make choice and comparison, because one attractive english novel must need have special theory to let readers to feel the author's creative mind to let readers to choose to read his/her story book more easily, before reader needs to spend time to choose which english novel to read.For exmaple, Hart Pover had about seven series. It can attract many readers to continue to read it. The reasons are due to this story author can touch readers' interesting to want to know that whether how the every story will continue happen in next step.So, when they read the serie one. They will hope this author continues to write the serie two in short time because they hope to know whether what will happen in this story step two. So, it explains that whether the story is attractive, it is the important factor to influence readers continue to read the author's story books. If the story is bore and it can not influence readers feel fun to know whether what the story will continue happen.

Then, it is difficult to influence the prior readers continue to pursue to read this next serie story. They will lose story pursuring desire

to continue to buy this author's next serie book to read. So, story content is very important to influence the readers' interest. If they

can feel the story is theory and fun and exciting when they read any stage in the story content of every chapter. Then, there are many

last serie readers , they will also feel reading need to read this story next serie, even more series. So, creative mind is very important

to influence the story author's success.

However, preparing a fiction to write, any fiction author needs follow these steps to prepare to write before. They may include:

Deciding on the idea(s) for your book, doing the research and creating an outline or structure for your book. Because one novel, you need

an ideastrong enough to carrythe reader through 300-400pages, and most ideas arenot that strong. You can combine more than one idea to produce multiple story-lines, and some authors have been very successful doing that, but the sum totalhas to be strong enough.How long would it take me to tell this story, and what kind of depth do I need from my characters to tell it?

I feel that one fiction author is similar to one non-fiction author, he needs to do the research. For example, one law or criminal author, he needs familiar these topics. If he has a background in the law or crimoinal investigation, or a particularfield of science. Then he can do less research tasks. Otherwise, when one fiction author plans to write one horror story. If he does not research any horror story authors' books to compare whether what their horror story contents are different and what the main contents which can attract or influence the readers to choose to read their books. So, he can compare some horror fictions whether what their attractive contents or

non-attractive contents are in order to avoid to create the non-attrative contents to let readers to read. So, researhing to read any last fictions , it will help the fiction author to avoid to write the bore contents to let readers to read in his new creative fiction.

The another obstacle to threaten any fiction author to be popular. It is how to discover the opinions between the living world and dream world to let readers to feel. It is one important factor to influence the fiction author's success. Because it is absolute that any fiction must be creative and dream. So, any readers will need to feel they are entering the dream world more than living world when they read any fiction or story. So, if the writer can give the living world actual opinions to let readers feel that it is possible to occur when they enter the dream world in their reading process. Then, it will bring exiciting feeling to let them to feel that this story seems to be occur in living world in possible. Hence, if the story' s content can let readers to feel it is not dream and it will occur in their living world in possible. Then, it will persuade them to continue to read again.

Successful scientistcs personal characteristics

Science job is exciting and fun and every scientist ought like this kind of job. Usually, scientists need to often research in lab. They

need to face unlimited fails in their research process and they also need to investigate and experiment, it aims to attempt to find any
not found discoveries to continue to carry on science research tasks. So, patience and continue researching and without fear failure attitude
must need to any one scientist. I shall indicate some similar characteristics to any one successful scientist as below:

Science training and experiment experiences are important factor to influence any one scientist's success , because any one scientist must need
to be taught to learn any kinds of science knowledge, such as space, earth, computer, biology, chemical, ocean, animal , engine etc. different kinds of science knowledge when they are university student. So, owning science training background must be one main factor to influence whether their science research can succeed. But, they can not also neglect the experiment experiences, because if they can have more times of experiment chances to let them to attempt to know whether why their every time experiment is possible failure. Then, they can improve their next experiment to avoid the errors occur again.

Learning and seeking or pursuring any new ideas that is also important to influence any one scientist's success. Because any new ideas will have chance to help them to solve the last or prior any problems. If they dislike to accept any new ideas or attempting to seek or discover any new ideas. Then, they will feel more difficulties to solve their any scientific problems and they can not achieve the researching success. So, learning and
seeking or pursuring any new ideas attitude can help the scientist to increase scientific research succeess chance.

They need have scientifical moral or ethic responsibility. The moral issue will influence any scientist's success. For medical science example,
when one biological cell engineering scientist does not consider moral issue. He does the experiment to attempt to apply pig cell to put in human body.
He aims to pursue whether what change to the person when he owns pig cell in his body. Although, he argues that this experiment can help human
to discover any new medicine to fight any diseases. But, in fact, his experiment can bring negative moral behavior to cause the person to die in possible. So, the death risk is high, even legal system is accept that it is legal experiment in the country. So, one successful scientist ought own high level moral standard to carrying on any experiments in his science research career any time.

Learning to enjoy the process of writing and presenting. Because every scientist needs to write any research to let anyone to know. So, he
must need to enjoy writing and then present hie presentation to let anyone to know his successful research. One attractive presentation must need
good writing skill to let anyone to understand how and why the experiment can succeed and what the experiment can attribute to human to enjoy. It is
one enjoyable new to anyone. So, if the scientist feel bore to write and present his final research result when he believe that his scientifical research is successful. Then, his research can not persuade anyone to believe his attribution is worth in society.

Finally, any scientist needs have much confidence. Because one confident scientist can have much successful chance to carry on any experiments. So, his successful chance time will be shorten. Otherwise, one lacking confident scientist will need long time to achieve his experiment in success because he lacks confidence will influence his experiment performance and judgement brings more errors. Then , long time experiment can also increase.

Internet method improve employee performance

Why do we improve to improve internet technology? What long term social benefits will benefits if scientists can improve internet speed and reseach any information function ? I shall research these questions to give suggestion as below:

Why does internet improvement make life better? Internet of Things Benefits In short, the scale of change that IoT technology offers can be scary. At the same time, the benefits of a well-executed IoT strategy can be more need for an organization: Safety, Comfort, Efficiency. Also, the Internet offers teens the ability to make friends with peers with whom they would not otherwise connect. With pop culture deteriorating into many distinct subcultures, teens' interests are more variable than they have ever been.With internet communication, employees can effortlessly communicate with one another at anytime from anywhere in the world. This allows employees situated in different parts of the world to give their opinion and voice their concerns. Through internet access, individuals in developing countries are able to gain access to more of the modern economy. With internet connectivity, those living in remote areas can now easily take out microloans, participate in e-banking and more. A large share of respondents predict enormous potential for improved quality of life over the next 50 years for most individuals thanks to internet connectivity, although many said the benefits of a wired world are not likely to be evenly distributed.

● How internet can excite young to learn?

Internet can learn youngs to learn much different new knowlege when they research any questions and find answers from internet channel.

As one major aspect of teen life is social environment, changes in how teens connect impact the ways in which teens develop social skills. ** Luckily, the Internet offers many social-skill enhancement opportunities for teens of all different personalities . One advantage the Internet brings that the standard school environment cannot is the ability for teens to adjust their amount of social interaction. Teens who are extremely outgoing can spend their free time in social environments both offline and online, making new connections and catching up with friends.For example, a teen who finds large amounts of face-to-face interaction to be intimidating can use the Internet to engage in conversations while reducing the potential for social anxiety. In a way, this trains less social teens to be more social . In the past, these types of teens did not have the advantage of this social training provided by the Internet.

● Internet can encourage Social Network Growth

The Internet offers teens the ability to make friends with peers with whom they would not otherwise connect. With pop culture deteriorating into many distinct subcultures, teens' interests are more variable than they have ever been. Whereas in the past, children at school might have discussed the current top 40 when discussing music, today's kids define their musical tastes as specific genres, such as post-industrial, dubstep or jpop. Today, it's harder for teens to find peers who share the same interests in their schools. But online, not so. The Internet's social networks help teens find communities of peers who share similar interests, allowing a teen to grow his social network in a way that is specific to him 2. Today's teens are increasingly willing to make friends with different groups of people due to the ability to actually meet them, and this can be useful when they reach adulthood, a time in which accepting people of different backgrounds and demographics is crucial to career and academic growth. The Internet offers teens the ability to make friends with peers with whom they would not otherwise connect.

Today's teens are increasingly willing to make friends with different groups of people due to the ability to actually meet them, and this can be useful when they reach adulthood, a time in which accepting people of different backgrounds and demographics is crucial to career and academic growth.But the Internet can help teens foster self identity through exposure to new people, communities, hobbies and concepts. As teens go through more experiences, they learn more about themselves. And as the Internet can offer teens a wealth of experience, it can play the role of hastening the development of self identity.For many teens, the hardest part of life is figuring out identity.But the Internet can help teens foster self identity through exposure to new people, communities, hobbies and concepts.

● What Are Main Benefits of Internet Communication speed improvement ?

It may include as below:

1 Makes communication easier

Doing business through phone or mail doesn't work well ? Before the internet came into existence, the only way to communicate was through a phone. Or if you needed to send a note you had to send letters via mail. With the arrival of the Internet, staff and team managers can connect instantaneously without leaving their work place. ezTalks Meetings, a one-stop internet communication provider, is a perfect example. With this platform, participants can communicate as if they were right next to one another thanks to its quality video and audio. The tool comes with a rich set of features like screen sharing, cross platform chat, innovative whiteboard, and more.

2 Enhances collaboration

Internet communication brings teams together across the globe. Staff can collaborate easily without limitations and make more informed decisions instantaneously. This leads to reduced project timelines, cutting back on the time required to launch a new product/service. This piece of technology is also useful in education. Not only can students collaborate with foreign students, they can share ideas and learn about the diverse cultures out there. Parents can also become actively involved in their kids education by linking their children school with libraries, homes, and more. Millions of schools around the world are already using this technology to enhance learning.

3 It is cost effective

The cost of internet communication is significantly low when compared with other means of communication like face to face meetings and mail delivery. The technology connects you to your partners, colleagues, clients and suppliers from just about any location for a fraction of the cost required to host a one-on-one meeting. And as technology continues to become more efficient, the cost of online communication continues to drop significantly. With the traditional face to face meeting, you need to spare time, cash to travel and so on. Internet communication allows you and your team to connect without having to leave your offices.

4 Improves work relationships

Building a good relationship between workers spread around the globe is not easy. Business trips can negatively affect life– work balance. Team members can burn out fast if they have to make business travels that deny them the chance to participate in crucial events with friends and family. With internet communication, employees can effortlessly communicate with one another at anytime from anywhere in the world. This allows employees situated in different parts of the world to give their opinion and voice their concerns. Therefore, internet communication is an important business asset, particularly for companies that have tapped into global markets.

5 Increases productivity

While the companies of yesteryear might not have treasured effective communication, modern workplace requires both the management and the staff have the tools to effectively communicate internally and externally. This is because effective communication is important in increasing productivity as it directly impacts the behavior of the employees and how they perform. Internet communication plays an integral role in getting stuff done fast and efficiently which ultimately improves productivity. Poor communication can have a negative effect on productivity as the staff may not get the adequate info to accomplish a job they have been assigned.

6 Increases accountability

Errors slow down productivity and so it is tempting to punish or fire employees who repeatedly make errors. One major advantage of internet communication is that it helps to decrease these errors. This piece of technology pinpoints errors and how staff can avoid them. In workplaces that don't make use of various forms of internet communication, those mistakes go unnoticed. With internet communication, there is no room for mistakes as employees feel liable for their actions and safe to point out mistakes. They also feel secure expressing their ideas and suggestions in a group setting.

● Why does internet improvement can help any industries services or efficiencies improvment?

Internet improvement will revolutionize the world and lead to groundbreaking changes in transportation, industry, communication, education, energy, health care, communication, entertainment, government, warfare and even basic research. For example, self-driving cars, trains, semi-trucks, ships and airplanes will mean that goods and people can be transported farther, faster and with less energy and with massively fewer vehicles. Automated mining and manufacturing will further reduce the need for human workers to engage in rote work. Machine language translation will finally close the language barrier, while digital tutors, teachers and personal assistants with human qualities will make everything from learning new subjects to booking salon appointments faster and easier. For businesses, automated secretaries, salespeople, waiters, waitress, baristas and customer support personnel will lead to cost savings, efficiency gains and improved customer experiences. Socially, individuals will be able to find AI pets, friends and even therapists who can provide the love and emotional support that many people so desperately want. Entertainment will become far more interactive, as immersive AI experiences come to supplement traditional passive forms of media. Energy generation and health care will vastly improve with the addition of powerful AI tools that can take a systems-level view of operations and locate opportunities to gain efficiencies in design and operation. AI-driven robotics (e.g., drones) will revolutionize warfare. Finally, intelligent AI will contribute immensely to basic research and likely begin to create scientific discoveries of its own. So, it implies that internet improvement ought assist any kinds of industy service or efficiency improvement.

● Internet may become any organizational digital assets

On an individual basis, we will think about our digital assets as much as our physical ones. Ideally, we will have more transparent control over our data, and the ability to understand where it resides and exchange it for value – negotiating with the platform companies that are now in a winner-take-all position. Some children born today are named with search engine-optimization in mind; we'll be thinking more comprehensively about a set of rights and responsibilities of personal data that children are born with. Governments will have a higher level of regulation and protection of individual data. On an individual level, there will be greater integration of technology with our physical selves. For example, I can see devices that augment hearing and vision, and that enable greater access to data through our physical selves. Hard for me to picture what that looks like, but 50 years is a lot of time to figure it out. On a societal level, AI will have affected many jobs. Not only the truck drivers and the factory workers, but professions that have been largely unassailable – law, medicine – will have gone through a painful transformation. It seems entirely reasonable that a great deal of our digital lives will be focused on habitable environments: identifying them, improving them, expanding them.

Significant, often highly communication and computation technologically driven, advances in day-to-day areas like health care, safety and human services, will continue to have a significant measurable improvement in many lives, often 'invisible' as an unnoticed reduction in bad outcomes, will continue to reduce the incidence of human-scale disasters. Advances in opportunities for self-actualisation through education, community and creative work will continue. So, I believe that future many organizations may apply internet communication tool for their digital assets.

● Internet improvement may assist robotic development

Most of the focus on technology and particularly AI and machine learning developments these days is limited to virtual systems (e.g., apps for travel booking, social networks, search engines, games). I expect this to move, in the next 50 years, into networking people with machines, remotely operating in a myriad of environments, such as homes, hospitals, factories, sport arenas and so on. This will change work as we know it today, as it will change medicine (increasing remote surgery), travel (autonomous and remotely-guided cars, trains, planes), entertainment (games where real robots, instead of virtual agents, evolve in real scenarios). These are just a few ideas/scenarios. Many more, difficult to anticipate today, will appear. They will bring further challenges on privacy, security and safety, which everyone should be closely watching and monitoring. Beyond current discussions on privacy problems concerning 'virtual world' apps, we need to consider that 'real world' apps may enhance many of those problems, as they interact physically and/or in proximity with humans. So, future historians will observe that, in many ways, the rise of the internet over the next few decades will have improved the world, but it hasn't been without its costs that were sometimes severe and disruptive to entire industries and nations as well as improve robotic development.

This is similarly valid for AI.Living longer and better lives is the shining promise of the digital age. Many respondents to this canvassing agreed that internet advancement is likely to lead to better human-health outcomes, although perhaps not for everyone. As the following comments show, experts foresee new cures for chronic illnesses, rapid advancement in biotechnology and expanded access to care thanks to the development of better telehealth systems. Life will improve in multiple ways. One in particular I think worth mentioning will be improvements in health care in three distinct ways. One is significantly better medical technology related to cancer and other major diseases. The second is significantly reduced cost of health care. The third is much higher and broader availability of high-quality health care, thereby reducing the differences in outcomes between wealthy and poor citizens. So, when hospitals can improve internet communication , if the hospital can apply robots to assist doctors and nurses to serve patients. Then, internet communication can help them to cooperate more efficient.

● Internet improvement to assist 5G laptop development

Many of the technologies we see commercialized today began in government and university research labs. Fifty years ago, computers were the size of walk-in closets, and the notion of personal computers was laughable to most people. Today we're facing another shift, from personal and mobile to ambient computing. We're also seeing a huge amount of research in the areas of prosthetics, neuroscience and other technologies intended to translate brain activity into physical form. All discussion of transhumanism aside, there are very real current and future applications for technology 'implants' and prosthetics that will be able to aid mobility, memory, even intelligence, and other physical and neurological functions. And, as nearly always happens, the technology is far ahead of our understanding of the human implications. Will these technologies be available to all, or just to a privileged class? What happens to the data? Will it be 'willed' as a digital legacy to future generations? What are the ethical (and for some, religious and spiritual) implications of changing the human body with technology? In many ways, these are not new questions. We've used technology to augment the physical form since the first caveman picked up a walking stick. But the key here will be to focus as much (or more) on the way we use these technologies as we do on inventing them. All of above factors will be influenced to future 5G mobile phone by internet improvement?

Our homes, transportation, appliances, communication devices and even our clothes will be constantly communicating as part of a digital network. We have enough pieces of this today that we can somewhat imagine what it will be like. Through our clothes, doctors can monitor in real time our vital signs, metabolic condition and markers relevant to specific diseases. Parents will have real-time information about young children. The difference in the future will be the constant sharing of information, data updates and responses of all these interconnected devices. The things we create will interact with us to protect us. Our notions of privacy and even liability will be redefined. Lowering the cost and increasing the effectiveness of health care will require sharing information about how our bodies are functioning. Those who opt out may have to accept palliative hospice care over active treatment. Not keeping track of children real-time may be considered a form of child neglect. Digital will do more than connect our things to each other – it will invade our bodies. Advances in prosthetics, replacement organs and implants will turn our bodies into digital devices. This will create a host of new issues, including defining 'human' and where the line exists between that human and the digital universe – if people are always connected, always on are humans now part of the internet?

● How internet improvement influences AI provides medical service to hospitals?

Similarly, AI embedded in devices or wearables can be applied to predict and ameliorate many mental health illnesses. However, there is potential for there to be huge inequalities in our societies in the ability of individuals to access such technologies, causing both social disruption and new causes for mental health diseases, such as depression and anxiety. On balance, I am an optimist about the ability of human beings to adjust and develop new ethical norms for dealing with such issues.Surveillance technology, especially that powered by AI algorithms, is becoming more powerful and all-present than ever before. But to look at that and say that technology won't help people is absurd. Medical technology, technology to help people with disabilities, technology that will increase our comfort and abilities as humans will continue to appear and develop.The digital revolution will bring benefits in particular for health, providing personalized monitoring through Internet of Things and wearable devices. The AI will analyze those data in order to provide personalized medicine solutions.The most noticeable change for better in the next 50 years will be in health and average life expectancy. At this pace, and, taking into account the developments in digital technologies, I hope that several discoveries will reduce the risk of death, such as cancer or even death by road accident. New drugs could be developed, increasing the active work age and possibility maintaining the sustainability of countries' social health care and retirement funds. Another area AI can have impact is in creating the framework within genomics, epigenomics and metabolomics can be used to keep people healthy and to intervene when we start to deviate from health. Indeed, with AI we may be able to hack the brain and other secreting cells so that we can auto-generate lifesaving medicines, block unwanted biological processes (e.g., cancer), and coupled to understanding the brain, be able to hack at neurological disorders."

Thus, I believe that future hospitals were able to utilize internet technology to solve human health problems to make citizens' lives better and improve their access to care and services to improve their health outcomes. The benefits of the internet in the health care industry have continued to improve access to care and services, particularly for elderly, disabled or rural citizens. Digital tools will continue to be integrated into daily life to help the most vulnerable and isolated who need services, care and support. With laws supporting these groups, benefits in these areas will continue and expand to include behavioral health and resources for this group and for others. In the area of behavioral health in particular, digital tools will provide far-reaching benefits to citizens who need services but do not access them directly in person. Access to behavioral health will increase significantly in the next 50 years as a result of more enhanced and widely available digital tools made available to practitioners for delivering care to vulnerable populations, and by minimizing the stigma of accessing this type of care in person. It is a more affordable, personalized and continuous way of providing this type of care that is also more likely to attain adherence.

● The cyborg generation: Humans will partner more directly with technology when internet is popular to be used in any where

The inevitable 'Singularity' will result in changes to humans and will increase the rate of our evolution toward hybrid 'machines.' I also believe that new and modified materials will become 'smart.' For instance, new materials will be 'self-aware' and will be able to communicate problems in order to avoid failure. Ultimately, these materials will become 'self-healing' and will be able to harness raw materials to manufacture replacement parts in situ. All these materials, and the things built with them will participate in the connected world. We will see continued blurring of the line between 'real' and 'virtual' life." For exaple, artificial general intelligence and quantum computing available in a future version of the cloud connected to individual brain augmentation could make us augmented geniuses, inventing our daily lives in a self-actualization economy as the conscious-technology civilization evolves. Implants in humans that continuously connect them to the web will lead to a loss of privacy and the potential for thought control, decline in autonomy.

● Everyone agrees that the world will be putting AI to work, when internet is improvement to raise robotic efficiency and performance improvement

The technology visionaries surveyed described a much different work environment from the current one. They say remote work arrangements are likely to be the rule, rather than the exception, and virtual assistants will handle many of the mundane and unpleasant tasks currently performed by humans. The shooting is done by a drone guided by a smart guy/gal working a 9-to-5 job in an air-conditioned office in a nice town. Garbage could be picked up, sorted, recycled, all by robots with AI. Tedious surgery completed by robots and teaching via YouTube would leave the humans to the interesting and exciting cases, not the redoing of same lessons to yet more patients/students. Humans could live well on a 20-hour work week with many weeks of paid vacation. Having a job/career could become a positive, not just a necessity. With 24/7 learning and just-in-time capacity, people could change areas or careers many times with ease whenever they become bored. This positive outcome is possible if we collectively manage the creation and distribution of the tools and access to the use of new emerging tools. Thus, future everyone will have hundreds of digital workers working for them. Our cognitive mediators will know us in some ways better than we know ourselves. Better episodic memories and large numbers of digital workers will allow expanded entrepreneurship, lifelong learning and focus on transformation.

Thus, our future social development already small world will shrink further as remote collaboration becomes the norm, resulting in major social changes, among them allowing the recent concentration of expertise in major cities to relax and reducing the relevance of national borders. Furthermore, deep learning and AI-assisted technologies for software development and verification, combined with more abstract primitives for executing software in the cloud, will enable even those not trained as software engineers to precisely describe and solve complex problems. I believe the question we're facing is not 'When will machines surpass human intelligence?' but instead 'How can humans work together with machines in new ways?' Rather than worrying about an impending Singularity, I propose the concept of Multiplicity: where diverse combinations of people and machines work together to solve problems and innovate. In analogy with the 1910 High School Movement that was spurred by advances in farm automation, I propose a 'Multiplicity Movement' to evolve the way we learn to emphasize the uniquely human skills that AI and robots cannot replicate: creativity, curiosity, imagination, empathy, human communication, diversity and innovation. AI systems can provide universal access to sophisticated adaptive testing and exercises to discover the unique strengths of each student and to help each student amplify his or her strengths. AI systems could support continuous learning for students of all ages and abilities. Rather than discouraging the human workers of the world with threats of an impending Singularity, let's focus on Multiplicity where advances in AI and robots can inspire us to think deeply about the kind of work we really want to do, how we can change the way we learn and how we might embrace diversity to create myriad new partnerships. So, future AI and internet technoloy will become new partners to assist any business development, even any organizations and social development. Hence, internet improvement must be needed in order to let any businesses can apply robots to raise efficiencies and improve performance more effectively. For example, free internet-connected devices will be available to the poor in exchange for carrying around a sensor that records traffic speed, environmental quality, detailed usage logs, and video and audio recordings (depending on state law). There will be secure vote-by-internet capabilities, through credit card or passport verification, with other secure kiosks available at public facilities (police stations, libraries, fire stations and post offices, should those continue to exist in their current form). Internet and 24/7 real-time connectivity will no longer be viewed as a 'thing' independent from daily life, but integral, like electricity. This has profound psychological implications about what people assume as normal and establishes baseline expectations for access, response times and personalization of functions and information. Contrary to many concerns, as technology becomes more sophisticated, it will ultimately support the primary human drives of social connectedness and agency. As we have seen with social media, first adoption is noncritical – it is a shiny penny for exploration. Then people start making judgments about the value-add based on their own goals and technology companies adapt by designing for more value to the user . Technology is going to change whether we like it or not – expecting it to be worse for individuals means that we look for what's wrong. Expecting it to be better means we look for the strengths and what works and work toward that goal. Technology gives individuals more control – a fundamental human need and a prerequisite to participatory citizenship and collective agency. The danger is that we are so distracted by technology that we forget that digital life is an extension of the offline world and demands the same critical, moral and ethical thinking.

In future 50 years every aspect of our life will be connected, organized and hence, partly controlled, as technology platform and applications businesses will take this opportunity. A few global players will dominate the business; smaller companies (startups) will mostly have a chance in the development sector. Many institutions, such as libraries, will disappear – there might be one or two libraries that function as museums to show how it used to be. People who experienced today's world will definitely value the benefits and amenities they have through technology (human-machine/AI collaboration). If technology becomes part of every aspect of our lives we will have to give up some power and control. People thinking in today's terms will lose a certain amount of freedom, independency and control over their lives. People born after 2030 will probably just think these technologies produced changes that are mostly for the better. It has always been like this – people have always thought/said 'in the old days everything was better. The free, open internet that represented a set of decentralized connections between idiosyncratic actors will be recognized as an aberration in the history of the internet. Today's internet giants will probably be the internet giants of 50 years from now. In recent years, they've made substantial progress in curtailing innovation through acquisitions and copying. As the industry matures, they will add regulatory capture to their skill sets. For many people around the world, the internet will be a set of narrow portals where they exchange their data for a curtailed set of communication, information and consumer services. Thus, digital tools will be part of our body inside and remotely, and will assist us in decision- making constantly, so it will become second nature. Nonetheless, physical feelings will still be exclusively 'physical,' i.e., there will be a significant difference between the 'sensor-based feelings' and real body feelings, so human beings will still have some advantages over technology. This, I believe, will last forever.

V

Improving human development history method

Why do we need to concern new health medicine drugs discovery? I believe that human will face any new kinds of diseases that we had not encountered or contacts in my past. If we lack any new kinds of health medicine drugs discovery to fight any kinds of new diseases in my future. Then, we must face death very easily, such as COVID 19 is one kind of new disease, the another person or other persons can be contacted to cause this kind of COVID 19 disease by the patient's cloths, shoes, hands, even air, mouth of hs body and things. Thus, it had caused many people die in global nowadays. So, medicine or drug or bio-scientists need to spend much time to do any experiment to attempt to discover any new kinds of medicines or drugs to fight any future new kinds of diseases. Otherwise, human will die very easily in soon.

● Why do we need drug discovery?

In the fields of medicine, biotechnology and pharmacology, drug discovery is the process by which new candidate medications are discovered. Historically, drugs were discovered by identifying the active ingredient from traditional remedies or by serendipitous discovery, as with penicillin. More recently, chemical libraries of synthetic small molecules, natural products or extracts were screened in intact cells or whole organisms to identify substances that had a desirable therapeutic effect in a process known as classical pharmacology. After sequencing of the human genome allowed rapid cloning and synthesis of large quantities of purified proteins, it has become common practice to use high throughput screening of large compounds libraries against isolated biological targets which are hypothesized to be disease-modifying in a process known as reverse pharmacology. Hits from these screens are then tested in cells and then in animals for efficacy.

However, modern drug discovery involves the identification of screening hits, medicinal chemistry and optimization of those hits to increase the affinity, selectivity (to reduce the potential of side effects), efficacy/potency, metabolic stability (to increase the half-life), and oral bioavailability. Once a compound that fulfills all of these requirements has been identified, the process of drug development can continue. If successful, clinical trials are developed. Modern drug discovery is thus usually a capital-intensive process that involves large investments by pharmaceutical industry corporations as well as national governments (who provide grants and loan guarantees). Despite advances in technology and understanding of biological systems, drug discovery is still a lengthy, "expensive, difficult, and inefficient process" with low rate of new therapeutic discovery. For example, in 2010, the research and development cost of each new molecular entity was about US$1.8 billion In the 21st century, basic discovery research is funded primarily by governments and by philanthropic organizations, while late-stage development is funded primarily by pharmaceutical companies or venture capitalists. However, discovering drugs that may be a commercial success, or a public health success, involves a complex interaction between investors, industry, academia, patent laws, regulatory exclusivity, marketing and the need to balance secrecy with communication. Meanwhile, for disorders whose rarity means that no large commercial success or public health effect can be expected, the orphan drug funding process ensures that people who experience those disorders can have some hope of pharmacotherapeutic advances.

● Where do new drugs come from? Why does it take so long to get a new drug approved? Why are drugs so expensive?

The medicines we ingest, inject, and inhale are often complex therapeutic compounds. The drugs are usually mixtures of chemicals made from starting materials or drug sources. Depending on the sources from which the drugs were created, the drugs can be categorized as natural, synthetic, or semi-synthetic. Natural drugs are made from compounds found in nature. The most prevalent natural drug sources are plants. The field of science that studies the relationship between people and medicinal plants is known as medicinal ethnobotany. Some examples of medicine that come from plants are morphine (from opium), digoxin (from flower, Digitalis lanata), and aspirin (from willow tree bark). Less prevalent natural drug sources include animals, microbes, and minerals. The first kind drug source is for example, synthetic drugs come from starting materials that are not found in nature. Instead, they are produced by man from smaller chemical building blocks. An example of synthetic medicine is the experimental anti-malaria drug, arterolane. Another kind drug source is semi-synthetic drugs are neither completely natural nor completely synthetic. They are a hybrid. Semi-synthetic drugs are generally made by converting starting materials from natural sources into final products via chemical reactions. Examples of semi-synthetic medicine include the antibiotic, penicillin, and the chemotherapy drug, paclitaxel. To make the chemotherapy drug, paclitaxel, 10-deacetylbaccatin is extracted from yew needles and undergoes a 4-stage synthesis process. They both are the main kinds of drugs manufacturing sources.

● Why does human need new drugs discovery ?

The reason of global health needs demand new approach to drug discovery, the pharmaceutical industry has made enormous strides in the production of potential therapies and medicines. But even today, close to 90% of candidate drugs that enter Phase 1 trials fail to make it to the market place. This is a system beset by duplication of effort and hence wastage of resources. No one lab or institution can do this on its own. We must urgently pool resources and expertise, minimise duplication, explore new drug targets, biomarkers, and technologies in order to generate new, effective, and more affordable drugs for patients more quickly.

Discovey of any one kind of new drug, it needs long time to experiment. It must come up with new ways to accelerate our drug discovery process. Alternatively, we must entirely rethink how we treat illness. This is not just limited to bacterial infections. We need to invent better ways to combat all forms of disease. The process of discovering, testing, and approving a drug for commercial use can take 20 years and over of 1 billion dollars. Obviously, decreasing both the time and the cost of developing these drugs can save many lives. There are some new technologies which are already helping to ramp up this process. For example, computational modeling of drugs has massively sped up the screening process for drugs. We can now take thousands of potential drug candidates and narrow them down to a couple viable options. But there are more ways we can expedite this process.

A recent estimate states that we now know the molecular cause of over 4,000 diseases — but we only have drugs for about 250. How can we do better? The FDA approval process is long and arduous. Even for compounds that have been approved in other countries, FDA trials can be drawn out for years. The FDA approval process can be responsible for about 25% of the cost of a drug and can delay the arrival of a drug over 10 years. There is even data that suggests that the FDA kills many more by not approving drugs than it ever saves by approving drugs (for more on the harmful effects of the FDA, see Cato, Forbes, The Independent Institute, and LifeExtension). By delaying good drugs that can save lives, and by doing little to stop bad drugs, the FDA is often an inhibitor to the medical process. We need to rethink the FDA if we want to streamline the drug discovery process. If we can change many FDA policies, we will see more drugs created for those 4,000 known targets.

● The process of new drug experiment success time evaluation

Any new kind of drugs experiment success, they must experience these processes. They may include:

1 Drug testing and licensing

All new drugs and treatments have to be thoroughly tested before they are licensed and available for patients. A new drug is first studied in the laboratory. If it looks promising, it is carefully studied in people. If trials show that it works well and doesn't cause too many side effects, it may be licensed. You may hear this process called 'from bench to bedside. There is no typical length of time it takes for a drug to be tested and approved. It might take 10 to 15 years or more to complete all 3 phases of clinical trials before the licensing stage. But this time span varies a lot. There are many factors that affect how long it takes for a drug to be licensed.

2 Factors that affect how long trials take

The type of cancer drug success experiement needs time

Clinical trials for rarer cancers often take longer because there are fewer patients available to take part. Research teams from several different countries may need to collaborate so there are enough patients. This can mean the trial takes longer to organise and set up. But international trials can often recruit people more quickly and so are likely be quicker in the long run.
Researchers running clinical trials for more common cancers are generally able to find enough people to take part more easily.

3 The type of treatment

Trials that use new methods of giving treatment, such as a new way to give radiotherapy for example, may take longer to set up and run. This is because the research teams need specialist equipment and extra training. These trials may only be able to run in a small number of hospitals compared to trials using standard ways of giving treatment. How long treatment takes can also affect the results. It is likely to be quicker to get results for a trial looking at a single dose or short course of treatment, compared to a treatment that lasts for months or even years.

4 The type of trial

Some trials look at treatments to prevent cancer or ways of screening for cancer. Screening means testing for cancer in people who don't have any signs or symptoms. People who join these trials haven't been diagnosed with cancer. The research team will often want to follow them for many years to see who develops cancer and who doesn't. They will then compare the different trial groups to see if a particular treatment can help prevent cancer or whether a test can help to diagnose it early.These trials often take a long time to get results compared to treatment trials. It can take years to see a clear difference in the number of people in the different groups who go on to develop cancer. So, any new kinds of drug research experiements, they depend on the number of patients needed in order to decide whether how drug quality level, how many drugs manufacturing supply number, drug price in global market.

Statistics experts look at what the research team want to find out and the design of the trial, and then work out how many patients are needed. If there aren't enough patients taking part, the results may not be reliable. The number of people they need to get reliable results will depend on how many treatment groups there are and exactly what the research team want to find out.

5 The follow up period

Research teams look at how well people are doing for some time after they have treatment as part of a trial. This is to see how well the treatment works over a longer period of time, and to find out more about long term side effects. Follow up periods can range from a few months to more than 10 years, depending on the type of treatment and the group of patients. Or maybe longer for a trial looking at screening or prevention.

6 Any problems with the new treatment

There may be problems with new drugs or treatments that the researchers don't know about until they run the trials. There could be unexpected side effects or reactions to treatment. Or there may be difficulties in giving the treatment to patients. Problems with the new treatment may mean the trial takes longer to complete.

Thus, any kinds of new drug experiement need long time to be attempted to carry on, every new kind of drug experiment is evaluated about 10 to 20 , even more time. So, future drug scientists have responsibilities to evaluate whether which kinds of diseases will cause in order to concentrate on spending time to carry on researching the kind of new drug experiment. It aims to use limited resource and time to let patients to get health.

Improving living environment method

What are the disadvantages if we do not concern how to improve our global living environment? I shall explain as below:

● reasons to improve living environment

Nowadays, as population on the earth keeps expanding, human needs increase endlessly causing more global environmental problems to proliferate globally. Global environmental crisis has become an unequivocal fact that can affect our livelihood and it is capable of changing the current landscape drastically. Hence, people hold the responsibility to tackle current global environmental issues to make this world a better place. With destructive natural disasters like flash floods or snowstorm as well as the changing of weather patterns, the earth is poised at the precarious verge of severe environmental crisis. Human intervention has caused many dysfunctions to the environment, some of which have left damages on the ecosystem that eliminates other sources of necessity to other living things. Ever since humans start to harvest the Earth's resources, many landscapes have been altered to fit the lifestyles of countless inhabitants. So people ought to be aware of other types of environmental challenges that the planet is facing. Some of the challenges that the planet is facing include overpopulation of human beings that leads to natural resources depletion, deforestation and loss of biodiversity, acid rain and ocean acidification, pollution and waste disposal. Thus, it seems that global living environment and pollution have close relationship. I mean that air and water and paste and chemical pollution will reduce if we can keep our global living environment more clean, safe and without more rubblishs are allowed to keep in our living places, even gardens, public places anywhere.

One of the key ethical questions is whether a life-extension pill would extend our healthy years or simply prolong frailty towards the end of life. Better health and longer life would certainly be an attractive prospect for many people. If we were healthier for longer then perhaps we could achieve more of our ambitions and engage in the things we enjoy for longer. But some people worry that our lives may be extended in a state of low quality of life rather than health. Although this is not the goal, critics worry that it might be an unintended consequence of intervention in ageing and longevity. As with all pharmaceuticals, both health benefits and risks need to be considered. If life span could be extended a great deal – perhaps to more than 100 years or even longer – then some other interesting issues might arise. For instance, would we simply run out of things to do and become bored? Even things that we enjoy may become stale after several centuries. How long would we have to work for? If our lives were 200 years long then it is unlikely that many people could afford to retire at 65. However, this may also present new opportunities such as having several different careers within a lifetime. If our future earth can not provide a health and clean living environment to let human to live, then our quality of living must be worse to compare nowadays, it will cause our next generation can not be health to live ot they will have many different kinds of disease, such as COV19 disease , or future there are many kinds of serious disease to compare COV19 disease , they will bring threats to influence our next generation to live in anywhere health places in our earth. It is very disappointment to us, such as our next generation's parents, we have not feel responsibilities to keep our living environment to be improved to let our next generation to live in global anywhere clean and health living environment. So, we need to concern how to improve our living environment nowadays.

However, I shall suggest these methods how to improve our living environment to be better. If we can be habit to do environment protection behaviors every day, then our living environment must be influenced to improve more easily and rapidly, in society, individual sand businessmen and our governments have resposibilities, they may include as below:

● Individual and businessmen and governments how to improve living environment

Individual responsibilities to improving living environment

1. Use Reusable Bags

Plastic grocery-type bags that get thrown out end up in landfills or in other parts of the environment. These can suffocate animals who get stuck in them or may mistake them for food. Also, it takes a while for the bags to decompose. Whether you are shopping for food, clothes or books, use a reusable bag. This cuts down on litter and prevents animals from getting a hold of them. There are even some stores (such as Target) that offer discounts for using reusable bags! These bags are useful for things other than shopping as well. I have heard of people using reusable bags when they move! If you forget your bags at home, buy a new one. Better yet, keep a couple bags in your car so you never leave home without them (just make sure you remember you put them there)! If you are in a position where you need to use the plastic bags, reuse them the next time you go shopping, or use them for something else. Just do not be so quick to throw them out!

There are some states that are outlawing or charging extra for using plastic bags. Using reusable bags helps the environment AND your budget!

2. Print as Little as Necessary

We have all had that teacher that wanted us to have a copy of every single reading when we come to class, or that professor who wanted a hard copy of the ten-page paper that is due next week. These are fine but it seems as if they do not understand that using so much paper is detrimental to the environment. What can you do? Ask your teacher if you can bring a laptop or an e-reader to class so that you can download the reading onto that and read it from there. If not, print on both sides of the page to reduce the amount of paper used. If you need to turn in a long paper, ask the professor if it is okay to print on both sides of the page and explain why you're asking. Most teachers care about the environment as well and would be willing to allow you to do so.

3. Recycle

Recycling is such a simple thing to do, but so many people don't do it. Many garbage disposal companies offer recycling services, so check with the company you use to see if they can help you get started! It is as simple as getting a bin and putting it out with your trash cans for free! Another way to recycle is to look for recycling cans near trashcans. Instead of throwing recyclables in the trash with your non-recyclables, make a point to take an extra step to locate recycling cans around your campus.

4. Use a Reusable Beverage Containers

Instead of buying individually-packaged drinks, consider buying a bulk container of the beverage you want and buying a reusable water bottle. Not only will this help the environment, but it will also help you save money since you are buying a bulk container. Many campuses offer water fountains designed for drinking as well as for refilling reusable water bottles. Make use of these fountains throughout the day when you finish off the initial beverage.

Along these lines, many restaurants offer reusable containers for drinks. If you go to a certain place a lot, consider buying one of these containers to help minimize waste. A lot of coffee shops even offer a discount to customers who use a reusable container for their drinks. Starbucks, as an example, offers a small discount for customers who do this. Saving the environment and money?

5. Save Water

Water is wasted more frequently than we can see. Turn off the faucet as you are brushing your teeth. Don't turn your shower on until you're ready to get in and wash your hair. Limit your water usage as you wash dishes. Changing old habits will be good for both the environment and your wallet!

6. Avoid Taking Cars or Carpool When Possible

Cars are harmful to the environment. Taking public transportation, walking, or riding a bike to class are better options that help the environment and your budget, as well as getting some exercise in! If you do need to use your car, compare schedules and places of residency with those in your classes. You can split the cost of gas and have alternating schedules for who drives when. This is cheaper than everyone driving separately and you'll be closer with friends!

Businessmen responsibilities to improving living environment

Instead of individuals have respobsilities to improve our living environment. Businessmen have also responsibilities to improve our living environment. I shall indicate mining businessmen example to explain how mining businesses may influence our living environment to be worse. The disadvantages of mining include harm to air pollution, water pollution, loss of usable land, destruction of animal habitat, and harm to local communities and the miners themselves. While mining produces the resources needed for fuel, electronics, and other items as well as jobs, companies often don't factor the harm mining can do into their decision making. Below factors may influence our global living environment to be worse as below:

Air Pollution

Lead, arsenic, cadmium, and other harmful substance As are often exposed by mining and picked up by the wind, causing allergies and breathing problems in local people. Mining machinery uses fossil fuels and releases large amounts of carbon dioxide and other substances that contribute to global warming.

Water Pollution

Mining can cause metal contamination and acid mine drainage that makes water unsafe for plants and animals. Sediments released by mining choke streams and erode soil. Both of these problems also cause problems for farming and the water people drink.

Loss of Usable Land

Mining, especially open pit mining, destroys land that can be used for farming, houses, and other human purposes, often permanently. Entire mountains and rivers can be destroyed. Loss of soil and deep underground excavation can also make land unstable and collapse.

Destruction of Animal Habitats

Mining also has disadvantages for plants and wildlife. It destroys homes and food sources for animals and leads to less diverse plant and animal life. Endangered species that are already sensitive to changes in their environment are especially at risk. Because mining releases toxins that linger for years later, the damage to plants and animals often isn't fully understood until after mining has ended.

Harm to Miners

Mining is dangerous for the people who do it, especially for miners who work underground. Breathing in mineral dust can cause deadly diseases like pneumoconiosis or black lung, while the machinery used often causes hearing loss. Back injuries and other physical problems are also common in miners. While big disasters often show up in the news, many of the miners who are killed or injured on the job never receive media attention. In 2010, almost 2,500 miners died from causes other than major accidents.

Consequences for Local Communities

Mining is also harmful to the communities that support mines. Mining can lead to loss of homes, land, and clean water, and it often releases chemicals into the environment that cause health problems for locals. Mines also need large amounts of water to operate, which leaves less for people to drink or farm with. It also causes less obvious problems. Because only some people in an area benefit from mining, but everyone faces at least some of the disadvantages, mining can divide communities. It can also lead to harassment or abuse from corporate or government officials who care more about the profits of mining than the people it affects. The secrecy around mining and who makes money from it often makes this disadvantage even worse.

Thus, ourselves and businessmen can not neglect our any activities can influence global living environment to be worse. We need to learn how to avoid to do any bad behaviors to influence our future global living environment to be worse, even the worst.

Governments responsibilities to improving living environment

Any country's government needs to concern social responsibility before it decides to implement any sustainable development. Because although sustainable development may bring some benefits to some countries, but it can also bring disadvantages to themselves countries. What Are Disadvantages of Sustainable Development? It may brins these disadvantages as below:

Increased Costs

Because sustainable development relies on newer technologies and materials that cost more to produce, the overall costs are often more than that of traditional construction. The higher cost of materials is passed on to developers. Developers pass it on to property owners, who pass it on to tenants. Future development will include tools that haven't even been invented yet. The trial and error of using new materials and ideas can also bring costs up for everyone.

Lower Quality of Life for Some Elements of Society

Sustainable development will shrink or do away with certain job sectors. This will lead to job loss for some workers. The fossil fuel industry could see plants close and employees lose jobs as sustainable development relies on new energy sources. The rising costs and less robust power of alternative energy can also lead to a lower quality of life for people who live in sustainably developed areas.

Resistance to New Methods

When people try to implement new ideas, there's naturally a certain amount of resistance. People in general are set in their ways and don't want to change their lives radically. As more governments and companies attempt to put sustainable development into practice, more resistance will follow.

Some of the resistance will come in the form of people who initially adopt the idea of sustainable development with enthusiasm, but their commitment shrinks as they start to put new ideas into practice. Contractors and tenants may resist a specific initiative because it forces them to change the ways they work and live.

Increased Regulation

Sustainable approaches will naturally lead to increased regulation on construction and the daily operation of businesses. A greater commitment to the environment will lead to tighter controls on how people live their lives. Stricter building codes and tougher emission standards are likely. While some people will accept a greater burden of regulation because they see the overall benefit, many people will disagree with government intruding into their lives.

Political Struggle

In addition to the public resistance, there's a political cost to committing to the environment. The deep political divides in society mean that some political powers won't want to commit to sustainable initiatives. Certain industries will try to influence politicians via lobbyists. Some politicians will be completely against sustainable development.

Is It Worth the Trouble?

People and organizations that are in favor of sustainable development believe that it's worth moving past these disadvantages to work on the environment. Advocates say that sustainable development is an investment in future generations. The biggest defenders of these initiatives are working on ways of overcoming the hurdles.

Thus, ineffective or poor sustainable development may also bring poor living environment, due to wrong sustainable development to the country. For example, if Afria government only concern how to find mining lands for sustinable development, but it neglects to keep clean and health and natural land living environment to African to continue to live. Then, it will reduce African quality of living to be worse. So, any countries governments need to keep balance to bring social benefit when they decide to do sustainable development in themselves countries.

Improving social welfare major mthod

Do you feel our nowadays social welfare is enough? What factors can influence our social welfare to be better or worse? Do we need to improve our social welfare to let our next generations feel comfortable and without difficulty to live? What feeling will influence to our future next generation if we do not plan to improve our social welfare? I shall explain why we need to concern how to improve our social welfare in order to let our next generation won't difficult to live as below:

● Why do we improve future social welfare ?

Why do we need to improve social welfare? Firstly, I shall explain why we need social welfare. Then, I shall explain why we need to improve social welfare. Social welfare may be explained that it is one kind of social protection has the potential to reduce insecurity for workers and help to bring employment contracts. Also, it is an investment in human capital for economic growth as successful economic depend on the quality of their workforce.

Why do we need social welfare? As a social welfare system offers assistance to individuals and families in need with such program as health care assistance, food providing and unemployment compensation. Lesser knon pasts of a social welfare system include disaster reief and educational assistances. What is the importance of welfare? When the welfare state has played aim important role to any countries in reducing socio-economic inequalities and proetcting people from various forms of handship , such as unemployment and ill health , as also proverty be an important social problem for economic development.

What is the purpose of social welfare policies? Social wefare policies mean providing especially assistance and social insurance benefit, traditionally have been conceived as instruments of social protection and redistribution. At a minimum, social welfare policies should protect individuals form proverty and relative deprivations So, it brings this question: who benefits from social welfare? The most common types of programs provide benefits to the elderly or retired, the sick or invalid, dependent survivors, mothers, the unemployed, the work-injured, and families. Methods of financing and administration and the scope of coverage and benefits vary widely among countries may be implemented in popular.

Nowadays, our societies believe that social welfare is an important tool for redistribution, social protection which has to be at the heart of the construction of the European project. If social and labour market policies are conceived in an appropriate manner, they help to promote both social justice and economic efficiency and productivity, instead of providing education, medical retired etc. welfare to the low income, low educational level social group as well as to achieve reducing poverty and inequality aim. Thus, it explains why our societies need to learn how to improve our global future social welfare to be be better , even the best social welfare system.

On conclusion, why was social welfare needed to create? Our society's population had been increasing rapidly and human's age had been prolonging, due to medical improvement, enough food provision. However, global has may dependent children and poor old people would gradually need as employment improved, retired assistance, unemployment assistance, educational assistance, and those over 65 age began to collect social security pensions. So, if we can not improve our societies to have the best social welfare to assist, these the most need of social assistance group. Consequently, the difference of rich and poor group must increase . It will be unfair to those low education and old age and low income families group in global. Thus, our future society must need to implement safe feeling to let anyone feel ourselves countries are suitable to us to live for our next generation. Hence, learning how to improve social welfare must be need to every country nowadays.

● Can improve social welfare to influence economy growth?

How social welfare impact any country itself economy? Does it has relationship between social welfare and economy? When it comes to public discourse the term "welfare state" is most often used in a derogatory way. For many people who hear the term welfare state, it means money being handed to people in poverty who don't deserve it because they aren't working to earn their income. The prevailing logic is that everyone knows hard workers are rewarded with higher income. However, that term means something different to actual economists who have dedicated their lives to studying economic systems and their impacts on broader society. In fact, the welfare state doesn't only apply to allocating resources to those living in poverty. It also means allocating resources to corporations. Any time the government allocates resources to any recipient in society, it is considered part of the welfare state. Capitalism lends itself naturally to economic cycles. The economy tends to swing severely between booms and busts. Without any kind of social insurance though, a capitalist economy may not recover from the bust end of a cycle. Even if it does, it would take much longer to recover than it would with social insurances in place. It is not in the best interest of the economy or society for a bust to last too long. The health of the economy is dependent on the economic health of the members of society.

However, Any type of government intervention is viewed as against a pure capitalist system. However, capitalism on paper has not worked out as well in practice without some government intervention on behalf of the greater good of society. Sometimes this has looked like a low level of resource distribution to those less fortunate and sometimes it has taken the form of resource distribution to corporations. Even an example such as farmers getting subsidies is a form of the welfare state. The guiding principle of welfare economics should be bringing all shareholders of the economy to a state of equilibrium where all groups share in the feeling of economic well-being.

However, the equilibrium doesn't happen all by itself. It requires public policy through government regulation and intervention to guide the economy in the direction of widespread well-being without sacrificing growth. Welfare economics can't end the bust end of the capitalist economic cycle. What it is meant to do, though, is mitigate the negative impacts of economic recessions. Welfare economics is meant to ensure that the bust end of the cycle isn't too severe and doesn't last too long. We should not be looking to cause undue economic suffering for any members of society.

I beleive that social welfare can impact economy growth. It means that the country can have better economy growth improvement, if it can provide good welfare to itself country. Otherwise, the country can have worse economy growth, if it can not provide good welfare to itself country. The reaons are becaure welfare can include any corporate (company) it's income as well as social individual both. There are two major types of welfare in the welfare state: social welfare and corporate welfare. While there are people in both types of welfare that do take advantage of the system, both are important tactics for stabilizing the economy.

1. Social Welfare

Social welfare encompasses programs such as social security, Medicare/Medicaid, food stamps, unemployment, the Affordable Care Act and other similar programs. The idea of these programs is to help safeguard people from poverty. The vast majority of the people who need to use these programs are either children, or they've worked their entire lives in our economic system. Fraud is extremely rare in these programs.

2. Corporate Welfare

Corporate welfare comes in a few different forms as well and is very much a type of welfare state. It is tax money that is given to corporations. It can also come in the form of tax cuts to corporations and it can also look like subsidies in certain industries. The purposes of using corporate welfare are usually to help grow a certain industry, to help stabilize a certain industry, or to help a certain industry avoid financial ruin. An example of corporate welfare is the auto-industry bailout. It is believed that corporate welfare actions such as these prevent an even worse economic disaster. Sometimes though, it seems corporate welfare moves make little sense. An example is the most recent Trump tax cuts. The economy has been growing for the past 8 years and is still doing well. Injecting government funds to booming industries through a corporate welfare action like the Trump tax cuts does not seem to fit any of the usual categories for stimulating the economy or preventing a downturn. It is unclear what the effects will be, but the move has been widely controversial among economists.

Hence, if the country has good social welfare system to provide itself country any company sale increasing chance. Then, when the country has many companies can earn high income, when many customers buy their products or consume their lesiure services. Consequently, the country's economy may be influenced to grow rapidly. The corporate welfare side of the welfare state can have some benefits. For instance, the automobile industry bailout saved jobs and a possible worse recession. By the government investing in budding renewable energy programs, it can generate economic growth in areas with innovative solutions to head off an energy crisis. Corporate welfare money doesn't always have that same effect on the economy. There should be greater scrutiny over how corporate welfare is used and whether it contributes significantly to economic growth. All corporate welfare programs should provide benefits to the whole economy.

On the other side, countries such as Norway have found that social welfare boosts their economies and capitalism. Economics professors in Norway have discovered that despite the short-term sacrifice of providing higher wages for their upper-class citizens, in the long term their social welfare programs have resulted in better equality, smaller gender wage gaps, and improved education across the nation—just to name a few examples given by Science Nordic.

Do welfare states boost economic growth ? If in the future human labour is less needed, keeping societies stitched together may require us to reinvent the welfare state. The laws of economics say social welfare should be in accordance with the economic development level of a country. Welfare programs that are beyond a country's development level are not good for economic development, as has happened in Greece. On the other hand, if the economy develops rapidly without corresponding improvement in people's living standards and public welfare, people will not feel a "sense of gain", which in turn will have a negative impact on economic development.

First, excessive welfare beyond a country's development level will impede accumulation and harm welfare programs in the future. In economics, production is the top priority and it decides consumption. A society has to improve its production level if it wants to improve its consumption level. Production here refers to extended production, because only expanding the scale will breed competition and provide unfailing supply. The expansion of scale should be high-quality and high-level expansion of production through innovation and improvement of the industrial structure. Second, welfare at any level needs economic support. High levels of welfare in countries such as Sweden depend on high taxation and high deficit. But the high-level welfare in Greece depends on high debt. High welfare supported by high taxation reduces development funds for enterprises, impeding the development of enterprises. And if enterprises lose energy, the entire economy will suffer. High taxation also affects individuals' desire and capacity for consumption and thus undermines people's enthusiasm to expand production. Third, excessive welfare will breed dependence and result in waste of social resources. Although high welfare comes from individual taxpayers' contribution, it seems like a public welfare provided by the state. It will result in many social problems, such as waste of social resources, voluntarily unemployment and retirement in advance. Once people get used to this kind of dependence, economic development will be undermined. economic development will also be undermined if the authorities fail to provide enough welfare for the people.

For China economy development example, China social welfare and itself economy deveopment has exact close relationship. There is a lesson to be learned here from the planned economy to China economy growth and its social welfare can be improved nowadays. China's social welfare level today is not high; there is much room for improvement. So to strike the right balance between welfare and economic development, we should abide by the following principles:

One, it has to be clarified that the basic and final goal of China's economic development is the well-being of the Chinese people. And since China is the world's second-largest economy, it should pay more attention to improving public welfare. The Fifth Plenum of the 18th Communist Party of China Central Committee said the national GDP and urban and rural residents' incomes have to be doubled by 2020 compared with the 2010 level, and hence the authorities should focus on coordinated development to improve public services.

Two, the distribution of public welfare should be fair and transparent. The public welfare different social groups enjoy today is unbalanced, especially when it comes to urban and rural areas. Therefore, the authorities should make efforts to rectify the imbalance.

Three, the authorities should take measures to prevent unfairness and corruption from creeping into redistribution of welfare.

And four, they should not forget that China is still a developing country, and development is key to solving social economic problems, and only further development can guarantee sustainable and high-level welfare. More importantly, development problems should not be used as an excuse to reduce public welfare.

On conclusion, I believe that improvment to any country itself social welfare, it can impact the country itself economy growth or recession significantly. Thus, any country needs to concern how to improve itself social welfare in order to improve economy growth, instead of improvement social poor problems for our future generation.

World peace improving method

One important issue that human must need to concern if we hope our future societies can develop or improve in success. This issue is that " our world must need to keep peace. Why and how our word must need to keep peace ? The reason is very simple. If our future countries aim to only to be the world top leader, every leader only concentrates on finding the best method to become world top leader, he/she neglects to concern how to make himself/herself country to develop technology, medicine, construction, social welfare etc. different social aspect issues. His/her time only concentrates on war aspect, so peace world is the major key to help our next generation can have safe, clean and good economy social environment to work and live in our world anywhere. The question is : How to keep peace world to avoid war? Ambitious leader must not respresent that he/she must be the top leader that he/she has effort to dominate any countries matter. He/she ought need to know peace is the most important factor that when every country can cooperate to do any matter in order to solve any social challenges, due to cooperation can help any country leader to reduce time to find the best solution when any county leader faces difficulties. So, leader cooperation must need to keep world peace in our future society, moreover, any country improvement must need any country leader cooperation to sit down to discuss any important issues together. It is the best method to build global the most safe society in order to let any country citizen to feel comfortable and safe to live in themselves countries. I shall explain how we can keep peace world as below:

Why do we need to achieve world peace? The reason most scoff at the notion of achieving world peace is because if you buy the principle that individual human revolution is the real solution, then literally some billions of people would need to actively embrace the notion of devoting themselves to continual self-reformation.Peace, as we all know, is very important in our lives and it is essential to our overall well-being. However, this is something that has, regrettably, eluded us for years and years in this world.We will be able to lead others into Peace, rather than getting drawn into their conflict and the endless cycle of action and reaction that only leads to more and more violence. There is increasing evidence to suggest that being peaceful, for example through yoga, tai chi or focused meditation, can have a direct and measurable impact on the world.It matters because we have an opportunity to break the cycles of violence, fear, and hatred- to help one another to wake up. By keeping our hearts and minds open we model how not to walk blindly down paths that lead towards only more hate and revenge. Be the peace you want to see in the world.

What does military strategy mean ?

Military strategies are methods of arranging and maneuvering large bodies of military forces during armed conflicts. It may include concept and different kinds of strateges as below:

Economic concepts in military may include:

Salaries – Always pay your troops on time.

Asymmetric costs – ensure the cost of enemy losses (or objectives) is at least an order of magnitude higher than the costs of attacking.

Budget like a business – Ensure there is sufficient funds and revenue streams to finish the war.

For example, Intentional insufficient Funding(Rcoined) - ensure you make the funds less than the return, if a cost of logistics costs X\$ in delivering army collateral, and supplies. By only closing a canal or an route, using sea denial strategy then the price becomes (X\$)*4= 4x\$.

Strategic concepts in military may include:

Center of gravity (military) – The hub of all power and movement on which everything depends, the point at which all energies should be directed.

Decisive point – A geographic place, specific key event, critical system, or function that allows commanders to gain a marked advantage over an enemy and greatly influence the outcome of an attack.

Moral ascendancy – Moral force is the trump card for any military event because as events change the human elements of war remain unchanged.

Decision-making occurs in a recurring cycle of observe-orient-decide-act. An entity (whether an individual or an organization) that can process this cycle quickly, observing and reacting to unfolding events more rapidly than an opponent, can thereby "get inside" the opponent's decision cycle and gain the advantage

Why do leaders feel war need, the reasons my include:

Principles of war, Objective (Direct every military operation towards a clearly defined, decisive, and attainable objective).Offensive (Seize, retain, and exploit the initiative). Mass (Concentrate combat power at the decisive place and time). Economy of Force (Allocate minimum essential combat power to secondary efforts).

There are both kinds of defensive and offensive strategies for war. They may include:

1. Defensive strategies

Boxing maneuver – A strategy used to "box in" and force an attack on all sides at once.

Choke point – A use of strategic geography, usually in a narrow area, intended to concentrate the enemy into a confined area where the defender can maximize his forces.

Defence in depth – A strategy to delay rather than prevent the advance of the attackers by buying time and causing additional casualties by yielding space so that the momentum of the attack is lost and the attacking force can be attacked on its flanks.

Elastic Defense - A strategy to flexibly absorb then repel the advance of attackers through carefully planned integrated fighting positions, perfected by the German Army in WWI.

Fortification – A semi-permanent or permanent defensive structure that gives physical protection to a military unit.

2. Offensive strategies

Air supremacy – A degree of air superiority where a side holds complete control of air power over opposing forces. Control of the air is the aerial equivalent of Command of the sea.

Attrition warfare – A strategy of wearing down the enemy to the point of collapse through continuous loss of personnel and material. Used to defeat enemies with low resources and high morale.

Bait and bleed – To induce rival states to engage in a protracted war of attrition against each other "so that they bleed each other white", similar to the concept of Divide and conquer.

Battle of annihilation – The goal of destroying the enemy military in a single planned pivotal battle.

Bellum se ipsum alet – A strategy of feeding and supporting an army with the potentials of occupied territories.

Blitzkrieg – A method of warfare where an attacking force, spearheaded by a dense concentration of armoured and motorised or mechanised infantry formations with close air support, breaks through the opponent's line of defence by short, fast, powerful attacks and then dislocates the defenders, using speed and surprise to encircle them with the help of air superiority.

Blockade / Siege / Investment – An attempt to cut off food, supplies, war material or communications from a particular area by force, usually taking place by sea.

Thus, any countrys need to learn different kinds of strategies in order to protect themselves country safety more easily. When they know their enemy had prepared to attrack them by air, land or sea weapons. However, I mean that any one country ought not choose to find the most suitable weapons to attack another country. It only need to find the best strategy to avoid the another country attack because it is only way to avoid war in our future society. So, negotiation or cooperation aims to discuss any social or country challenge, it is the only way to avoid any war in global.

WHAT IS THE TRUE CAUSE OF WAR?

The leaders of countries go to war. They marshal their reasons, stir up the public, dehumanize the enemy (as I wrote about in an earlier post, The True Cause Of Cruelty), and send out their forces. The number of people actually responsible for the decision to go to war can usually fit comfortably inside a single large-sized room. Leaders, of course, only occasionally represent the best of what humanity has to offer so they usually exhibit the same failings and weaknesses as the rest of us. They get angry when they shouldn't, let their egos motivate them more than they should, and are entirely too concerned with doing what's popular rather than what's right. They suffer from the same three poisons as the populations they lead: greed, anger, and stupidity.

The true cause of war lies in the unchecked rampaging of these three poisons through the hearts of individual people. Though the situations confronting world leaders that lead them to decide to wage war often seem complex, the only way in which they're different from conflict that erupts between two people standing in a room is that they occur on a larger scale. But if in civilized societies we expect people to work out their differences amicably (whether themselves or with the help of the courts), why don't those same expectations apply to differences between civilized countries?

In a world in which tyranny continues to exist, war may in fact sometimes be justified. In the same way it's necessary to fight to defend oneself when attacked, so too it's sometimes necessary to go to war to put down injustice, or even the possibility of injustice when its likelihood is great enough. Rarely, however, is this given as a primary reason. Even democracies seem to be roused to war only by self-interest.

Avoiding war methods:

1. Leaders can not be dominated by anger emotion or feeling very earily

In fact, I believe that expert human beings who do not like to bring war very earily. They To achieve world peace—to create a world in which war ceases to break out—seems impossible because of the sheer number of people who haven't yet mastered themselves, who haven't tamed their ambition to raise themselves up at the expense of others, and who haven't learned to start from today onward, letting past wrongs committed by both sides remain in the past. In short, it seems an impossible dream because we're in desperately short supply of human beings who are experts at living.

article continues after advertisement

An expert at living isn't a person who never experiences greed, anger, or stupidity but rather one who remains in firm control of those negative parts (which can never be entirely eliminated), who's able to surmount his or her darkest negativity, and displays a peerless ability to resolve conflict peacefully. What generates this expert ability to resolve conflict? Wisdom and joy. Wise people are happy people, and happy people are wise. If enough people in the world's population became happy and wise, violence would be used far less often to solve conflict. If this pool of experts at living became large enough, we'd start seeing some of our leaders being picked from among them. And if enough leaders were experts at living, war, too, would be used far less often to solve conflict and further the interests of nations.

However, the most significant obstacle to achieving world peace isn't the extraordinary difficulty involved in becoming a genuine expert at living, though. It's that those most in need of reforming the tenets they hold in their hearts, who most need training in how to be an expert at living, are those least interested in it, a point well articulated here. The only real lever we have to pull with such people is their desire to become happy. We must convince them to follow our lead by becoming so happy ourselves—so ridiculously, genuinely happy—that they decide on their own they want to be like us, that they want what we have. And then we have to show them how to get it. Good ideas are our weapons. When people come to deeply believe in notions that promote peace, peace will follow like a shadow follows the body. So, any leaders must believe that weapons are not the best solution to achieve leader person success. They must believe that if they can cooperate to any country leaders which must be the best solution ,because it is the only way when they can sit down to spend time to discuss how to solve any social argument, then they can help themselves to decide the most method to solve any social , even country challenges. So, weapons are the foolish tool , it represents the foolish leader whose personal choice in nowadays society. Negotation or cooperation to avoid argument between leaders this strategy must be the best method to avoid war. I shall indicate these different psychological methods to leaders as below:

1. Require the leaders who promote and support war to personally participate in the hostilities. This would provide a critical threshold of personal commitment to war by requiring some actual personal sacrifice of leaders.

2. Show the faces and tell the stories of the children of the "enemy" until we can feel the pain of their deaths as though they were the deaths of our own children. It is much more difficult to slaughter an enemy who one recognizes as being part of the human family.

3. Give full support to the establishment of an International Criminal Court so that national leaders can be tried for all egregious war crimes at the end of any hostilities. All leaders who commit egregious crimes must be held to account under international law as they were at Nuremberg, and they must be aware of this from the outset.

4. Impeach any elected leaders who promote or support illegal, preventive war, what was described at the Nuremberg Trials as an "aggressive" war. It is the responsibility of citizens in a democracy to exercise control over their leaders who threaten to commit crimes under international law, and impeachment provides an important tool to achieve this control.

5. Rise up as a people and demand that one's government follow its Constitution, cut off funding for war and find a way to peace. US citizens must demand that Congress not give away or allow the president to usurp its sole authority under the Constitution to make the decision to go to war. Citizens should also demand that Congress exercise its power of the purse to prevent war, including not giving financial support to a president attempting to bribe other countries to participate in an illegal war.

6. Preventing nuclear war methods may include: In order to help prevent it, it's helpful to first take some time to learn about the consequences of such a war and how it would affect the entire world. Once you're armed with knowledge, you can start contacting your local representatives to encourage them to take action in preventing nuclear war.Show up to town hall meetings, if applicable. If you have the opportunity to go to a town hall meeting in your city or town, use this as a chance to voice your concerns about the threat of nuclear war. The representatives at this meeting will be able to hear your message, as well as others attending the town hall meeting.

7. Prepare what you're going to say before attending the meeting.

Use the information you gathered in your research to support your argument. Send an online message to your representatives. Many times, you can email the specific representative from your district by finding their message page. Type in something like "Find my representative" followed by your location. This should lead you to your representative's site which will often have a contact option.

Use the contact option to send your representative a message. Make your message as personalized as possible—representatives are more likely to take action if they feel the issue is truly important to you. Your message could say something like, "I strongly urge you to push for negotiations regarding the use of nuclear weapons," and continue talking about how the threat of nuclear war affects you and others around the world.

8. Write a letter to personalize your message. A hand-written letter asking your representatives to prioritize the threat of nuclear war is a helpful way of taking action. When writing the letter, use facts and information you've gathered about why it's so important to prevent nuclear war, and keep it to about 1 page.

9. Call your representatives to encourage them to take action. Taking the time to call your representatives shows that you're passionate about the topic and want your voice heard. Keep your message or talk short and specific, and use a polite tone to give your argument authority and value.

10. Ask your representatives for an in-person meeting. Call your representative's office to see if you can schedule a meeting to talk with them. Since they're super busy people, you may have to wait several weeks, or get a meeting with one of their aides instead. Prepare what you want to talk about ahead of time so that you're ready.

On conclusion, it is bad enough if a conflict between major powers erupts because of intractable grievances over crucial substantive issues. But it is even worse if such a tragedy occurs because rivals engage in ill-considered, symbolic posturing. Unfortunately, that appears to be the trend in both East Asia and Eastern Europe. It would be wise for all parties involved to reduce the level of risk and renounce such conduct.

Learning Human past development history method

● What is the timeline of human prehistory?

History is the study of the past in order to understand the meaning and dynamics of the relationship between cause and effect in the overall development of human societies.This timeline of human prehistory comprises the time from the first appearance of Homo sapiens in Africa 300,000 years ago to the invention of writing and the beginning of history, 5,000 years ago. It thus covers the time from the Middle Paleolithic (Old Stone Age) to the very beginnings of world history.Human evolution, the process by which human beings developed on Earth from now-extinct primates. Viewed zoologically, we humans are Homo sapiens, a culture-bearing upright-walking species that lives on the ground and very likely first evolved in Africa about 315,000 years ago.This is the oldest human permanent settlement that has yet been found by archaeologists. 21,000 years ago: artifacts suggest early human activity occurred in Canberra, the capital city of Australia. 20,000 years ago: oldest pottery storage or cooking vessels from China. 20,000–10,000 years ago: Khoisanid expansion to Central Africa.

Human history, also known as world history, is the description of humanity's past. It is informed by archaeology, anthropology, genetics, linguistics, and other disciplines; and, for periods since the invention of writing, by recorded history and by secondary sources and studies. As agriculture advanced, most humans transitioned from a nomadic to a settled lifestyle as farmers in permanent settlements. The relative security and increased productivity provided by farming allowed communities to expand into increasingly larger units, fostered by advances in transportation.

The first humans emerged in Africa around two million years ago, long before the modern humans known as Homo sapiens appeared on the same continent.There's a lot anthropologists still don't know about how different groups of humans interacted and mated with each other over this long stretch of prehistory. Thanks to new archaeological and genealogical research. First things first: A "human" is anyone who belongs to the genus Homo (Latin for "man"). Scientists still don't know exactly when or how the first humans evolved, but they've identified a few of the oldest ones.

One of the earliest known humans is Homo habilis, or "handy man," who lived about 2.4 million to 1.4 million years ago in Eastern and Southern Africa. Others include Homo rudolfensis, who lived in Eastern Africa about 1.9 million to 1.8 million years ago (its name comes from its discovery in East Rudolph, Kenya); and Homo erectus, the "upright man" who ranged from Southern Africa all the way to modern-day China and Indonesia from about 1.89

million to 110,000 years ago.In addition to these early humans, researchers have found evidence of an unknown "superarchaic" group that separated from other humans in Africa around two million years ago. These superarchaic humans mated with the ancestors of Neanderthals and Denisovans, according to a paper published in Science Advances in February 2020. This marks the earliest known instance of human groups mating with each other—something we know happened a lot more later on.

● Why do we need to develop and learn human history ?

History helps us develop a better understanding of the world. You can't build a framework on which to base your life.History helps us understand ourselves. To understand who you are, you need to develop a sense of self. History helps us learn to understand other people. History is not just an essential introduction to your own country. However, studying history is important because doing so allows us to understand our past, which in turn allows us to understand our present. If we want to know how and why our world is the way it is today, we have to look to history for answers.

Moreover, to study history, rather than merely to memorize lists of battles, however, is to look into the causes of and relationships between important events. Historians do not merely record what took place, but try to work out why. This is why the study of history includes historiography and philosophical theories of history. It also includes epistemology. Historians weigh different types of evidence in a forensic manner, trying to establish which accounts are reliable and corroborated. The study of history, therefore, is important both because it helps students to understand the past, and therefore the present, and because it teaches vital skills for discovering the truth. In addition to these points, history is an inevitable part of every other academic discipline. Scientists study the history of science, literary scholars study the history of literature. An in-depth understanding of any subject requires the study of history.

● past medical development

The Past, Present and Future of Healthcare ought how develop ? Economy, social standards, and general thinking models have always been a massive influence on pretty much every industry mankind has dealt with. Healthcare makes no exception , so we have created an infographic to show you just how much healthcare has evolved across the ages. Lessons from the past medical (health care) development, the patient should be at the center of the healthcare system should always and not the other way around, where instead of implementing patient-centered solutions, the system is complicating and worsening an already challenging situation for the patient.

How past medical development

Mainly thanks to the continuous technological progresses in the industry, healthcare has transformed significantly in the past few years. A lot of things nobody would have thought possible a few years back are now practicable and they're actually saving lives. Evaluating, diagnosing and treating patients from a distance is nowadays possible thanks to telemedicine.

Thus, nowadays, collecting, storing and managing patient data while achieving HIPAA compliance is of great significance within the healthcare industry. That is precisely why various solutions to manage data collection processes faster and in a more secure way had to be implemented. Electronic medical records allow physicians to access records online and store them securely in order to give their patients access to their personal health records as well. It is come from our past medical development.

In our past medical development history, it is difficult to explain when vaccines became an accepted practice, mostly because the journey to discovery was long and complicated. Beginning with an attempt by Edward Jenner in 1796 to use inoculations to tame the infamous smallpox virus, the usefulness and popularity of vaccines grew very quickly. Throughout the 1800s and early 1900s, various vaccinations were created to combat some of the world's deadliest diseases, including smallpox, rabies, tuberculosis, and cholera. Over the course of 200 years, one of the deadliest diseases known to man – the small pox – was wiped off the face of the earth. Today, vaccines continue to save millions of lives each year - including jabs that protect against deadly flu strains and can help prevent some cancers.

Before the first use of a general anaesthetic in the mid-19th century, surgery was undertaken only as a last resort, with several patients opting for death rather than enduring the excruciating ordeal. Although there were countless earlier experiments with anaesthesia dating as far back to 4000 BC – William T. G. Morton made history in 1846 when he successfully used ether as an anaesthetic during surgery. Soon after, a faster-acting substance called chloroform became widely used, but was considered high-risk after several fatalities were reported. Over the 150 years since, safer anaesthetics have been developed, allowing millions of life-saving, painless operations to take place.

The first medical imaging machines were X-rays. The X-ray, a form of electromagnetic radiation, was 'accidentally' invented in 1895 by German physicist Wilhelm Conrad Röntgen when experimenting with electrical currents through glass cathode-ray tubes. The discovery transformed medicine overnight and by the following year, Glasgow hospital opened the world's very first radiology department.

Although originally discovered many years before, began being used for medical diagnosis in 1955. This medical imaging device uses high frequency sound waves to create a digital image, and was no less than ground-breaking in terms of detecting pre-natal conditions and other pelvic and abdominal abnormalities. In 1967, the computed tomography (CT) scanner was created, which uses X-ray detectors and computers to diagnose many different types of disease, and has become a fundamental diagnostic tool in modern medicine.

The incredible potential of stem cells was discovered in the late 1970s, when they were found inside human cord blood. Two specific characteristics make stem cells remarkable: they are unspecialised cells that can renew themselves through cell division even after being inactive, and under certain conditions can be used to make any type of human cell. This discovery has enormous potential and stem cell therapy has already been used to treat leukaemia and other blood disorders, as well as in bone marrow transplantation. Research is currently ongoing to use stem cells to treat spinal cord injuries and a number of neurological conditions such as Alzheimer's, Parkinson' and strokes. However, due to the ethical issues surrounding the use of embryonic stem cells, researchers are likely to face many obstacles when developing stem cell-based therapy.

The next major medical imaging technology was discovered in 1973 when Paul Lauterbur produced the first magnetic resonance image (MRI). The nuclear magnetic resonance data creates detailed images within the body and is a crucial tool in detecting life-threatening conditions including tumours, cysts, damage to the brain and spinal cord and some heart and liver problems.

● past transport development

The history of transport is largely one of technological innovation. Advances in technology have allowed people to travel farther, explore more territory, and expand their influence over larger and larger areas. Even in ancient times, new tools such as foot coverings, skis, and snowshoes lengthened the distances that could be traveled. As new inventions and discoveries were applied to transport problems, travel time decreased while the ability to move more and larger loads increased. Innovation continues as transport researchers are working to find new ways to reduce costs and increase transport efficiency. However, international trade was the driving motivator behind advancements in global transportation in the Pre Modern world, there was a single global world economy with a worldwide division of labor and multilateral trade from 1500 onward.The sale and transportation of Textile, silver and gold, spices, slaves and luxury goods throughout Afro-Eurasia and later the New World would see an evolution in overland and sea trade routes and travel .

Road transport development, the first earth tracks were created by humans carrying goods and often followed trails. Tracks would be naturally created at points of high traffic density. As animals were domesticated, horses, oxen and donkeys became an element in track-creation. With the growth of trade, tracks were often flattened or widened to accommodate animal traffic (hollow way or drover's road). Later, the travois, a frame used to drag loads, was developed. Animal-drawn wheeled vehicles were probably developed in the Ancient Near East in the 4th or 5th millennium BC and spread to Europe and India in the 4th millennium BC and China in about 1200 BC. The Romans had a significant need for good roads to extend and maintain their empire and developed Roman roads.

Rail transport development, the history of rail transportation dates back nearly 500 years and includes systems with man or horsepower and rails of wood (or occasionally stone). This was usually for moving coal from the mine down to a river, from where it could continue by boat, with a flanged wheel running on a rail. The use of cast iron plates as rails began in the 1760s, and was followed by systems (plateways) where the flange was part of the rail.

However, with the introduction of rolled wrought iron rails, these became obsolete.

past technology developemnt

Technology runs our lives these days. Smartphones, tablets and computers – we really can't seem to function without them. In a very short amount of time, technology has exploded in the market and now, many people cannot imagine a life without it. To understand how we left the dark ages (which really wasn't all that long ago) to where we are today, it is important to understand how technology evolves and why it matters.

Purpose Drives Technology Forward

All technologies are born out of purpose. For example, search engines were created to sort through the massive amounts of data online. With each new upgrade technology compounds existing technologies to create something better than what was previously used before.

With the lightning speed of technological evolution, it is no wonder many people have struggled to keep up. To be fair, the scope of technology's expanse is so great, wrapping everything up into a single blog post is practically impossible.

The Past: World, Meet The Internet

Looking back to the 1990's, the Internet was a new commodity many, but not all, households and businesses began to gain access. For people living during that time, the sound of the painfully slow dial up signal connecting to the Internet is a not-so-fond memory.

past construction development

Construction is an ancient human activity. It began with the purely functional need for a controlled environment to moderate the effects of climate. Constructed shelters were one means by which human beings were able to adapt themselves to a wide variety of climates and become a global species.

The history of construction overlaps many other fields like structural engineering and relies on other branches of science like archaeology, history and architecture to investigate how the builders lived and recorded their accomplishments. Those fields allow us to analyse constructed buildings and other structures built since prehistory, the tools used and the different uses of building materials. History of building is evolving by different trends in time, marked by few key principles : durability of the materials used, the increasing of height and span, the degree of control exercised over the interior environment and finally the energy available to the construction process.

● past education development

Past Education System Education was strong in ancient days also. In ancient days, the education system has changed based on periods such as Vedic, Brahmanical, Muslim, British periods. In Vedic periods schools were becoming boarding and students were handed over to the teacher.

Education in the Past:

Education in early, medieval, and the British periods has to be viewed in:

(a) The perspective of historical growth, and

(b) Its philosophic significance.

From the latter point of view, in the Vedic period, schools were boarding schools where a child was handed over to the teacher at the age of about eight years, and he was imparted knowledge for developing ideal behaviour and not for its utilitarian end. Knowledge, it was felt, was something that lent meaning, glory, and lustier to life. The teacher took personal interest in the life of his students. Education was all comprehensive.

For example, physical education was compulsory. Students were taught to build up a strong and healthy body. Training was given in the art of war, including archery, riding, driving, and in other allied fields. School education began with phonology, including study of grammar. After that, study of logic was taken up which dealt with the laws of reasoning and art of thinking. Then came science of Arts and Crafts. Lastly, came the discipline of life which was concerned with sexual purity and chastity in thought and action, including simplicity in food and dress, emphasis on equality, fraternity and independence, and respect for the teacher. Thus, language, logic, craft, discipline and building up character formed the basics of education in early India.

In the Brahmanical period, the Vedic literature formed the chief subject of instruction. The main aim of education was the learning of the Vedas. But the Sudras were excluded from the right to education. Education was given on the basis of caste rather than ability and aptitude. Women also were debarred from education.

In the Muslim period, the objectives of education changed. It was more to teach the three R's and train in religious norms. The higher education was imparted through schools of learning while the vocational and professional training was given within the caste structure. Sanskrit and Arabic or Persian was the mediums of instruction.

In fact, any country past education teacher indivdual income source comes from pupils mainly, but many vocational training institutions , they are the main school organizations in any past education industry development. The teachers' remuneration was paid by the rulers through grant of land, presents from pupils, allowances paid by wealthy citizens, and payment in the form of food, clothes or other articles. The financial position of the schools was not very strong. They did not have special buildings of their own. In many cases, schools were held in local temples or mosques or teachers' houses. The schools were conducted almost exclusively by Maulvis (priests) for the Muslim students and by Brahmins for the Hindu students. Vocational training was provided by father, brother, etc. to the child. Thus, the caste system provided vocational training and transmitted skills from generation to generation and also provided gainful employment. There was no emphasis on physical education, developing thinking ability, or teaching some craft. Chastity, equality, simplicity were not the ideals of student life. The specialisation of professional roles had not reached a stage at which a separate class or caste could take up education work as a specialised function. Education was more practical.

In the British period, education aimed at producing mainly clerks. Education was student-centred rather than teacher-centred. Unlike today, education in this period never aimed at freedom of individual, excellence of individual, equality amongst all people, individual and group self-reliance, and national cohesion. Christian missionaries engaged in imparting education gave considerable importance to conversion of religion. Education in schools and colleges was not productive which could break down the social, regional and linguistic barriers. It never aimed at making people masters of technology. It also did not focus on fighting injustice, intolerance and superstition.

● past traditional work model changing

Is the traditional workplace over? The traditional workplace is over, and by 2030 it will look and feel totally different. According to CBRE, workplaces solutions will help workers with productivity, with an increased emphasis on communal workspaces. The traditional work environment is quickly changing. The rapid rise in coworking, defined as "the use of an office or other working environment by people who are self-employed or working for different employers, typically so as to share equipment, ideas, and knowledge," has started to change the way we work. What are the benefits of traditional workplace culture? Companies with traditional workplace cultures are often bureaucratic, and on the bright side, this can mean that they benefit from stability, structured communication, central authority and decision-making, and consistency.

Each new generation in our workforce is a catalyst for change in workplace culture. The inevitability of each new generation becoming the majority in our workforce, and therefore becoming the most influential demographic group in the corporate world, has been one of the primary catalysts for change in the dynamic of workplace culture for some time now. The exponential growth in technology and its subsequent innovations, paired with the growing millennial influence, has put productivity in the workplace environment.

We can see a lot of new, nontraditional practices in workplace culture. In older, larger corporations, in which change is difficult, slow, and often discouraged, traditional practices still dominate. What if your company isn't a startup or tech-based company that's parallel to the Silicon Valley trajectory, but also isn't a huge global corporation that's been around for half a century? Balancing traditional and nontraditional practices in workplace culture becomes an issue that's not only important, but crucial to employee productivity, and ultimately, your business's success.

Traditional Practices: What They Are, and Their Benefits:

These days, it's easier to identify traditional culture characteristics and practices from their potential drawbacks than it is to conduct a simple online search. Companies with traditional workplace cultures are often bureaucratic, and on the bright side, this can mean that they benefit from stability, structured communication, central authority and decision-making, and consistency. Within such companies, there is a certain level of professionalism when it comes to work hours, personal space, and work-related responsibilities and communications.

While 9-to-5 workdays and cubicles are disappearing in favor of flexible hours and open-office layouts, established corporations are still finding success in traditional office spaces and uniform work hours and even dress codes. When your employees are expected to arrive at the office on time, maintain a professional appearance and conduct their work within their designated work areas and with respect to their coworkers, which ultimately amounts to an organized and respectful workplace, companies stand to gain. How? Such traditional organizational cultures and practices feature highly efficient and productive employees that thrive in a relatively stress-free environment. Furthermore, valuing traditional practices based on professionalism have been seen to trickle down to clients and customers, and it's no secret that this is the key to success for your business.

Nontraditional Practices: What They Are, and Their Benefits:

Nontraditional practices in workplace culture don't necessarily mean the opposite of traditional practices. What it means, for the most part, is that these practices are employed to accommodate a company's geographic barriers, per its digital workplaces, as well as its employees' individual and collective needs, be it from diversity or otherwise.

The key to nontraditional practices in workplace culture is flexibility. Being flexible with your culture refers to granting some or all of your employees the freedom to organize their schedules and work hours to meet their needs as long as their work is completed on time, flexibility in holidays and days off, and opening most or all workspaces to allow employees the freedom to create an environment that fosters collaboration and productivity. Some companies even go so far as to provide a full kitchen, including food, beverages, and snacks.

One of the most successful companies at implementing this type of nontraditional workplace cultures and practices is Google. It's Mountain View, California headquarters features Wi-Fi enabled shuttles, free healthy meals, laundry and fitness facilities, and on-site childcare. Certainly a progressive work-life balance will be needed to change from past working model. For example, Google internet company organizational culture and practices, while they've proven to be wildly successful, provide a sound framework for the fundamental structure of how nontraditional practices in workplace culture can foster productivity. This structure includes practices such as working from home, private rooms for designated activities, wellness programs, evolving workspaces, and equal opportunity in regards to diversity.

Indeed, these nontraditional practices contribute to the success of modern companies worldwide, via employee engagement, satisfaction, and productivity, but much is lost in the way of professionalism. Is it worth the potential costs? Let's assume your company's workforce is comprised of equal-parts baby boomers (Gen A) and millennials (Gen B). How do you balance the needs of two generations, of which the age gap pits traditional and nontraditional practices against each other? It may be easier said than done, but flexibility is the answer, and of course, exceptional leadership.

Here's a list of several characteristics and practices with which to be flexible, and the role that leadership plays in helping create a (healthy) balance of professionalism and productivity:

Work hours: While older, tenured employees may be used to and dependent on routine work days and hours, younger employees tend to benefit from dynamic hours. Great leaders will ensure that a company's needs are met first and foremost, while bridging the gap between employee practices in work hours. Professionalism is the key to creating an understanding across all employees, no matter how flexible a work schedule they require to be their most productive selves.

Coworking Spaces: Is it possible to have closed offices and cubicles, but also open rooms and non-assigned desks and rooms? Certainly. To reduce costs and benefit most from flexible office layouts, your company might need to designate certain spaces and offices to certain employees, tasks, and meetings, while allowing a free-flowing, open-office layout in other areas. As a leader within your company, this means setting and enforcing certain rules and regulations, especially when it concerns noise levels, personal space, and personal items.

Management: Traditional practices in management feature the bureaucratic top-down approach. Millennials don't seem to enjoy the layers this seems to add in communication, and are deterred by the "command and control" element it adds to workplace culture. While digital collaboration platforms, which companies have had no choice but to adopt, have assisted in the way of opening lines of communication, your company's management needs to restructure its policies towards task-delegation, communication, and other relevant issues. In regards to leadership, leaders must be more approachable, cooperative, and willing to individualize management policies and practices to fit the needs of each employee.

Learning Human present development process

● Human right development history

The belief that everyone, by virtue of her or his humanity, is entitled to certain human rights is fairly new. Its roots, however, lie in earlier tradition and documents of many cultures; it took the catalyst of World War II to propel human rights onto the global stage and into the global conscience.

Throughout much of history, people acquired rights and responsibilities through their membership in a group – a family, indigenous nation, religion, class, community, or state. Most societies have had traditions similar to the "golden rule" of "Do unto others as you would have them do unto you." The Hindu Vedas, the Babylonian Code of Hammurabi, the Bible, the Quran (Koran), and the Analects of Confucius are five of the oldest written sources which address questions of people's duties, rights, and responsibilities. In addition, the Inca and Aztec codes of conduct and justice and an Iroquois Constitution were Native American sources that existed well before the 18th century. In fact, all societies, whether in oral or written tradition, have had systems of propriety and justice as well as ways of tending to the health and welfare of their members. Global human right development had been experiencing mature stage from non human right development stage.

Global human rights and development (GHRAD) Human rights and development aims converge in many instances and are beneficial only to the government and not the people although there can be conflict between their different approaches. Today,when? a human rights-based approach is viewed by many as essential to achieving development goals. Historically, the "minority clauses" guaranteeing civil and political rights and religious and cultural toleration to minorities were significant acts emerging from the peace process of World War I relating to a peoples rights to self-determination. Overseen by the League of Nations Council the process allowed petitions from individuals and was monitored under the jurisdiction of the Permanent Court of International Justice. The 'clauses' are an important early signpost in both the human rights and development histories.

● Reasons we need need to develop human right

1: Human rights ensure people have basic needs met

Everyone needs access to medicine, food and water, clothes, and shelter. By including these in a person's basic human rights, everyone has a baseline level of dignity. Unfortunately, there are still millions of people out there who don't have these necessities, but saying it's a matter of human rights allows activists and others to work towards getting those for everyone.

2: Human rights protect vulnerable groups from abuse

The Declaration of Human Rights was created largely because of the Holocaust and the horrors of WII. During that time in history, the most vulnerable in society were targeted along with the Jewish population, including those with disabilities and LGBT. Organizations concerned with human rights focus on members of society most vulnerable to abuse from powerholders, instead of ignoring them.

3: Human rights allow people to stand up to societal corruption

The concept of human rights allows people to speak up when they experience abuse and corruption. This is why specific rights like the right to assemble are so crucial because no society is perfect. The concept of human rights empowers people and tells them that they deserve dignity from society, whether it's the government or their work environment. When they don't receive it, they can stand up.

4: Human rights encourage freedom of speech and expression

While similar to what you just read above, being able to speak freely without fear of brutal reprisal is more expansive. It encompasses ideas and forms of expression that not everybody will like or agree with, but no one should ever feel like they are going to be in danger from their government because of what they think. It goes both ways, too, and protects people who want to debate or argue with certain ideas expressed in their society.

5: Human rights give people the freedom to practice their religion (or not practice any) Religious violence and oppression occur over and over again all across history, from the Crusades to the Holocaust to modern terrorism in the name of religion. Human rights acknowledges the importance of a person's religion and spiritual beliefs, and lets them practice in peace. The freedom to not hold to a religion is also a human right.

6: Human rights allows people to love who they choose

The importance of freedom to love cannot be understated. Being able to choose what one's romantic life looks like is an essential human right. The consequences of not protecting this right are clear when you look at countries where LGBT people are oppressed and abused, or where women are forced into marriages they don't want.

7: Human rights encourage equal work opportunities

The right to work and make a living allows people to flourish in their society. Without acknowledging that the work environment can be biased or downright oppressive, people find themselves enduring abuse or insufficient opportunities. The concept of human rights provides a guide for how workers should be treated and encourages equality.

8: Human rights give people access to education

Education is important for so many reasons and is crucial for societies where poverty is common. Organizations and governments concerned with human rights provide access to schooling, supplies, and more in order to halt the cycle of poverty. Seeing education as a right means everyone can get access, not just the elite.

9: Human rights protect the environment

The marriage between human rights and environmentalism is becoming stronger due to climate change and the effects it has on people. We live in the world, we need the land, so it makes sense that what happens to the environment impacts humanity. The right to clean air, clean soil, and clean water are all as important as the other rights included in this list.

10: Human rights provide a universal standard that holds governments accountable

Human right development had a two-fold purpose: provide a guideline for the future and force the world to acknowledge that during WWII, human rights had been violated on a massive scale. With a standard for what is a human right, governments can be held accountable for their actions. There's power in naming an injustice and pointing to a precedent, which makes the UDHR and other human right documents so important.

● present medical development

Nowadays, artificial intelligence can assist medical health service to improve patient medical service performance in order to let they feel more medical satisfaction. Having been in gradual development over the past decade, artificial intelligence has already produced impressive technologies that have significantly altered the healthcare landscape. Life science companies and research institutions are teaming up with pioneering technology giants such as Google, IBM and Apple to invent smarter and faster ways to diagnose, treat and prevent diseases. These innovative technologies range from diagnostic tools that can detect malignant tumours invisible to the naked eye, to cognitive computing systems that produce tailored treatment plans for cancer patients. So, it seems that impact artificial intelligence is having on healthcare service to bring patients to feel more health care service satisfaction.

What does present medical mean? During the 19th century, economic and industrial growth continued to develop, and people made many scientific discoveries and inventions. Scientists made rapid progress in identifying and preventing illnesses and in understanding how bacteria and viruses work.

However, they still had a long way to go regarding the treatment and cures of infectious diseases. During the 19th century, the way that people were living and working was changing dramatically. These changes affected the risk of infectious diseases and other conditions. In our nowadays medical industry innovation, it may include these factors to influence its innovation in success.

Industry: As more manufacturing processes became mechanized, various work-related diseases became more common. These included lung disease, dermatitis, and "phossy jaw," a type of jaw necrosis that affected people working with phosphorous, usually in the match industry.

Urban sprawl: Cities started to expand rapidly, and certain health problems, such as typhus and cholera, became more common as a result.

Travel: As people traveled between various parts of the world, they carried diseases with them, including yellow fever.

Meanwhile, scientific advances at that time started to make new treatments possible. Scientific breakthroughs: As "germ theory" developed, scientists began to test and prove the principles of hygiene and antisepsis in treating wounds and preventing infection. New inventions included the electrocardiograph, which records the electrical activity of the heart over time.

Communications: As postal services and other communications improved, medical knowledge was able to spread rapidly.

Political changes: Democracy led to people demanding health as a human right.

However, the 19th and 20th centuries saw breakthroughs occurring in infection control. At the end of the 19th century, 30 percent of deaths were due to infection. By the end of the 20th century, this figure had fallen to less than 4 percent. So, nowdays medical innovation can reduce more patient death number in global hospitals.

● present transport development

In the reconstruction of a region or a nation, transport systems invariably play a vital role. The growth and development of transportation provides a medium, contributing to the progress of agriculture, industry, commerce, administration, defence, education, health or any other community activity. Many of the regional characteristics that are influencing the layout of the existing transformational system are the creation of their antecedent transformational features. However, the present-day transport network has evolved out of the past framework because as trail evolves successfully into the pioneer dirt road, then into the improved farm road and finally, into the present day paved highways with heavy motor traffic. Many factors are involved in the development of a transport system. The present-day transport system of a country or a region cannot be explained by one factor alone.

Below these factors are influencing our future transport systems how change , they may include:

1. The historical factor – this involves the location and pattern of systems, technological development, and institutional development and settlement, and land-use patterns.

2. The technological factor – the technological characteristics of each major transport mode are considered together with a discussion of the effects of technological advances.

3. The physical factor – this includes physiographic controls upon route selection, and geological and climatic influences.

4. The economic factor – the structure and nature of transport costs are examined, together with service quality and methods of pricing and charging.

5. Political and social factors – these include political motives for transport facilities; government involvement in capital, monopolies and competition, safety, working conditions and coordination between modes; transport as and employer and the social consequences of transport developments.

The above mentioned factors affect transport in different ways, influencing each other as well as affecting transport systems directly and indirectly. Transport systems themselves, together with the physical environment within which they are set, also influence all these different areas of human activity. Each factor may operate in a positive, negative or neutral way; each may affect transport on different scales, from the local to the global; and two basic dimensions time and space are involved.

present technology developemnt

Technology development is a manifestation of scientific progress. This strong shift in the world of technology, which is represented in several aspects, advanced by information technology, as well as technology related to devices and inventions, etc. Technology has become a feature of the modern era, and the necessities of life, so hardly one can dispense with it, it is present in educational institutions, in medicine, in the media, in communication, and in agriculture, etc. The technology development has gone through several stages until it reached what it is now, keep reading to discover together the different stages of technology development.

We distinguish 4 stages of technology development:

The first stage called the emerging technology stage. It is the acquisition of a production process, infrastructure, skilled labor, mastery of management systems, and product quality. This stage was marked by a high level of risk in it, due to its lack of use before; there are no previous experiences related to it. As the risk and failure rate is advanced, this stage spent a long time until the safety of technological tools was confirmed, and it can be trusted.

The second is a process of adaptation to more sophisticated technologies allowing to market products adapted to local or foreign demand. It is called rapid technology stage and characterized by fast progress and spread and met with great acceptance due to the reliability of the technology and the success of the experiences related to it. The technology of this stage was used in establishments and institutions, as well as in the services of SMS messages and related to cellular devices.

The third stage of technology development is the introduction of the first degree of innovation. That allows the firm to improve its productivity and competitiveness. It has its own research laboratory and begins to produce its own licenses.

The stage of the basic technology. In this stage, technology has become one of the main pillars upon which enterprises depend. Such as the presence of the Internet, where enterprises and companies depend on most of their business, and without them, they will lose their productive and competitive role.

present construction development

How technology is transforming the construction industry?

The construction industry has a vast potential, and companies should focus on implementing digitalisation, innovative technologies, and new construction techniques to improve productivity and efficiency. For example, in India, the construction industry is an important indicator of the state of the economy as it is one of the largest employment generators in the country. With strong linkages to industries such as cement, steel, chemicals, paints, tiles, etc., the sector serves as one of the strongest propellers of private sector involvement in the country's built environment. Between now and 2050, rapid social and economic changes will significantly increase India's population and the size of its cities, creating a huge demand for the construction industry. India will soon have one of the largest shares of the world's building stock, consisting mainly of new developments.

As the operation dynamics of the real estate business in India are evolving and innovating at a pace much faster than envisioned, it is almost imperative that innovations be applied to the most basic as well as most important step in the value chain – construction techniques. Today, new technologies in construction are being developed; and what seemed like future tech 10-20 years ago—connected equipment and tools, telematics, mobile apps, autonomous heavy equipment, drones, robots, augmented and virtual reality, and 3D printed buildings—are here, being deployed and used on jobsites across the world. It is also expected that there will be wider use of technology in construction and construction management in the future as companies realise the long-term efficiency and cost savings of such techniques.

Technology in the construction space has coincided with growing demand for faster construction and world-class quality. Some of the trends that we foresee playing a pivotal role are as follows: Real-time information through software and mobile apps: Today, there are software and mobile solutions to help manage every aspect of a construction project. Mobile technology allows for real-time data collection and transmission between the jobsite and project managers in the back office. Cloud-based solutions enable on-site employees to submit timecards, expense reports, requests for information (RFIs), work records, and other verified documentation. This can save hundreds of hours per year in data entry, and automatically organises critical files. Nowadays, construction industry applies smart phones technology to bring real time data collection response in order to achieve construction workers cooperation efficiently. Real-time information through software and mobile apps: Today, there are software and mobile solutions to help manage every aspect of a construction project. Mobile technology allows for real-time data collection and transmission between the jobsite and project managers in the back office. Cloud-based solutions enable on-site employees to submit timecards, expense reports, requests for information (RFIs), work records, and other verified documentation. This can save hundreds of hours per year in data entry, and automatically organises critical files.

Hence, smartphones may bring these advantags to construction industry. Smartphones and mobile apps have made communication and collaboration on projects easier. By integrating solutions that sync in real time, allowing different stakeholders to add notes, change drawings and responds to RFIs instantly and then share that information among everyone involved with the project at the same time, without interrupting the day's work. Transforming product development through offsite construction Offsite construction is typically used on projects with repetitive floorplans or layouts in their design such as apartment buildings, hotels, hospitals, dormitories, prisons, and schools. Offsite is performed in a controlled environment and it works like an auto manufacturing plant. At each station, workers have all the tools and materials to consistently perform their task, whether that be constructing a wall frame or installing electrical wiring. This assembly plant method of construction reduces waste and allows workers to be more productive. Use of construction technologies to bring down construction cost It is expected that there will be a wider use of tech in construction and construction management in the future as companies realise the long-term efficiency and cost savings of such techniques. Tech in construction space has coincided with a growing demand for faster construction and world-class quality.

Digtial technology can also bring these advantages to construction industry. Technologies such as aluminum formwork, tunnel formwork, prefabricated buildings, building information modelling (BIM), among others, can assist in significant savings if adopted. With the use of BIM, developers can incorporate digital representations of buildings in 3D models to facilitate better collaboration among all stakeholders on a project. This can lead to better designing and construction of buildings. Tunnel framework makes use of steel fabricated forms to cast beams, walls and columns in one go. As the steel formwork can be used repetitively, it lowers labour costs and saves time as the walls and slabs do not need finishing work, thereby improving construction efficiency. In addition to this, by implementing prefabricated technologies, developers can avail of benefits such as site safety, waste reduction, improved air quality, and quality management. Disruptive and exponential technologies to accelerate innovation Construction firms are now using data to make better decisions, increase productivity, improve jobsite safety, and reduce risks. With artificial intelligence (AI) and machine learning systems, firms can turn the data they have collected over the years to predict future outcomes on projects. Furthermore, they gain a competitive advantage when estimating and bidding on construction projects as well. AI can also improve worker productivity by reducing the amount of time wasted moving about the construction site to retrieve tools, materials and equipment to perform certain tasks. With virtual reality (VR), workers could get exposure to environments such as confined spaces or working at height in a safe, controlled environment. VR simulators have been used for years to train soldiers, pilots, and surgeons and could be used in the same way to train workers on everything from operating cranes and excavators to doing welding and masonry work. Augmented reality (AR) is another technology that can greatly improve safety on the construction site. Whether it's allowing for a more detailed safety plan to be developed or providing training on heavy equipment using actual equipment on real sites with augmented hazards, there are several ways that AR can be deployed on the jobsite. In addition to this, companies are also relying on bricklaying robots or rebar tying robots. Once set up, these robots can work continuously to complete tasks faster than human workers without needing to take breaks or go home. Use of drones and site sensors for fast-track surveying With the advent of drones in the construction industry, developers can quickly conduct jobsite inspections and identify potential hazards each day. They can also be used to monitor workers throughout the day to ensure everyone is working safely. Drones are being used to take photos of as work progresses to create as-built models of jobsites to keep everyone informed of the changing work conditions each day. The construction industry has a vast potential, and companies should focus on implementing digitalisation, innovative technologies, and new construction techniques to improve productivity and efficiency. By using technologies such as BIM, AI, IoT, mobile applications, among others, companies will be able to streamline their project management, thereby enhancing the quality and safety of projects. With digitisation paving ways in the construction industry, companies across the spectrum will have to make concerted efforts to enhance their skills.

- present education development

What is the definition of education discipline to contine develop future education system to be better ?Education, discipline that is concerned with methods of teaching and learning in schools or school-like environments as opposed to various nonformal and informal means of socialization (e.g., rural development projects and education through parent-child relationships).

Education in the Present Period:

Education today is oriented to promoting values of an urban, competitive consumer society. Through the existing education system, India has produced in the last five decades number of scientists, professionals and technocrats who have excelled in their fields and made a mark at the national and international levels. The top scientists, doctors, engineers, researchers, professors, etc., are not those who were educated abroad but had got their entire education in India. If these experts and all those people who have reached the highest level have come through our present educational system, how could we deny the positive aspects of the education system as it is found today? Thus, while we cannot totally criticise our present education, there are some issues which need our urgent attention, if we are really concerned with a better future.

The question relates not to the past or to the present but rather to the future education innovation. How are we going to prepare the experts in various fields to meet the challenges of the newest and latest technology of the twenty-first century? It is not a question of the extent to which education provides or fails to provide employment to people but it is a question of education providing modern technology for the benefit of the poor and deprived people. It is a question of the quality of education. Instead of merely viewing the growing population as a liability, we should change the population into an asset and strength along with trying to control its growth.

This can be done only by education and human development. Merely giving a degree and a certificate to a young person that he is qualified for appointment is not enough. We have to make our younger generation think. The present education system does not encourage a person to think. He is taught a set syllabus which he is expected to reproduce during the examinations. This is deficient system. The youngsters have to be provoked to ask more and more questions which will not only help them to think but will also compel teachers to read and learn more. We have, thus, to change the examination system. We have to compel students to take learning more seriously. We have to wean them away from cutting classes, indulging in strikes, participating in students' politics, seeking admission only for contesting elections and offering courses only as a part-time study course. We have to build their character.

The three main deficiencies in the present education system may be described as follows:

(1) The present education does not generate or fortify the type of knowledge that is relevant to our changed society.

(2) Technology associated with a particular body of knowledge is inappropriate to our stage of development in terms of its employment potential or investment demands.

(3) Education has failed to provide value framework which may prepare committed politicians, bureaucrats, technocrats, and professionals on whom our nation can depend for sophisticated system of support services to be useful in taking the country to the highest level.

● present work model changing

COVID-19 has brought unprecedented human and humanitarian challenges. Many companies around the world have risen to the occasion, acting swiftly to safeguard employees and migrate to a new way of working that even the most extreme business-continuity plans hadn't envisioned. Across industries, leaders will use the lessons from this large-scale work-from-home experiment to reimagine how work is done—and what role offices should play—in creative and bold ways. Changing attitudes on the role of the office. When will the COVID-19 pandemic end? How and why can COVID-19 disease impact business work model changes ? Before the pandemic, the conventional wisdom had been that offices were critical to productivity, culture, and winning the war for talent. Companies competed intensely for prime office space in major urban centers around the world, and many focused on solutions that were seen to promote collaboration. Densification, open-office designs, hoteling, and co-working were the battle cries. But estimates suggest that early this April, 62 percent of employed Americans worked at home during the crisis, 1 compared with about 25 percent a couple of years ago. During the pandemic, many people have been surprised by how quickly and effectively technologies for videoconferencing and other forms of digital collaboration were adopted. For many, the results have been better than imagined.

According to McKinsey research, 80 percent of people questioned report that they enjoy working from home. Forty-one percent say that they are more productive than they had been before and 28 percent that they are as productive. Many employees liberated from long commutes and travel have found more productive ways to spend that time, enjoyed greater flexibility in balancing their personal and professional lives, and decided that they prefer to work from home rather than the office. Many organizations think they can access new pools of talent with fewer locational constraints, adopt innovative processes to boost productivity, create an even stronger culture, and significantly reduce real-estate costs. These same organizations are looking ahead to the reopening and its challenges. Before a vaccine is available, the office experience probably won't remain as it was before the pandemic. Many companies will require employees to wear masks at all times, redesign spaces to ensure physical distancing, and restrict movement in congested areas (for instance, elevator banks and pantries). As a result, even after the reopening, attitudes toward offices will probably continue to evolve.

But is it possible that the satisfaction and productivity people experience working from homes is the product of the social capital built up through countless hours of water-cooler conversations, meetings, and social engagements before the onset of the crisis? Will corporate cultures and communities erode over time without physical interaction? Will planned and unplanned moments of collaboration become impaired? Will there be less mentorship and talent development? Has working from home succeeded only because it is viewed as temporary, not permanent?

However , the reality is that both sides of the argument are probably right. Every organization and culture is different, and so are the circumstances of every individual employee. Many have enjoyed this new experience; others are fatigued by it. Sometimes, the same people have experienced different emotions and levels of happiness or unhappiness at different times. The productivity of the employees who do many kinds of jobs has increased; for others it has declined. Many forms of virtual collaboration are working well; others are not. Some people are getting mentorship and participating in casual, unplanned, and important conversations with colleagues; others are missing out.

Predicting Human future development trend
  ● Why do we need to predict how our future development ?

In our ruminating and decision-making we are constantly looking forward, trying to decide the best course of action to achieve our goals and avoid potential discomforts. If we can predict accurately, then we will make good decisions and be successful in meeting our goals and objectives. Being able to predict is about connecting cause and effect. However, people who spend more time predicting future will become futurists, although all humans have this art. Futurists are always there predicting the future that they could not possibly see in their lifetime. Their predictions are verified only by their future generations.

Why do psychologists predict the future? Defends the failure of people to predict the future. Confusion between prediction and hindsight; How psychologists predict an outcome. New Year's is a time when people attempt to predict how they will behave inthe coming months. Predicting the future is nearly impossible. So often we berate ourselves and others for failing to do so. Why do people make predictions? Sometimes it is for the person making predictions to feel in control over others. For some it's a warning. Your point: It will always be around, people making predictions no matter what the motive is behind it.

I shall indicate these nowadays threats that we shall feel difficulties to avoid problems occurences to influence our lives, if we do not plan to predict how our future development as below:

1. This is what 2030 could look like if we win the war on climate change.

Climate change causes serious environment pollution to influence our lifes in the future. I suppose that one day morning, you walk out of your door in the morning into a green and liveable city. You can choose to call upon a car. An algorithm has calculated the smartest route for the vehicle, and it picks up a few other people on the way. Since the city council has banned private cars in the city, tons of new mobility services have arrived. It is cheaper for you not to own your own car, and it reduces congestion, so you arrive at your destination more quickly and don't have to spend time looking for parking. There are a lot fewer cars on the streets and the rest are electric. All electricity is green by the way.

Thus we need to learn how to keep healthy meals easy to cook. Single use plastics are a distant memory. When you buy stuff, you buy something that lasts. But because you buy a lot fewer things, you can actually afford better quality products. "Refuse, reuse, reduce, recycle" is the new way of looking at things. Because citizens have buying so much stuff, they have more money to spend on services: cleaning, gardening, laundry help, healthy meals easy to cook, entertainment, experiences, fabulous new restaurants. All of which brings the average modern person more options and more free time. Picking up the mantle against climate change may not be so bad after all.

2. We may face any organizational form of violences

The first step to halving violence by 2030 is to have a clear sense of how it is distributed in time and space. Take the case of lethal violence. There is a misconception that more people die violently in war zones than in countries at peace. While total levels of violence oscillate from year to year, it turns out that the reverse is true. The UN Office for Drugs and Crime estimates that the ratio is roughly 5:1. Put simply, many more people are dying violently as a result of organized and interpersonal crime in countries like Brazil, Colombia and Mexico than in internal conflicts in countries such as Afghanistan, Syria and Yemen. This is not to say that one type of lethal violence is more important than the other, but rather to ensure a more fact-based diagnosis.

For Middle East violence example, after two decades of devastating wars in the Middle East, 2020 marked a turn-around leading to the formation of a new regional security forum by 2030 supported by key global powers, including the United States, China and Russia. The forum did not replace traditional regional rivalries or end all conflict, but leading global and regional powers recognized the risks of growing instability and the value of a region-wide mechanism for conflict prevention and management.Until 2030, the Middle East was the outlier in the world, being the only region to lack a forum for security dialogue. Regional alignments were largely based on the balance of power logic with cooperation limited to containing common external threats, most notably Iran. No venue existed where all regional parties could exchange threat perceptions and engage in confidence-building on areas of common concern. The short-lived Madrid process in the early 1990s had achieved some limited success but was too narrowly linked to progress on Israeli-Palestinian peace, which sadly did not come to pass.
Shifting regional alignments and a dangerous escalation led global powers to see common interests in stabilizing the region through a multilateral forum. At the same time, regional leaders become more open to alternatives that favored diplomacy over conflict, particularly as they faced difficult socioeconomic pressures at home to meet the demands of their rising youth populations. This confluence of global and regional interests provided an opening to launch a new cooperative security dialogue.

Hence, it seems that we need to find any methods to avoid any violence countries attack ourselves countries easily in order to avoid our hurt, even death occurrence easily. The only way to make a serious dent in violence is by acknowledging its full scope and scale together with the factors that drive it. This must be accompanied by sustained investment in reducing the risks and improving the protection of affected areas and populations, and investing in solutions with a positive track record. In the US, for example, research suggests that a focus on reducing lethal violence in the 40 cities with the highest rates of homicide could save more than 12,000 lives a year. In Latin America, reducing homicide in just the seven most violent countries over the next 10 years would save more than 365,000 lives.

3. Learning future mobile technology for any new functions, instead of phone call function.

The year is 2030. Imagine this: a young man lives in India. In his teens, he experienced an episode of depression. So when, as a new undergraduate, he was offered the chance to sign up for a mental healthcare service, he was keen to do so. This India child chose a service that used mobile phone and internet technologies to enable him to carefully manage his personal information. He would later develop clinical depression, but he spotted that something wasn't right early on when the feedback from his mental healthcare app highlighted changes in his sociability (he was sending fewer messages and leaving his room only to go to campus.) Thus, we need to prepare to learn future new mobile techniques.

Shortly thereafter, he received a message on his phone inviting him to get in touch with a mental health therapist: the message also offered a choice of channels through which he could get in touch. Now in his mid-20s, Ajay's depression is well under control. He has learned to recognise when he's too anxious and beginning to feel low, and he can practice the techniques he has learned using online tools, as well as easily accessing high-quality advice. His progress through the rare depressive episodes he still experiences is carefully tracked. If he does not respond to the initial, self-care treatment, he can be quickly referred to a medical professional. Ajay's experience is replicated across the world in low, middle and high-income countries. Similar technology-supported mental illness prevention, prediction and treatment services are available to all.

4. Learning how to avoid to pollute our natural environment

After a decade of interventions, of activists and policy-makers fighting side by side, clean air is recognized as a basic human right and cities like we see blue skies throughout the year. What changed from those dark days of 2020 to today, is the early recognition of health impacts of air pollution by governments, which spurred action around the globe. The urgency of the situation was recognized by 2020 and governments in some of the most polluted geographies came together to share knowledge and practice on how to lower emissions. Industries took the lead in looking at their own value chains, sectors like energy and transportation became leaders in cutting out carbon and other toxic pollutants from their factories. The steep decline of the fossil fuel industry by mid-century gave way to technology and innovation in these traditionally carbon intensive sectors. Today emissions pricing has made pollution pricey – it is cheaper and more profitable to be cleaner.

5. Learning how to use our internet platform to work at home.

The Internet today is growing at an incredible speed in ways that have enormously expanded people's work and living spaces. Cyberspace has become a new homeland for human beings, a place where all countries are getting increasingly interdependent, and a community of intertwined interests and shared future.While digital technology increases the welfare of the general public, it will also lead to unequal development opportunities in different regions and different groups due to the imbalance of Internet development in different countries and the lack of skills of individual citizens.Therefore, in order to get to my vision for 2030 that features inclusiveness and balanced development, we need to work together to narrow the digital divide.

First, we need to speed up building global Internet infrastructure that is accessible to all. Second, we need to promote inclusive development on a truly global scale. It is important to enhance Internet capacity in developing and underdeveloped countries to support the UN 2030 Agenda for Sustainable Development. Third, the protection of women, children, and other vulnerable groups should be strengthened in cyberspace.

The platform cooperativism movement shines a light on some of the real potentials for worker owned- and managed-platforms for every possible service. We can also think about running platforms as civic utilities. gig workers in platform economy 2030. However, in many places, platforms are becoming utilities. Think for instance of Uber's desire to become an operating system for the city. Our cities will undoubtedly need operating systems. But we should ask ourselves if we want a privately managed operating system run by an unaccountable company based in another country. Or a locally-managed, locally-owned, democratic, and accountable one. Thus, we aren't going to be able to turn back the clock to a world with no platforms. But by looking to strategies that involve transparency, accountability, worker power, and democratic ownership, we have in front of us the tools to move towards a less exploitative and more just platform economy.

The platform economy in 2030 could be one in which consumers know more about their impacts, regulators are enforcing minimum standards, workers are exercising their collective power, and we have all found ways of building, supporting, and using democratically run and accountable platforms. Thus, online platform work which will be future our new working trend at home for any office employers. So, we ought attempt to learn how to apply online platform to work at home. I believe that many employers believe it can help employees to raise efficiency or improve performance, it is not only due to COVID 19 disease influences employers feel fear many workers can have COVID 19 disease when they work in offices. If COVID 19 disease disappeared, global will have many employers feel their employees ought to apply online platoform to work at home because they will feel that onlinr platform work must raise employees efficiencies and improve working performance to compare that they work in offices together.

6. We create cities where you can walk to everything you need

Politicians love big infrastructure projects, but do we need them? Clearly new infrastructure for expanding cities is important, but maybe there is a more important question to ask: How well are we using our existing infrastructure?

In the 1980s, when the baby boomers arrived in large numbers at universities around the world, most campuses simply expanded at great expense. One key exception was Cape Town University. Unable to expand its footprint, the university asked the above question and was surprised to find how little its infrastructure was being used. Lecture theatres, for example, were only being used for 17% of the available hours. Over the next 30 years, Cape Town University trebled its numbers on the campus without any major building programmes, simply by reprogramming its timetable. The result was a more vibrant campus and big savings in expenditure. Much of the infrastructure in our cities is equally underused. Freeways are designed for peak hours; schools have one session per day, usually in the morning, leaving the afternoon and evening free; and the list goes on.

A study entitled Transforming Australian Cities showed that if all future development was contained within existing metro boundaries, cities would save $110 billion in infrastructure costs over 50 years for every 1 million people added. Our scientists vision for 2030 is a world where cities make better use of the infrastructure they have, before building new projects at huge financial and environmental cost. This would see people living in closer proximity with good access to essential infrastructure such as public transport, social services and high quality public spaces, as was the case in cities prior to the motor car and urban sprawl; cities, in other words, where walking is the dominant form of transport and the street is the dominant location for public life.

In year 2030 over 60% of the world's population will live in cities, have an urban mindset and a community-based reality. Good life choices can be made based on information and data enabled systems that allow freedom of choice combined with proactive service delivery from city to people.

Climate action required a major paradigm shift in cities and impacts the way city life is organized. By combining new technology, AI and systemic change cities are able to provide a sustainable environment that leaves room for individual choice. People will adapt to the new conditions by a combination of public and private products and services that make life functional, secure and fun. Societies based on trust will flourish.One of the most pressing global challenges is how to provide energy in a sustainable manner. Energy impacts all city life. Holistic leadership needs to be paired with individual behavioral change in order to find solutions for post-carbon life.

Successful cities in year 2030 utilize scalable solutions from around the world. Urban reality will become a global family of cities that deliver the optimal combination of functionality and fun.

Also,in 2030, buildings and cities will be naturally responsive to their immediate environmental and cultural context as well as the occupants' physiological, psychological, sociological and economic needs. An extraordinary outdoor and indoor environment quality that enhances happiness, health and well-being will be achieved with super low energy intelligent systems that is adaptive and resilient.

Innovative buildings.The construction industry that delivers these infrastructures will be highly integrated and innovative, motivated by sustainable propositions rather than short term business financial interests. It will offer a win-win-win platform (people, profit, planet or triple bottom line) for all stakeholders in government, industry, the workforce, and research and development, to allow everyone to live in an environment that supports health.

7. Clean electricity will dominate the energy sector

Scientists indicate that if we get things right, by 2030 the global carbon concentration will drop to 350 parts per million from 407 parts today. By then, the energy sector will largely be electricity, and at least half of the electricity is from renewable resources. Deep de-carbonizing efforts will be demonstrated by governments and corporates, and yes, even the ordinary members of the public.

By 2030, electricity will also be democratized and people will be empowered with choices and they will choose energy sources that sustain life. Power generations will also shift from centralized structure to greater distributed renewable generations. The electricity system will be defined by further digitalization, enabling the concept of sharing economy in the energy space. By 2030, trading of excess solar electricity with neighbours and sharing of electric vehicles within the community will be the way of living. Children will be taught to live in harmony with the environment. All these did not happen by chance. It happened because there was sufficient willpower to deliberately shape the future of energy. It happened because the need to preserve the future of our children finally matters.Thus, we need to avoid to waste to use any electricity nowadays because scientists believe that electricity will have many new functions for our future. If human wastes to use more electricity, then will not get any advantages when future any new functions are needed to use electiricty, but electricity can not be provided to satisfy human future any new function needs. So, we need to learn how to avoid to waste electricity nowadays.

8. Streets are made for people not cars, walking is needed more than driving cars when we can spend little time to anywhere.

The future of transportation, as most of us imagine it, is dominated by driverless cars - but to truly build a sustainable future for our cities, we need to reduce the numbers of cars on the roads full-stop. This can be achieved through a fairly simple, practical and proven strategy: temporarily taking cars off our streets altogether.

Why ought people use the streets on bicycles instead of cars ?

In the mid-1970s, the Colombian capital Bogotá saw the birth of what would become a global movement called Ciclovia, often known as 'open streets' in English-speaking countries, which entails the creation of car-free routes throughout the city every Sunday and public holiday. As well as improving public health, both by encouraging people to take exercise as well as reducing traffic pollution, Ciclovia fosters a sense of inclusion and ownership of their city among its participants. It has even helped to erase barriers between historically segregated communities. This model has been replicated all over the world, especially in other Latin American countries and in cities the length of Africa. To ensure sustainable cities all around the world, we must move away from our over-dependency on the automobile. Temporary interventions - like car-free days - work with existing assets and focus on shifting people's perception, which will ultimately shape how we view and exercise sustainable urban planning in the long term.

9. We need to learn how to use technology supports the challenges of our ageing populations.

Many developed countries are facing a combination of declining birth rates and increased longevity. This poses challenges to many social systems that have taken a pyramid-shaped population structure - a broad section of younger people supporting a small pinnacle of the elderly - for granted.

Some of the problems, such as pensions and health insurance systems, are well recognized and may be solved by redistributing benefits and costs under political initiatives. But there are other issues that cannot be solved this way. health of aging population. One example is the shortage of blood for transfusion. Tens of millions of patients receive blood transfusions worldwide every year thanks to blood donors - most of whom are from younger generations. In Japan, 80% of the patients receiving blood transfusions are over the age of 60, whereas 90% of blood donors are younger than 60. By 2030, a more than 10% shortage of blood for transfusion is expected, and this gap will continue to worsen. A shortage of blood is something redistribution cannot solve even with a social consensus. To compensate for this expected shortfall, a project to mass-produce platelets and other blood components from induced pluripotent stem cells (iPSC) is currently under development at my biotech start-up, Megakaryon, which I founded with the support of the Japanese Government.

Hence, there are other areas where technological innovation may offer solutions to the challenges presented by our ageing populations, such as robotics assisting in caring for older people. These challenges, however, are unavoidable and technological moon shots need time. The next 10 years will be critical for our preparations. We will only find out who is swimming naked when the tide goes out in 2030. Japan is set to be the first country where the population tide goes out and can be considered as a showcase for the problem. We to learn difficult kinds of new technology to help human to solve any global problems if they occured in future one day.

Thus, we must stop thinking of technology as a threat. The world has an immense opportunity to leverage new technologies in a way that takes advantage of its strengths.Reforming the way we govern and manage technology is instrumental to doing the right thing in several battles we have waiting for us. To make sure that artificial intelligence and machine learning do not replicate bias. To have a digital identity that does not undermine privacy. To fight the threat of terrorism without building surveillance states.

Humans being monitored. Because of this, governance of new tech needs to move beyond the state and subscribe to a more inclusive model — this certainly doesn't mean that governance should be handed over to the private sector.

It's time for us to reconsider our social contract: is it really the state that we should be handing over some of our rights to? How should the role of states change in a world where private companies have outsized power to shape our everyday lives? A new type of human-centered governance requires transparency and redress at every step and with every actor that poses a threat to our human rights—and our ability to be human. Human-centered governance means that we move away from centralized power in the sovereign state model to a much more adaptive, multidirectional, and multistakeholder governance setup.

10. Any countries need to concern how to provide enough social welfare to 'Old age' care starts when you're young, even you also become for the old aging in future.

If old age represents the accumulation of every advantage and disadvantage built up throughout a person's life, whether economic, social, environmental or behavioural, then surely the solution to healthy ageing lies in a whole-life approach. However, concerns about a patient's financial, social and emotional health often emerge too late, and well after a serious medical diagnosis. A holistic, multi-disciplinary and person-centred model of care can ensure dignity, comfort and well-being during the final phase of a patient's life.

It is important that these comprehensive and wellness-oriented aspects of care are integrated much earlier in each person's life, and become part of primary care. As the global burden of disease shifts towards non-communicable diseases, much more can be done around the world to enhance the capacity of the primary care sector to care for a person's overall welfare. This approach would include addressing socio-economic constraints and their impact on lifestyle choices (such as diet, exercise, alcohol and tobacco consumption), mental health issues such as depression, stress and loneliness, and other social or environmental barriers, all of which are proven to have significant repercussions for the ageing process. As an easily accessible point of contact the healthcare system for millions of people, primary care providers hold the key to shaping the ageing process for the better. Beyond preventative healthcare and screening for early disease detection and management, how can sound policies empower primary care providers to offer services like lifestyle counselling or tailored care plans that promote better health proactively? It is time for policymakers and industry leaders to reimagine the way societies structure, finance and deliver primary care to promote healthy ageing for all.

11. Learning how to Cut poverty in half with information technology

In 2030 the diversification and sophistication of productive activities, enabled using information and communication technology (ICT), will have contributed to a 50% reduction of poverty around the world.

more children using IT, resulting in increased GDP. The first decade of the 21st century showed us that the use of ICT has positive effects on the productivity of individuals, households and the economy in general. The World Bank found that, for developing countries, an increase of 10% in the fixed internet penetration rate was associated with an average increase of 1.38% in the GDP growth rate between 1980 and 2006.

Other studies, meanwhile, have found that when broadband is introduced, GDP per capita is between 2.7% and 3.9% higher than when it has not yet been introduced. Inspired by these international results, Colombia's National Planning Department (DNP) found in 2018 that increasing the average download speed in Colombia by 1 Mbps is associated with a 2.9% increase in GDP per capita. With this purpose, progress has been made in broadening the access, use and appropriation of ICT. Public efforts to do so were focused on the poor and other vulnerable populations, as well as on rural and remote areas.Therefore the rapid progress made in closing the digital divide and ensuring the almost half of the world's population who lacked access to the internet in 2019 were connected, was the key element in leading social and economic development up to 2030. This allowed us to enhance the great capacity of innovation, generation of added value and diversification of human ingenuity that - supported by technologies such as artificial intelligence - increased its efficiency and effectiveness. All this was achieved by making sure no one was left behind.

Thus, I believe that future new digital technologies are currently shaping and transforming whole societies. Increasing access to data and digital technologies empower people. However, the digital divide still exists and it plays out along different dimensions. By 2030, I envision an inclusive world where divisions have been reduced - especially the gender divide. For this to work, we need to make sure three things happen. First, strengthening digital technologies skills and lifelong learning to include everyone, notably women and low-income individuals. Second, we will need to tackle risks like cybersecurity risks and the misuse of information. Third, we will need to use the digital technologies such as Artificial Intelligence and Machine Learning to help us addressing collective challenges like improving healthcare and curing diseases.

12. AI Technology in space underpins privacy security on earth

By 2030, the combination of space technology and AI will have helped us deal with global challenges like deforestation, oil spills, farming, cross-border terrorism and migration flows, and will continue to provide insights that are meaningful at a local level for the economy. For this to happen, we need to make sure three things happen. First, we will have to apply common ethical standards to the way big data and AI are used. Second, we will need to design AI systems to guarantee privacy and data protection, as well as ensuring transparency to ensure people know when they are interacting with AI. And third, accountability must be established with internal and external independent audits, especially for AI systems whose use affects fundamental rights.If we get this right, integrated satellite and terrestrial networks will ensure secured communications that make governments and societies less prone to destabilization.

13. Healthcar, Precision medicine is for everyone, not just the rich

It would be amazing to think that by 2030, everyone has access to technologies that enable them to make better health decisions. In this future, precision medicine and personalized medicine can become part of everyone's health options - not just the rich. Everyone is able to acknowledge and balance the limitations of biotechnologies. We know much more about humanity and diseases. Most of all, biotechnology and medicine have not intruded into people's lives and medicalized the 'normal' course of life. People are still able to say no to certain interventions, because health and well-being do not come at a cost of relinquishing rights, choice and freedoms.

How do we get there? As we learn more about pregnancy, screening services can add to knowledge of one's life course, predicting health outcomes before the child is even born. However, as pregnancy testing and screening services are currently developed with increased genetic sequencing, whether and how we can use this new knowledge will be determined by what society currently considers normal – and the application of these technologies is contested in many societies. Without balanced views, pregnancy screening can harm society, but it does not have to.First of all, we can harness knowledge from low and middle-income countries, to integrate different perspectives. In these parts of the world we are more in tune not just with our bodies, but with our environments. We realise that life is a complex set of inter-dependencies. Social justice and respect for others underpin all our decisions. Finally, we work respectfully and transparently in every decision we make to alleviate suffering based on local needs and not imposed needs.

14. We'll get water from the moon to help fuel a new water place source in space.

By 2030, humans extract the first resource in outer space - this could be water on the moon. In addition to water, which can be used to drink and maintain agriculture, the water molecule (H_2O) can be separated into hydrogen and oxygen, as a clean fuel source. The extraction of water on the moon will not only enable human life to be sustained in space, but it will enable us to build and maintain the necessary space infrastructure, including satellites, to sustain and improve our quality of life on Earth.

An image of the moon, by doing so, we do not need to use the resources from our home planet, Earth. Further, our quality of life on will be significantly improved as a result of the innovations we achieve with a sustained human presence in deep space, as well as the extension of the Earth's economy into space and the subsequent creation of business and jobs. However, in order for all of this to be realized, one key piece of action that needs to be taken today is an international consensus on the rules of engagement for governments and commercial entities to utilize the resources which exist on our moon and in space. Proper governance of space resources is required for a sustainable and peaceful human future. If we can achieve this milestone at the political level, we can elevate our species to a new height.

● Technology development stage

A technology forecaster generally makes forecasts concerning how soon various types of technologies will be possible and what characteristics they may have. They do not focus on what the technologies will have, because the actual technology that will be used in the future depends on economic, social, and political considerations and these are normally beyond the province of the technology forecaster. For example, a technology forecaster might forecast that it will be possible by the year 2050 to produce electricity from nuclear fusion, but whether thermonuclear fusion will actually be used for that purpose may depend on a variety of non-technological considerations.

Scientists had developed stages of technological development. These are:

Scientific findings: Basic scientific understanding of some phenomenon has been developed.

Laboratory feasibility: A technical solution to a specific problem has been identified and a laboratory model has been created.

Operating prototype: A device intended for a particular operational environment has been built.

Commercial introduction or operational use: The innovation is not only technologically successful but also economically feasible.

Widespread adoption: The innovation has shown itself to be superior in some way to whatever was used previously to perform its function and begins to replace previous methods.

Diffusion to other areas: The innovation becomes adopted for purposes other than those originally intended.

Social and economic impact: The innovation has changed the behavior of society or has somehow involved a substantial portion of the economy.

Thus, our future energy will be caused to change from power electricity to nuclear electricity in possible.

● Future new technology product invention

Energy storing bricks house building

Scientists have found a way to store energy in the red bricks that are used to build houses.Researchers led by Washington University in St Louis, in Missouri, US, have developed a method that can turn the cheap and widely available building material into "smart bricks" that can store energy like a battery. Although the research is still in the proof-of-concept stage, the scientists claim that walls made of these bricks "could store a substantial amount of energy" and can "be recharged hundreds of thousands of times within an hour". The researchers developed a method to convert red bricks into a type of energy storage device called a supercapacitor. This involved putting a conducting coating, known as Pedot, onto brick samples, which then seeped through the fired bricks' porous structure, converting them into "energy storing electrodes". Iron oxide, which is the red pigment in the bricks, helped with the process, the researchers said.

Robotic guide dogs

A student at Loughborough University has designed a "robotic guide dog" that will help support visually impaired people who are unable to house a real animal. The product, designed by Anthony Camu, replicates the functions of a guide dog as well as programming quick and safe routes to destinations using real-time data. Theia, named after the titan goddess of sight, is a portable and concealable handheld device that guides users through outdoor environments and large indoor spaces with very little input.

Sweat powered smartwatches

Engineers at the University of Glasgow have developed a new type of flexible supercapacitor, which stores energy, replacing the electrolytes found in conventional batteries with sweat. It can be fully charged with as little as 20 microlitres of fluid and is robust enough to survive 4,000 cycles of the types of flexes and bends it might encounter in use.The device works by coating polyester cellulose cloth in a thin layer of a polymer, which acts as the supercapacitor's electrode. As the cloth absorbs its wearer's sweat, the positive and negative ions in the sweat interact with the polymer's surface, creating an electrochemical reaction which generates energy.

"Conventional batteries are cheaper and more plentiful than ever before but they are often built using unsustainable materials which are harmful to the environment," says Professor Ravinder Dahiya, head of the Bendable Electronics and Sensing Technologies (Best) group, based at the University of Glasgow's James Watt School of Engineering. "That makes them challenging to dispose of safely and potentially harmful in wearable devices, where a broken battery could spill toxic fluids on to skin.What we've been able to do for the first time is show that human sweat provides a real opportunity to do away with those toxic materials entirely, with excellent charging and discharging performance."

Self-healing 'living concrete

Scientists have developed what they call living concrete by using sand, gel and bacteria. Researchers said this building material has structural load-bearing function, is capable of self-healing and is more environmentally friendly than concrete – which is the second most-consumed material on Earth after water. The team from the University of Colorado Boulder believe their work paves the way for future building structures that could "heal their own cracks, suck up dangerous toxins from the air or even glow on command".

Living robots

Tiny hybrid robots made using stem cells from frog embryos could one day be used to swim around human bodies to specific areas requiring medicine, or to gather microplastic in the oceans. "These are novel living machines," said Joshua Bongard, a computer scientist and robotics expert at the University of Vermont, who co-developed the millimetre-wide bots, known as xenobots. "They're neither a traditional robot nor a known species of animal. It's a new class of artefact: a living, programmable organism.

All of above which are scientists prediction that these new technology products will be invented to succeed to provide human to use in possible.

● future medical development

Going back a few years, there was definitely a lack of a patient-centric approach in healthcare, not to mention the challenges of a paper-based system, too many bureaucratic tasks, the lack of investment in prevention, security incidents and the list can go on. Over the years, patient care, patient safety, privacy and data security have changed for the better and to this day, in many aspects, things continue to evolve in the healthcare world. Medical research is another rapidly evolving field and even though many aspects such as prevention and treatments development have been highly improved through research over the years, there will always be room for improvement.

What does the future medical changing? What future changes do you expect to see in the healthcare industry? So one thing is certain. The healthcare industry is changing and evolving at an extremely fast pace right now. Exciting times are ahead, whether we're talking about more technological changes such as advances in the medical research field, in mobile, wearable technologies and robotics or processing and analyzing healthcare data improvements.

1) Mixed reality opens new ways for medical education

Augmented, virtual, and mixed reality are all technologies opening new worlds for the human senses. While the difference between these technologies might seem arbitrary at first, it greatly determines how they could be used in healthcare. While AR lets users see the real world and projects digital information onto the existing environment, VR shuts out everything else completely and provides an entire simulation, and mixed reality is able to interact with the world while projecting information into it. Thus, AR can be used by surgeons for projecting potentially life-saving information into their eyesight during operations, VR can be used in psychiatry to treat phobias efficiently, and mixed reality is able to bring revolutionary novelties to medical education, or pre-operative surgical planning, among others. For example, the Microsoft HoloLens opens up radically new ways for medical education as it is able to project the human body in its full size in front of med students. Thus, the organs, veins or bones will be visible accurately in

3D, and future medical professionals will be able to analyze their shape, remember their characteristics more vividly than it is possible when studying from a book. There are already some universities who plan to introduce the new technology: Case Western opened its new health education campus in collaboration with the Cleveland Clinic in 2019, where students study anatomy from virtual reality rather than cadavers.

2) Brain-computer interfaces bring hope for the paralyzed

Research has geared up lately in the area of brain-computer interfaces (BCI). Dr. Gary Marcus, at New York University and Dr. Christof Koch at the Allen Institute for Brain Science told The Medical Futurist that brain implants today are where laser eye surgery was decades ago, but the field will advance significantly in the upcoming years. Imagine a retinal chip giving you perfect eyesight or the ability to see in the dark, a cochlear implant granting you perfect hearing or a memory chip bestowing you with almost limitless memory.

What if you could type into a computer with only your thoughts or control your entire smart house by sending out the necessary brainwaves?

Although that's really galactic leaps away, the first neuroprosthetics is already on the market: you can purchase cochlear implants, and retinal implants – the latter was approved by the FDA in 2013. Moreover, implants for people with Parkinson's disease send electrical pulses deep into the brain, activating some of the pathways involved in motor control. Rarer, but also in use, are brain implant therapies for people paralyzed by spinal cord injury or other neurological damage. A chip inserted into the brain reads off electrical signals that are translated by a computer to restore some movement and communication. Couple it with an exoskeleton, and magic will truly happen: lately, it made headlines that a 30-year-old paralyzed man, Thibault, was able to move all four of his limbs with the help of a 'mind-reading' exoskeleton. We expect more similar stories to come.

3) Might we all end up being recreational cyborgs?

There are already famous examples of real-life cyborgs, and I am truly convinced that such creatures will not only populate the terrain of sci-fi movies, but they will be everywhere around us in the very near future. The 'cyborg-craze' will eventually start with a new generation of hipsters who implant devices and technologies in their bodies just to look cooler.

Advances in future medical technology will not just repair physical disadvantages such as impaired eyesight but will also create superhuman powers from having the eyesight of an eagle to possessing the hearing of a bat. Hearing aids powered with artificial intelligence, earbuds making you multilingual, or RFID chips already point to that direction. While a patient wearing implanted defibrillators or pacemakers can also be added to the group of cyborgs, I expect to see more cases when patients ask for the implantation of a certain device without having medical problems.

4) 3D printing drugs in dinosaur shapes for kids

If guns, bars of chocolate, even entire houses can be 3D printed now, and the biotechnology industry is even working on printing out living cells; why would the appearance of 3D printed drugs be surprising? It's a logical sequel that's already happening.

5) New technologies bring along new diseases?

Regarding technological development, there is always a risk for the emergence of so far unknown illnesses and conditions. New types of diseases might appear due to the excessive use of virtual reality solutions, video consoles or smartphones. Examples include virtual post-traumatic stress disorder (v-PTSD), which might be the diagnosis for gamers who participate in large virtual battles wearing VR masks (such as Call of Duty) and experience similar symptoms as those soldiers who fought in real wars.

6) Artificial food as the hope against food shortages

Synthetic tea? Lab-grown meat? Artificial milk? Nutrients and vitamins in a protein shake? Sci-fi movies like the Matrix, Star Trek or The Hitchhiker's Guide to the Galaxy showed us a glimpse of the future of eating disconnected from Mother Earth. Some innovative solutions are already here, promising an option for alleviating the overstraining of natural resources and still providing food for millions of humans.

7) Voice as diagnostic and medical support tool

Researchers and medical professionals have noticed in the last years how useful voice-based solutions can prove to be in healthcare – both in diagnostics as well as in supporting their daily tasks, such as administration.

Scientists found that characteristics of patients' voices – or as medicine labels them, vocal biomarkers – reveal a lot about their health; and help in detecting serious diseases and health risks. For example, an Israeli company, Beyond Verbal deals with emotion analytics and provides voice analysis software. It has announced that its algorithms were successful in helping to detect the presence of coronary artery disease (CAD) in a group of patients. Another initiative, Sonde Health Inc., a Boston-based company develops a voice-based technology platform for monitoring and diagnosing mental and physical medical conditions, but we expect a lot more solutions to come in the future.

In fact, the same is true for the use of voice-based technologies for supporting medical professionals in their gargantuan fight against administration. Artificial intelligence-based voice to text technologies promise to turn the tables on the necessity of bureaucracy in the doctors' office: the physician and the patient could speak while a voice assistant listens in and puts down the interpreted text into the relevant columns in the EHRs. That's what we expect to happen in the future.

8) Patient empowerment as a consequence of the tech revolution

In the last decade, rapid technological advancement has resulted in a shift toward digital health in medicine. This shift is theorized as a cultural transformation of how disruptive medical technologies providing digital and objective data accessible to both caregivers and patients lead to an equal level partnership between physicians and patients with shared decision-making and the democratization of care. However, from the patients' side, the result is the evolution of the 'e-patient' – where the 'e' stands for 'electronic', 'equipped', 'enabled', 'empowered', 'engaged' or 'expert'. A patient who takes responsibility for their health, and actively engages in shaping their future – in a mutually beneficial partnership with their caregivers. Although this doesn't sound like technological advancement, which it really isn't, it is enabled and facilitated by wearables, health sensors, and any other innovations which make patients the point of care.

9) Digital tattoos for a more invisible healthcare

With the development in 3D printing as well as circuit printing technologies, flexible electronics and materials, applying so-called digital tattoos or electronic tattoos on the skin for some days or even weeks became possible. Some researchers use gold nanorods, others graphine or various polymers with rubber backing to apply the tattoo on the skin without causing irritation. Certain experts believe that these skin patches or tattoos are only the beginning, and in the future, other skin techniques such as henna, tanning, and makeup will also be tested. These flexible, waterproof materials impervious to stretching and twisting coupled with tiny electrodes are able to record and transmit information about the wearer to smartphones or other connected devices. They could allow healthcare experts to monitor and diagnose critical health conditions such as heart arrhythmia, heart activities of premature babies, sleep disorders and brain activities noninvasively. Moreover, by tracking vital signs 24 hours a day, without the need for a charger, it is especially suited for following patients with high risks of stroke, for example.

● future transport development

I believe that future transport innovations may include as below:

Self-driving drone taxis

Autonomous drone taxis that drive themselves are currently being tested before being released on the market. The drones, which look much like a regular helicopter, have 18 propellers. They can carry 2 passengers and are expected to be in service by July 2018.

Maglev trains

Maglev (short for "magnetic levitation") trains hover about 4 inches above their tracks and are propelled by electrically-charged magnets. Riders claim the trains are exceptionally comfortable and stable. Maglev trains have been recorded to travel at a rate of 375 miles per hour (mph). Maglev trains are already in operation in China and Germany and are expected to become a common mode of transportation throughout the world by 2030.

The re-occurrence of new technology over the years has helped us on how we live and carry out our day to day activities, and most of this development is as a result of inventing and creating a new ways to reduce our daily stress and live an improved life. The transportation industry is one of the important areas where new technological advancement takes place. We now see cars that drive themselves along predetermined routes. Trains that will use new magnetic rail systems. And an amazing new "hyperloop" train that will speed 800 miles per hour.

Transportation technology like Hyperloop has become well known as people know that it can transport many people to a great distance in a nick of time. But there are others as well which you may or may not be aware of. Developments in high-speed rail have historically been impeded by the difficulties in managing friction and air resistance, both of which become substantial when vehicles approach high speeds.

The vactrain concept theoretically eliminates these obstacles by employing magnetically levitating trains in evacuated (air-less) or partly evacuated tubes, allowing for speeds of thousands of miles per hour. All these innovations are not just a form of illusion, they are set to happen within the next coming years or have already started transporting us. This has increased the level of some industries like vehicle transport companies/car shipping carriers, truck production company, and fleet management to be more efficient.

High- Speed Rail Network

High-speed rail networks are generating tremendous interest all around the globe. Just of recent South Korea have started building a maglev train that will operate within the Incheon Airport, and China reportedly has a second maglev train in development. A planned maglev train will transport passengers over 200 miles between Nagoya and Tokyo in just 40 minutes, helping to free congested roads, reduce air pollution, and reduce accidents the main issue with maglev trains is the high cost of development. Because of the fast speeds, the trains have to be routed directly between destinations, said Enderle.

Hyperloop transportation systems

This transportation concept, conceived by Elon Musk, founder of Tesla Motors and SpaceX, is currently being designed and developed. Hyperloops are essentially transportation tubes that run pods of passengers or freight through a pressurized track at high speeds. Hyperloops run at an average of 600 mph; their top speed is 760 mph. There are several companies currently working to advance the technology. One company hopes to launch its first passenger service in 2021.

Satellite-based air traffic control systems

Air traffic control systems in operation today are ground-based, using technology that that dates back to the 1960's. Satellite-based control systems allow air traffic controllers to be more efficient. The U.S. is currently working on NextGen, a satellite-based air traffic control system that is being implemented in stages through 2025. GPS technology will be used to increase accuracy and shorten routes. NextGen is expected to save time and fuel, reduce air traffic delays, increase flight capacity and permit air traffic controllers to monitor aircraft with improved safety margins. Once NextGen is rolled out across America's airports, airplanes will be able to fly closer together, making it easier to take direct routes and avoid delays caused by "stacking" planes waiting for take-off. NextGen will reduce aircraft gridlock, both in the sky and in airports.

Self-driving electric buses

Automated city buses and shuttles will be in operation in the near future. Autonomous vehicles use cameras, radars and GPS systems to recognize and communicate with traffic lights and have impressive safety records. These buses of the future will reduce the impact on the environment because they are electric. Self-driving buses are already in operation in China and Germany, and are being tested in the U.S. Autonomous buses have a back-up mode where a human can take control of the vehicle if needed.

Elevated buses

While self-driving electric buses are making strides worldwide, China is working on a bus system that will reduce traffic congestion. The elevated bus is a vehicle that "straddles" traffic. It runs on a special track that allows regular vehicles to drive underneath. The Transit Elevated Bus (TEB) system is currently being designed in China and is expected to reduce traffic congestion by 30 percent.

Flying hotel pods

A fleet of drones that are portable hotels are being designed by a company in Canada. The hospitality concept, Driftscape, is a mobile, self-sustaining hotel that uses drone technology. Driftscape allows guests to travel while sleeping, roam or touch down in diverse locations. It is made up of several modular units that include food and beverage elements. Driftscape offers 360-degree views of the outside world and is particularly suited to have minimal impact on the environment, allowing the guest to travel to locations that are sensitive while preserving the integrity and authenticity of the location.

Smart roads

Roads are the foundation of the future of transportation, providing society with smart mobility. A typical smart road will be more animated, able to communicate with vehicles and people using sensors, data capture abilities and the ability to be responsive to changes in the environment. Roads will literally talk to traffic signs, bicycles and vehicles. Roads will virtually be alive.

Smart roads will be able to store solar energy and transfer that energy into electricity for vehicles and the infrastructure. They will glow in the dark using photo-luminescent powder that charges during the day. Smart roads will use motion-sensor lights to light up only the sections of road that are being used, providing night visibility while going dim when not in use.

Smart roads of the future will be able to melt snow and ice using electricity or hot water, reducing traffic accidents that cause injury and death. In addition, federal, state and local governments spend billions of dollars on the operation, maintenance and repair of highways and drivers lose billions of dollars annually due to corrosion-related repair costs and depreciation linked to chemicals used to treat roadways during the winter.

Ground level pedestrian lights

There has been a rise in the number of accidents involving foot traffic since the use of smartphones has increased. An innovation in transportation technology is a system that can be installed at pedestrian traffic lights that would light up the pavement in red or green to signal when it is safe or not safe for pedestrians to cross the street safely.

Bicycle share programs

Bicycle share programs allow riders to pay a small fee to ride a bike from one point to another, leaving the bike at the ride share station. This is a helpful program in urban areas where traffic can make it easier – and faster – to ride a bike than drive a car. Bicycles are good for the environment as they do not emit harmful emissions; bikes are an eco-friendly mode of transportation as well as giving riders the opportunity to get healthy exercise. Bicycle share programs are already in operation in several major metropolitan areas, and are expected to be become more common in the future. These ten innovations are in addition to electric vehicles and driverless cars, both of which are growing in popularity and pervasiveness. Electric cars are an excellent solution to the issue of the damage to the environment that current fuel sources create. Autonomous vehicles are reported to be safer and increase efficiency.

The future will bring dramatic technological improvements to the transportation sector, many of which are in unchartered terrain. The government may need to get involved and cooperate more closely with private investors, innovators and other stakeholders as an agent of public interest. Transportation has a rich history of both technical and policy innovation, a history that is likely to persist. Transportation is in an upheaval as it struggles to continue to support the prosperity and quality of life of our nation and others on the planet.

Whatever the future of transportation holds, it is clear that it will continue to play an intrinsic role in human history, making the world a safer and more interconnected place. With over 100 years of combined transportation industry experience helps MMA professionals understand and address specific challenges within the industry.

Stronger Global Positioning System (GPS) Will Change How We Commute

Nowadays, GPS are not a new phenomenon- we have been using GPS for more than a decade. But now, there is a huge difference when comparing the modern GPS devices to the earlier models that were found or use in the hardware. GPS devices were very limited in the past, they could only calculate mileage to provide an estimated time to a final destination of a vehicle. But nowadays GPS devices are more resourceful. Aside from the fact that they now fulfill the basic functionality of planning a trip, some auto transport companies now use GPS unit to make an adjustment to know when the weather is favorable to travel, to know the traffic condition of every route so as to decide the best route to take to deliver as fast as possible.

Water-Fueled Car invnetion

What do you think will happen if the rate of air pollution that is produced by a petrol powered car can be reduced? A water-fuelled car is an automobile that hypothetically derives its energy directly from water. Water-fuelled cars have been the subject of numerous international patents, newspaper, and popular science magazine articles, local television news coverage, and websites. The case of driverless cars that have been made into reality; water fueled car has been on trial by several scientists for a long period of time which I think will soon be made into reality and we will start to live a simple life.

String Theory Transportation Development

String theory is a set of attempts to model the four known fundamental interactions — gravitation, electromagnetism, strong nuclear force, weak nuclear force — together in one theory. You might hear about string theory in quantum physics, but have you ever heard about it in the transportation field?

The concept is based on the use of two strings with a wheeled vehicle riding on them. It is a new low-cost transport system, and it can go through everything water, deserts or forests, towers.

future technology developemnt

What are the future technology development advantages and disadvantages? I shall explain as below:

Advantages of Technology development

a. Business Efficiency: Things can be done almost instantly using technology. Commodity manufacturing tools have been greatly simplified, and this has caused a significant reduction in waste and reduced costs for consumers.

b. More jobs: Technology has created a tremendous amount of new jobs. In our world's economy as a whole new group of people is needed to work with, develop, and maintain new technology in homes and workplaces.

c. Better in communication: Keeping in touch is easier now than ever before. You can talk to, chat with, or collaborate with anyone in the entire world, and this has stimulated amazing things and a better understanding of other cultures.

d. Medical care: A lot of new technology is developing in the medical field. Surgical procedures and daily functions have become so simple and effective that the level of illness and accidents has decreased dramatically.

Disadvantages of technology development

a. The social gap: technology is expensive, and keeping up with the latest trends is almost impossible for a person who is not in the upper class. This has caused a large social gap between the people who can and cannot afford the cost of these technologies.

b. A generation of laziness: Since everything has become easier or fully implemented for us through the use of technology. People slowly but surely forget how to do things the old way and forget the good old hard work.

c. Things get old quickly: As technology development is new, faster and more efficient new versions are designed. This may be a problem because you may have the latest and best technology, but it will get old in a very short time, and this causes our landfills to fill with computers, mobile phones, and other things.

future construction development

What's the future of the construction industry digital development?

Unlike other industries, the Engineering and Construction sector has been slow to adopt new technologies, and has certainly never undergone a major transformation. As a result, productivity has stagnated over the last 40 years, or in some cases, even declined. This unimpressive record looks set to change very soon, and very dramatically. In fact, profound changes are already taking place – though not yet on a sufficiently wide scale – in many aspects of the construction industry. The writer William Gibson's famous phrase fits the industry perfectly: The future is here today – it is just not evenly distributed.

The key is digitalization. More and more construction projects are incorporating systems of digital sensors, intelligent machines, mobile devices, and new software applications – increasingly integrated with a central platform of Building Information Modelling (BIM).The challenge now is to achieve widespread adoption and proper traction. Wherever the new technologies have properly permeated this fragmented industry, the outlook is an almost 20% reduction in total life-cycle costs of a project, as well as substantial improvements in completion time, quality, and safety.

Construction reconstructed in all its phases

Technological advances are now revolutionizing almost all points in the life-cycle of a built asset, from conceptualization to demolition. The chart below shows the relevance of digital technologies along the engineering and construction industry's value chain. Digitalization is transforming all three major life-cycle phases of construction projects. Consider the following scenario – no longer futuristic, but "here today", though its building blocks are still distributed patchily over disparate projects.

During the Design & Engineering phase, BIM identifies potential design clashes and constructability issues, thereby averting costly corrective rework; and it improves the tendering process by making the information more transparent and accessible.vAn interesting example is that of Crossrail – one of the world's largest and most complex infrastructure projects, building a major new underground line across London: the designers and engineers are using a centralized set of linked BIM databases to integrate about 1.7 million CAD files into a single information model.

During the actual Construction phase, drones survey and inspect the construction site. 3D printers prefabricate many of the building components. GPS and radio-frequency identification (RFID) are used for tracking the materials, equipment, and workers, in order to then optimize flows and inventory levels. Robots and autonomous vehicles do much of the actual building work. 3D laser scanning or aerial mapping is used for comparing work-in-progress against a virtual model, thereby enabling prompt course corrections and minimizing corrective work. Take the case of a Japanese equipment manufacturer that has developed fully autonomous bulldozers, led by drones that map the area in real-time to provide data on the workload.

During the Operations phase, embedded sensors continue to monitor any given part of an asset, checking for deterioration, facilitating predictive maintenance, and continually updating a central database. Augmented reality is used for guiding maintenance crews. Big data – on traffic movements, electricity consumption, and so on – are collected digitally, and are subjected to advanced analytics, in order to optimize decision-making and generally boost operational efficiency. By way of illustration, consider the approach taken by the Japanese building service provider NTT Facilities to the inspection, maintenance and repair of their R&D premises: by integrating the BIM model into the building's facility- and asset-management system, and making intelligent use of this combined resource, the company was able to reduce the cost of operations and maintenance by an estimated 20%.

● future education development

The future system of education will give more importance to technical and professional education and skills development than moral education. It will give more importance to countries development, give more importance to training for students, help students build up professional qualities. Educated people are the main asset of a nation.

Education for the Future:

Our society is moving towards an unknown future. The crises that the contemporary society is encountering are likely to increase in their frequency and intensity. With rising population and dwindling resources, our country has to face new problems. To meet the challenges of this future, we will need knowledge and skills that may contribute to problem-solving capacity not only in the fields of science and technology but also in the fields of human relations and management. Unfortunately, the education system today is decaying more and more instead of responding creatively to the challenges of contemporary predicament. We need to reset our priorities. First, we accept the philosophy of 'education for self-reliance'. The emphasis must shift from higher secondary and higher education to primary and adult education.

Second, the content of education at higher secondary and college/ university levels needs serious consideration. Third, the problem is of management of education.

At present, bureaucratic styles persist. Bureaucrats are not sensitive and responsive to the changes in the environment of education. Low budgets, high indiscipline, administrative lapses and interference and political pressures make decision-making in the field of education hazardous. As such, management of education should be made free from bureaucrats' and politicians' interference. Fourth, the problem is of accountability of teachers, particularly in higher education. Many cases are reported where teachers fail to take classes for months and even years together. They rarely take interest in regularly going to libraries and reading journals and latest books. We have to restore purpose to education and determine suitable techniques of teaching. Then we have to regulate the factors that debase and vulgarise it. Control on teachers is the most important requisite in the educational system.

Fifth, the problem is that we have to create greater seriousness regarding studies among students, for whom acquiring knowledge is the most vital question. Education is believed to be mobility multiplier. It works for the perpetuation of status and privileges. But should higher education be open to all students? Many students seek admission to Law, Arts and Commerce courses only because they have to 'kill time' till they settle in life. Should they not be directed to technical and professional courses? Should education be not brought round to sub serving their interest? Sixth, the issue is that we have to give a push to vocational/professional education which has considerable demand in the open market. We have to assume that every educated person cannot become a specialist or an expert but has to equip himself with a skill which can help him earn his livelihood.

We have to think of the coming two or three decades and pay attention to the type of agriculture, type of developing industry, trade and commerce and new fields of service and employment that the future decades will throw up. This will help us in building education system which will give us better cultivators, better skilled workers, better mechanics, or whatever. Seventh, the issue is of linkages between various departments like Agriculture, Industry, Labour, Electronics, Law, Science and so forth so that universities, IITs and colleges know the type of skilled people required. What is needed is full education in each field which will prepare the individual to find employment of his choice and enable the employer to get a candidate of his liking. Eighth, the issue is of making all illiterate people literate. According to the available estimated figures for the year 1998, assuming that the literacy rate in India has gone up from 52.21 per cent in 1991 to 60 per cent in 1998, there are about 400 million people to be educated. This is a tremendous task. While it is a well-known fact that all state governments have schemes of raising literacy level, it needs to be emphatically stated that we require more than 25 years to achieve the set goal. Perhaps policies like compelling students to teach the illiterate during two months' vacation period will help in reducing the target period. Ninth, the point is of reducing the number of drop-outs at the primary level. The available figures show that the percentage of drop-outs in 1996 at different stages of school education among boys and girls was as high as 38 to 41 per cent.

- future work model changing

The Future Workplace: Will Where We Work Change? Traditionally, the workplace has been just that – a place we go to in order to work. Statistic indicated that with 8 in 10 company leaders planning to allow employees to work remotely some of the time, according to Gartner research, many are asking whether the days of the physical workplace are numbered. Will our workplace remain an office that we commute to work from, or could it simply be our living space or environment we choose to work?

While some organizations such as Twitter, Square, Facebook and Shopify have announced permanent work-from-home plans, not everyone is ready to dispense with the physical workplace. Working from home has allowed businesses to keep operating during the pandemic, and many employees have thrived, but there's a growing realization that remote working isn't for everyone. Some people have struggled with the isolation and loneliness of being apart from their co-workers, while others have had to cope with work-from-home arrangements that are far from ideal. Not everyone has a dedicated office, or even a dedicated working space, they can decamp to. Video calls have proven effective for communicating and collaborating but, arguably, they fall short when it comes to encouraging innovation and relationship-building. These are just some of the reasons why having a physical workplace is still important, though whether it is used in the same way as before remains to be seen. The signs are that post-pandemic, flexible working will become the new 'normal'; according to estimates from Global Workplace Analytics, 25-30% of the workforce are likely to be working from home multiple days a week by the end of 2021. If this is the case, why would companies spend more than they need to on costly premises or office space that will only be occupied some of the time?

In future, many businesses may decide that a smaller office better suits their needs, and their budget. So, rather than being a place where employees go to work every day, the workplace could become a central hub for employees to gather, collaborate, brainstorm and meet clients when they need to. If employees aren't travelling to the office every day, there is less of a need for them to live within reasonable commuting distance. Real estate agents are already reporting a growing trend for migration from large cities to more rural, less densely populated areas as people crave fresh air, a healthier lifestyle and bigger properties with more space for working from home.

As life and work become more rural, international architect and engineering firm BDP predicts that local neighbourhoods will take on a new significance and that businesses will spring up to serve the needs of local workers. This might include hubs offering office equipment such as printers and scanners so that people have what they need nearby. Mindful of the fact that keeping people physically connected is beneficial, some businesses may look to operate more regional outposts close to where employees live. These would allow employees to escape the confines of home and interact with others without having a long commute. Tech firm Fujitsu has already announced such a strategy in Japan; it plans to halve its office space in the next three years and set up a system of hub and satellite offices in areas where most of its workforce resides. And for businesses wanting even more flexibility, negotiating a flexible lease or membership with a co-working company like Regus, WeWork or The Office Group could give them access to the regional, national or even international office facilities they need.

Move to another country remote work trend

While 95% of remote jobs today require workers to be in a certain state or country, usually due to employment and tax laws, around 5% are location-agnostic, according to flexible job search site FlexJobs. As remote working rises in popularity, it is not unreasonable to expect that proportion to grow, which means that, for some people, the workplace could soon be virtually anywhere in the world.In a bid to make up for lost tourism due to the pandemic and boost their economies, these countries are hoping to lure remote workers with their beaches, lifestyle benefits or low living costs and (at the time of writing) low coronavirus infection rates. When travel restrictions ease, working in sunnier climes or experiencing a new culture could be an attractive option for many. Provided people are productive and willing to work across time zones, if required, there is no reason why employers shouldn't support it.

On conclusion, global remote global work trend will be influenced to cause. The physical workplace is unlikely to disappear altogether – at least not yet. There are advantages in bringing people together in a single place, even if less frequently than before. But it won't be the workplace as we know it today. As employers increasingly recognize that output is what matters, not how many hours people spend at their desks, there will be more flexibility in where people work. How much flexibility will depend on the nature of the work but, with the right technology and an Internet connection, it could potentially be anywhere they choose.

VI
How Society influences organizational behavioral change

What is psychological function

In general, psychology science is often mislead to explain what its functions wrongly by our society. Psychology English is come from " psyche" and " logos" two words consist. The prior word means " soul" and the later word means " theory" . So, psychological science is explanation of mind science. It is one kind of research human mind activities science or it is one kind of research human's behavioral science. Any kinds of human's Behaviors mean observation from environment influences. But, nowadays, psychological science of new explanation means human's mind and behavior observation both aspects research.

So, what does psychological science mean? In fact, anyone can be one part time (folk psychologist) . For example, any one child can own ability or knows how to predict any one's psychology or mind successfully, e.g. he knows how to keep his toy in not easy discovered or secret location in his house or school or any places, and he aims to make wrong direction to mislead his friends need to spend much time to find his toy. He aims to achieve none any his friends or patents can find or discover this toy easily consequently. It explains that any one adult , even child, he does not need to be taught, but he can have himself mind or ability to feel whether he ought need to how to do himself behavior to achieve his aim immediately. This kind of personal creative or own protective behavior or mind research that is psychologists want to find any answers to support and to explain why and how child can own this kind of psychological mind. It is one part of psychological research aim.

Why does psychologists know what you want easily or they can make more accurate judgement? In general, psychologists feel need to do any psychological science research aims, because they want to discover or find what are the thinking or mind about any one in order to make the absolute accurate judgement. Psychologists' duties need to research any one's psychological activities, why he/she feel happy or sad or satisfactory or any emotion, which factors influence he/she Has this kind of emotion and what the relationship is between of them. For example, the person assumes that he often feels difficult to sleep, he will attempt to buy any useful drugs or medicines to eat to help him to sleep easily. But, if he can not still feel that any kinds of drug can help him to feel enough sleeping after he eats it easily. Then, he has possible to find one psychologist to help him to find what factors cause him to feel difficult to sleep. SO, finding any factors to cause any one feels disappoint or failure or fear or difficult to do any thing etc. different negative emotion challenges, it may be any psychologist's duty to know how to find the main factor(s) to help to serve his patients satisfactorily.

Some people feel psychologists' duties are easy. It is wrong view point. In fact, they need spend long time to research any psychological topics and they are very difficult to research in order to conclude any results or answers.

I shall indicate both interesting cases , they concern how psychologists can help their patients successfully as below:

For bind people example, some bind or without enough eye sight seeing any thing people who can not see any thing long time, some psychologists can help them to see any things clearly when they are old age successfully in possible.

For another horse lotto win money participates case, there is one group people decides to invest money to participate this time horse lotto winning money competition. Before, every time horse competition, they share their opinions to concern every time horse lotto competition. And then, they will concentrate nervous to discuss and make group participation final decision to choose which numbers of horses, they decide to buy together. For every horse lotto competition, it has these three kinds of different level of decisions. The first kind is the least risk and prudential decision, it is without any investment money is needed to buy any hour number in the horse lotto competition. The another more risk decision is invested less money to some horses , they feel that they have possible to race in win and the final is the most risk decision is that to invest less money to some horses only, but they do not know that they have no possible to win money in the time horse lotto race competition with every participant personal average opinion comparison.

So, the participant's overall final decision may include three results: (1) more prudential decision result, (2) more risk decision result (3) without more prudential and more risk decision result.

So, psychologists can attempt to help them to apply psychological concept and theory to give recommendation how to raise chance to win this horse race lotto competition before he had gathered any horse past race experience and winning or lose times information to analyze every horse's winning chance rate. However, the psychologist must not guarantee they can win any horse race lotto in this competition. He can only give suggestion to help them to make more accurate judgement whether they ought choose which number of horse to buy.

What investigation methods as used by psychological science? For example, researching about how much violence level to the movie, you need to do surveys to enquire any participants whose feeling to this violence movie. Your investigating method is survey method. For another example, your participation to research the patients eat the drug how to influence their feeling or emotion, it is drug laboratory experiment method. For final example, you participate the activity and the psychologists use video camera to record your behavior, it is one observation method.

Some psychologists apply experiment psychological method to find what the main factors influence the student feels bore or difficult to learn anything. Some psychologists apply physical psychological method to find what factors cause close relationship between building biology process (stage) and human behaviors, e.g. How do our brains carry on analyzing our daily activities? Where are our brain part locations for our emotion, activity and mind leading functions? Has it same brain activity to learn between reading English and reading Chinese language? Some psychologists apply development psychological method to research how and why human's character causes and personal psychological mind development process, social behavioral development. Hence, psychological science research may be our whole person life development process research. From student stage, we have chance to encounter learning difficulties, when working age stage, we may encounter challenge how to cooperate to work with team members efficiently in any organizations, till to our old age stage, we may encounter our psychological and mental and physical health challenge. Hence, psychologists need to apply their professional psychological knowledge to help us to solve our any personal challenges , when we have chance to encounter in our different life stages

● What is psychological mind analysis function

Do you feel that your behaviors will be influenced by non-control or unknown factors influence? Do you ensure that your behaviors are careless causes? Psychological analysis function can be applied to these aspect: It can help us to know what myself actual ability owning to do any matters. For example, because we feel happy, so we will feel that we have this kind of ability to do this matter, even it is difficult to let us to feel to finish. Because happy feeling motivate us to attempt to do this matter, but it does not represent that we must own this kind of effort to succeed to finish this matter. It is only ourselves personal ability feeling or we have no own this kind of ability in fact. Otherwise, actual myself ability is between myself ability and exceeding myself super ability; actual myself ability represents logic and clever or talent that you own, they you're your protective ability. We can follow actual principles to choose to attempt to do any matters in order to achieve satisfactory feeling.

So, when we know what is actual ourselves abilities own, we will have more chance to finish the matter successfully. Because we have known whether what our actual abilities own to do the matter to achieve more successful chance. The final psychological mind analysis is that when we know what our social principle is and our life aim or goal or intention is, then we won't limit out actual owning abilities to attempt to achieve our any life aims or goals successfully in the end our life.

For example, some talent scientists, talent musicians, talent actors. They had known what their actual abilities in their life own. SO, they can have more confidence to attempt to do " exceeding themselves abilities behaviors" to achieve their life goals successfully. They have these personal characteristics: They had correct or right psychological mind analysis to know whether what they real need or hope to achieve as well as what their actual themselves " super owning abilities" that they ensure to own in order to accept to spend long time to learn how to raise their unique skills or techniques as well as doing owning super ability behaviors to achieve their life dreams. For some space scientists, actors, super sport people their abilities are seemed to own god helping, their super abilities are due to they had known whether what their unique owning abilities are different to general humans. So, psychological mind analysis function aims to let any people attempt to find or discover whether they have any unique abilities , they are unknown and psychologists need to help them to attempt to find any unique abilities in order to create their talent skills or techniques in possible.

What is behavioral mind?

In general, in our living environment, we attempt to apply basic learning principle to change our behaviors. It is very common situation. We can observe someone's behaviors in order to learn their skills. For learning basket ball , football playing sport skills example, the basket ball , football players must not need the basket ball, football coach leaders to teach them how to play. They can observe any one football or basket ball team players to learn how their skills to play in proficient very easily. They only need to spend long time to observe their skills in order to learn their skills in success. It is observation learning method, though these observations in order to learning their abilities in success. It is one interesting topic to psychologists' research concerns whether we can observe any person's skills or techniques in order to learn their same level skills or techniques in success.

The question is that whether observation is right or wrong learning behavior or method to any leaners. It is general psychologists have interest to research topic. In general, they believe that our behaviors can be caused by external and internal both factors. The potential environment seems to everyone to be same, but actual environment is ourselves behaviors how are created. For example, one meeting environment people treat themselves attitudes are the same, but one person behaves more rude and not polite and causes noise feeling in whole meeting environment, so his not polite behavior influences the meeting environment people treat him more punishment, but less appreciation. Otherwise, any other people perform their

same behaviors , such as polite and quite personal attitude in the meeting environment. So , many people can create more appreciation, but less punishment behaviors between them in whole meeting environment. It means that we can create chance to ourselves in different environment. It depends on whether how we perform our behavior and feeling to adapt the different environment needs. Such as this meeting environment, when many people perform their behaviors to like to listen other people what they are speaking in quiet personal attitude and they are polite to let any one speak to express his/her opinion in prior in the whole meeting environment. So, these kind of personal behavioral performance attitude is accpeted to whole members. Otherwise, the only one member, he often performs himself behaviors to argue and rude attitude and he also performs not like to listen any one personal opinion, he only believe his opinion must be the best among all of these members in whole meeting. So, he won't be appreciated his opinion performance and he will have punishment feeling from other members as well as he often feels arguement and he needs to spend much time to argue and support his opinions to other members' opposite opinions

in whole meeting process. Hence, in general any environment, we will be influenced to decide whether we ought choose to do ourselves behaviors in order to satisfy others people's acceptance more easily. Such as this meeting environment example, when some members feel their behaviors are appreciated or accepted , due to their performance and attitude are polite , liking acceptance to listen other opinions, without causing noise and argument, without performing perosnal attitude to let other feel himself/herself opinion must the best among all memebers.

In this meeting members' discussion time, this kind of polite and liking listening, liking acceptance other opinions personal attitude behavior will be appreciated. So, many memebers will feel to be appreciated among of them. Otherwise, the one member often perform rude and not polite personal attitude, and he only

likes others listen his opinion before anyone. He only feel that his opinion must be the best among of all members. However, he does not like to change his attitude to accept to listen other opinions before, he likes to cause arguement to discuss their opinions among of them and his behavior will let many members to feel rude. Due to he does not like accept to change his behavior in whole meeting environment. SO, he must feeling to be punished and without any appreciation in whole meeting

environment.

Hence, our behaviors ought be controlled or dominated by extrenal environment more than ourselves mind control if we hope our behaviors are accepted by many people in society in general. For example, if many the school class students hope to exam to pass this time examination more easily. Their mind will tell them that they will fail the time examination more easily, if they can not spend much time, e.g. one day spends at least 5 to 10 hours maximum per day and three months at least studying period to study hardly at home or school library. Then this class may have more than 50 percent students number will like to attempt to spend at least 5 hours hard to spend study in this three months studying period before this examination in order to achieve passing this examination successful aim or goal or intention.

So, this class student themselves mind is dominated by this classroom learning environment factor influence to persuade their hard studying learning

behavior. However, some lazy students will choose their mind more than learning environment acceptance, so they will still choose to spend less than 5 hours per day and it is only one month or two month studying period to carry on studying to follow their learning time table daily. Because they

do not feel that they will have high chance to pass this examination if they can spend longer time and longer learning period to gather any

information or teaching material from their school library as well as reducing leisure time and increasing studying time at home before this examination.

So, it explains that somethimes we need to choose to accept to follow to do any decision from either ourselves mind or our external environment as well as we also need to make judgement whether what factor will bring more benefit to us after we choose to do our final decision from either ourselves mind or our external environment factor influence. Because we do not know that whether ourselves mind or acceptance general external environment public mind which can help us to achieve our any goals more easily. So, it explains that why sometimes we needs to do psychological mind analysis between acceptance to ourselves mind more or acceptance to general public mind more in order to implement or

achieve some decisions more success consequently.

IN conclusion, on psychologists psychological mind analysis view points, they need to help patients to know how and why whether they ought follow external environment public mind more

or themsleves mind more in order to judge whether their patients' choice to be decided to do same matters whether it is right or wrong judgement, when their patients feel difficult

to do some decisions and they need their recommendation to indicate their psychological mind anlaysis assistance need in order to achieve their any decisions more success.So, psychological mind analysis function aims to help patients to know or find reasons tro explain that why they ought choose to do the kind of behaviors and help them to judge whether their behaviors choice or decision is right or wrong to be accepted to general society, even themselves.

Psychologist social service kinds of assistance

In our society, we have many different kinds of psychologists, e.g. criminal psychology, child , young, old age psychology, education psychology,

adult psychology, patient psychology, mental psychology, adult psychology, mental psychology, employee organizational psychology etc. However,

different psychologists will have themselves different psychological service to satisfy their patient mental health needs. In this chapter, I shall

introduce these different kinds of psychologists' tasks how to satisfy their patients' mental health needs. I shall indicate these different kinds

of psychologists' tasks how to satisfy their patients' mental health psychological needs. I also indicate some cases to explain what their tasks differences are.

Firstly, in psychology at work or organizational behavior or employee employee psychological research aspect, it concerns a large part of how people define who they are is by what they do. Work can be a key part of our social identity to build employees sense of themselves. IN special, employees organizational psychology

helpe organizations to solve employees mental health and how to bring a good job satisfactory feeling and it can promote psychological wellbeing when people are employed have lower rates of psychological health problems group target.

In psychology at work research aspect, it includes these organizational psychological assistance aspect: How to create a psychological healthy workplace to a meaningful work and what can keep people fulfilled and productive in their jobs ? It considers how to let employees to feel how to do work more attrative, rather than how to

make unemployment less attractive. As well as how improving on physical health and sickness absence to some lazy employees' negative mind psychological influence, how the organizational

psychological health of the workforce impacts on organizational health of the organizational performance, how to help organizations measure optimal levels of engagement at work

have significant benefits for the employee. Such higher levels of engagement are characterised by increased levels of angry, dedication, being strongly involved in one's work, experienccing a sense of significance, and being absorbed in one's work so time passes quickly.

So, how to designing work to encourage engagement is also needed to bring beneficial to the employers, helping organizations to attempt to find whether what of a number of key factors influence employees' psychological health and wellbeing in the workplace as well as seeking why and how some individual factors are other are linked to the work environment, e.g. finding what the main reason(s) whether it is/ they are the job insecurity or dissatisfaction or increased risk of low engagement or poor rewarded or long working hours time or feeling boreing etc. different factors influence a decreased productivity to bring a negative impact on the organization's employees.

Hence, employee organizational psychologists need to give their professional opinions to serve any organzations to help them to find what the main factor(s) influence(s) some or all employees' productive performance is(are) caused poor suddenly as well as finding the effective solutions or methods to attempt to help the organizations to recover or improve or raise their employees' productive performance effectively and efficiently in order to achieve the consequence to let all employees will feel happy or feel satisfactory to work in the organizations to avoid employees leaving turnover number increasing occurrence in possible.

Secondly, in concerning mental health and distress preventive psychology aspect, mental health psychologists need to let feeling mental distress hospital patients feel their mental disease or mental pressure can be changed to be health in possible. They need to help any mental patients to find what factors cause their mental sickness (illness), e.g. their mental sicknesses are caused from job stress or personal negative emotion, focus on distress or prior personal sad or unhappy past life experience. THeir mental health service aims to help their mental patients to solve any mental health problems are either illnesses or diseases. All these mental illnesses are assumed by a focus on distress as something

that is perhaps " in the mind". So, all mental illness patients , their mental illnesses are assumes to have cause and effect relationship to their " poor mind" illnesses.

SO, mental health psychologists will focus on their mind research to find why and how they have any mental illnesses suddenly. The term mental illness, for example, any mental

health psychologists will suggest that their walk will be illness, and it has a medical character, but that ill will also take a mentalistic or psychological focus. It is the different between a mental health psychologist and a nervous illness doctor how they view their mental illness patients, e.g. a nervous illness doctor will suggest the right

medicine (drug) to attempt to help the mental illness patient, but a mental health psychologist will apply psychological knowledge to attempt to help the mental illness patient to solve his mental problems. So, the mental health psychologist will feel psychological health treatment is more useful to compare medicine oe drug eating treamtment, and they will assume that the mental patient's problems is caused due to his psychological emotion factor more than his physical illness factor. For example, one person feels distress or mental pressure, mental health psychologist will feel his distress may be caused from overload job pressure, but a vervous illness doctor will feel his pressure is caused

by body physical illness factor more than poor or negative emotion influencing factor. So, one mental health psychologist is one mental health psychologist doctor to find whether what external environment or his/her personal psychological emotion is his main factor to cause his patient feels unpleasant or emotion pressure feeling suddenly in

order to solve his psychological illness problem successfully.

Hence, medical psychologists are well aware of the close link between physical disease and mental health. Frequently, psychologists are asked to see a patient who has been admitted to a general medical facility, due to a medical illness or disease that may have a psychological overlay. When providing clinical services to a medical patient in a general hospital, psychologists are finding that they are part of an interdisciplinary team. IN conclusion, any hospitals or clinics must nee medical

psychologists give medical psychological methods to solve patients' psychological challenges when he/she feels disappointed or fear himself or herself will die in possible in order to avoid he/she commits suicide easily. Hence, medical psychologist needs to help any patients to build positive emotion continue alive independence. Their role needs to assist

doctors to solve their patients' psychological health needs when they are living in hospitals, even they leave their hospitals in future one day.

Thirdly, for crininal psychology social function aspect, why does our society need criminal psychologists? IN our legal system of our society, it is a reflection of what is considered tolerable and intolerable behavior within that particular society, i.e. intolerable behavior is disapproved of by the majority. However, we must have people to

anti-social behavior to let our sosciety to know their dissatisfaction, it is their criminal intent major factor. IN fact, any legally wrong or immoral behavior, e.g.

burglary, fraud, killing theft, trespass, fighting are caused by the criminal people's negative psychological factor. In general, although many of them had known that they will be punished if they still do criminal behaviors in our society. But, they can not dominate or control themselves to do any criminal behaviors. So, it explains why that we still need criminal psychologists to help them to find why they do criminal behavioral reasons after they had done criminal behaviors as well as

they are punished to go to court to be judged consequently.

Criminal psychologists aim to let their criminal patients to know their errors and use professional acriminal psychological methods to help them to learn how to avoid to do any criminal behaviors again after they are free to go to society to prepare to find new jobs to do or beginning re-new life again. The criminal psychologists will make

a number of assumptions that any criminal people who have these similar characteristics. They may include as below:

The first assumption is that every individual's behaviors is due to their own interpretation of reality and real environment can influence how any why the person does criminal behavior in society.

The second assuption is that people will learn meaning by observing how other people react in society, both positively and negatively. SO, if the person often contact his friends who often react

negative social behavior, they will influence or persuade him to trend to do any criminal behavior more easily in society. The third assumption is that we evaluate our own behaviors according

to the meanings, we have learned and that we have acquired from others. So, we will learn any one's behavior and we will make evaluation whether we ought or ought not follow their behaviors

to do. For example, any one knows killing another person is a criminal act. However, in some suitations, for instance, when a peson kills in self-defence, when a legitimate killing because he needs to protect himself body to be attacked to cause hurt, even death as well as he feels that he has possible to be killed if he does not decide to kill the person in the environment immediately. So, criminal psychologists needs to help the killer to feel that he is not a actual killer in psychological view point, although he had killed the person in legal view point in orde to avoid that he commits suicide himself easily in any time.

Hence, any one criminal psychologist, he/she had learnt these criminal psychological knowledge to prepare how to help his / her owning criminal mind and doing criminal behavioral patients to solve negative psychological or negative emotion challenge after they had done criminal activites. Their criminal psychological knowledge may include these several aspects: Knowledge of key concepts and psychological models of criminal behavior, capacity to identify the different perspective on human nature under the theoretical development and research of any criminal behavioral causes, familiarity with research methodologies commonly employed in the field of criminal psychology, as well as a capacity for analyzing their strengths and weaknesses , a biosocial fame of reference included, ability to examine critically specific offences and apply psychological models of criminality to case studies, awareness of the different prevention, treatment strategies for working with offenders, a range of presentation skills. They need to do face to face contact to spend some time, e.g. one day one to two hours, five days within every week time to talk to the criminal person is prison in order to find whether whar his/her negative psychological or negative emotion factor(s) can cause or influence his/her decision to make any kinds of criminal activities consequently as well as finding the methods to let they feel positive emotion or positive psychological reflection to avoid to do any similar criminal activities again after he/she leave the prision in orde to protect our social safety, due to their criminal activities occurrence again and reducing criminal rate raising occurrence easily in our society .

Forthly, I will explain what the educaiton psychological function is. Education psychologists may give recommendation to teachers how to encourage their students to themselves learning interest to be raised by their teachers' teaching methods influence or themselves psychological learning method influence both as well as how to improve their school classrooms teaching -learning environment in order to influence their students feel happy to learn in their classrooms to achieve aim to help them to get high grade results consequently. It is helpful in instructional strategies and provides basis for the selection of appropriate methods, techniques, approaches , tools to satisfy and fulfil the need of learners that results in better learning, with the help of educational psychological teacher is able to create positive learning environment in the clasrooms resulting in effective learning. So, the educational psychologist plays an important role in making learning easy, joyful and interesting process. Likewise also conflict classroom management strategies may be used in teaching, learning leading towards better ways of delivering information to the learners in the classroom.

Finally, I shall explain what child psychology is? Every child stage development is important to influence his/her personal behavior when he/she grows up to be adult. So, child psychologists need to give opinions to their any ons child patient's partents and help their every child patient's patients to know why to teach their child/children in positive teaching and learning way, when they are living at home daily. Because every child whose patients wll influence his/ her behavior when he/she is adult and he /she needs to work in society.

For example, how to create or develop the child's unique skill or technique if the child is one one talent child to be needed to find whether he/she owns which kinds of skills , which need their patients help him/her to discover. Then the child can concentrate on training to upgrade the kind of undiscovered skills to hel him/her to become one talent child as well as attributing his/her human intelligence to our society's benefit. For another example, the educational psychologist needs to give opinions to the child's parents to teach them how to persuade the child to follow learning disciplines to raise learning ability when they contact at home, the child ought first to be presented with problems and methods and only later with disciplines.

In conclusion, all of above these different kinds of psychologists, they have different professional psychological knowledge and skill to help our
social different stakeholder patients to solve their mental problems and satisfy their mental health service nees in order to let our society can
have many positive psychological mind people feel happy to live in our society.

Definition of crime behavior

In psychology, there are three theories to explain crime behavior. First is the consensus view, which indicates the legal system of the society is a reflection of what is considered tolerable and intolerable behavior within particular society, i.e. intolerable behavior is disapproved of by the majority. Before a crime can be said to have occurred, it has to be committed. So, without an action, there can be no crime. The act must be legally forbidden. It is not enough to just be anti-social behavior, and the act must also have a criminal intent to commit to act. For example, if a banker helps the bank's client to invest to cause loss, carelessly, who has not proved to help whose client to invest to cause loss intentionally. Then, who has no criminal intent to commit the act. The staff's behavior must be legally wrong, may not be morally wrong only. For example, the bank teller is proved to steal whose bank employer's clients' saving account money for himself/herself to steal to use. This is legally wrong behavior. Otherwise, the bank teller neglect to help the bank clients to keep to save box carefully. Then, it is morally wrong behavior, because who has no intentional stealing behavior. Thus, business crime needs the person has crime behavior, not only moral in behavior only. Second is the conflict view, it is the direct opposite of the consensus view. In society, some group of people believe different groups of people, such as students, professionals, unions, businessmen etc. These groups are in conflict with each other in a range of ways, due to the inequality of the way that wealth is divided. There will be some poorer people, some wealthier people, some power, some with no power. Thus inequality leads to a society based on conflict, which is thought to then promote crime. For example, poorer people, e.g. no job people or unemployed people who will commit crimes, such as theft, burglary, murder, when middle class people may commit crimes, such as theft from employers when collar crime, fraud. The upper classes may commit crimes such as environmental pollution, and damage which may not be considered crime in same way as burglary, for example. Third is the interactionist view, it maintains that there is no moral right or wrong, rather changes in moral standards affect the legal standards. For example, killing another person is a criminal act. However, in some situations, for instance, when a person skills in self-defense, it is considered as legitimate killing.

What are social psychological crime reasons? Why does working environment influence staff individual crime decision? What do legal procedure strike staffs as fair? In criminal cases, psychological factors may influence decisions involving arrest, prosecution, bargaining etc. criminal behavior.

When making arguable social judgement, e.g. whether the staff have crime intent to do whose behavior, it means innocent behavior, e.g. stealing office cash or computer's behavior. Would this defendant commit such as offence or intentionally? Facts are not all that matter. In the types of staff's individual crime, in the status, age, sex and race of the defendant, it's hard to isolate the factors that influence the employer's judge. The fact includes physical attractiveness, for example, when employers asked individual staff to judge the guilt of baby -aced and mature-faced of the staff defendant. The Baby-faced adult (staff with large, round eyes and small chins) seemed most native and were found guilty more often of crimes of negligence and less often of intentional criminal acts in office. It convicted, unattractive staffs also strike people as more dangerous, especially if who are sexual offenders in working environments.

Any ethical concern is about scientific jury selection, experiments reveal that the staff individual attitudes and personal characteristics don't always predict how and when and why whose crime behavior caused. There are no magic questions to be asked, not even a guarantee that a particular survey will detect that a particular survey will detect useful to the criminal staff individual attitude-behavior and personality-behavior relationship for whose criminal intention.

Does the criminal staff who subject to the social influence to cause whose criminal behavior decision in office? e.g. stealing office cash or computer or any office properties . For example, a bank counter staff steals whose bank employer whose withdraw one client's saving account money to provide himself/herself to use or doing false office documents to earn personal bank loan borrowing benefits for whose one bank client to earn personal benefit illegal behavior.

To patterns of either minority influence, or even to majority group staffs think to do office criminal behavior. All in office environment, one individual staff who has criminal intention, usually who is usually by minority or majority group influence by whose colleagues. It is possible that who decide to plan to do office criminal stealing behavior together. So, when the staff steals the valuable thing in office, who will sell the valuable thing to exchange interest to share this illegal cash earns with whose colleagues to enjoy together. Thus, although it seems that this stealing behavior is belong to this staff one person to do, but the fact, it is possible the minority or majority group colleagues had planned to arrange when and how and where to encourage who have confidence to attempt to do this criminal behavior in the office first time. Because who feels whose employer won't know who will steal this office property and when this office property will be stolen and where any office property will be stolen. However, it is a hypothetical situation to let this office staff and whose other colleagues to feel whose employer doesn't know this stolen matter will happened. So, it causes who have more confidence to attempt to do this stealing criminal psychological behavior in office. Otherwise, if who feel whose employer will know this stealing matter will happen. It means that the employer will know who will steal his one kind of property and where this property is located and when this property will be stolen in office. Then, I believe who don't choose to attempt to plan to do this criminal stealing behavior in office.

Is the process to motivate the staff's criminal behavior by which certain minority or majority group of the staff individual colleagues and to guide or persuade him/her to encourage whom to attempt to whose stealing criminal behavior in office? One example of the power of the staff individual criminal behavior in office is leadership. The process by which is certained the individual staff is mobilized and is guided by whose minority or majority colleagues group in office. Some office leaders are formally appointed or elected by their minority or majority colleagues group in office; others emerge informally as the criminal group interacts in office. What makes for good office criminal group leadership often depends on the situation, the best colleague relationship person (staff) to lead the criminal colleagues team may not make the best criminal leader of the sales force, e.g. criminal stealing office property behavior. Some staffs excel or task leadership at criminal organizing work, setting criminal guide and focusing on criminal goal attainment in office. Others excel at social leadership, at building criminal teamwork, mediating solving conflicts and being supportive with colleagues (staffs) in office.

In office, social leaders (criminal behavior leaders) often have a democratic style, one that delegates authority and welcomes input from criminal staff team members in office. Many experiments reveal that such leadership is good for morale, e.g. office morale. To office, minority or majority colleagues group criminal behavioral members who usually feel more satisfied when who participate in making criminal behavioral decisions in office. If a office criminal behavioral leaders can control or plan or lead over whose criminal behavioral task or steps, the team of criminal colleagues also become more motivated to achieve stealing behavior more successful in office. So, the office criminal behavioral leaders who value good criminal behavioral team feeling and take pride in achievement therefore criminal behavior is encouraged to cause under democratic leadership. Any effective office criminal leadership styles, we now know, vary with the situations in office environments. So, the most effective office criminal supervisors in coal mines, banks and government organizations etc. environmental offices score high on tests of both criminal task and social relationship. They are actively concerned for how criminal work is progressing and sensitive to the criminal behavioral needs of their subordinates in office. Thus, it will encourage office criminal behavior causing more easily. Studies also reveal that many effective office criminal leaders of laboratory groups, work teams, and large corporations exhibit office criminal behaviors that promote or encourage minority or majority colleagues to influence criminal behaviors occur in office. Otherwise, sometimes, to be sure, office criminal teams also influence their criminal leaders. In trying to under staffs, employers wonder why who act and way to do criminal or immoral behavior in office. For example, if worker productivity declines, does the employer assume the workers are getting lazier? Or has their equipment become less efficient? When a salesperson says that outfit really looks nice on the client, does this reflect genuine feeling or telling immoral lie to give wrong message to persuade the client to feel this shirt is beautiful or comfortable when who wears it to choose to buy misleading.

It is attributing causality to the staff or the working
situation. Employer endlessly analyze and discuss why office immoral, even criminal behaviors happen as who do, especially when something negative or unexpected occurs. Attribution theory analyzes how we explain people's behavior, such as how employers explain staffs' behavior. The variations of attribution theory share some common assumptions that we (employers) seek to make sense of our world (office environment), then we (employers) attribute people's (staff's) individual actions to internal or to external causes, and that we (employers) do so in fairly logical, consistent ways.

The theory of how people (staffs) explain others' (colleagues') behavior, for example, by attributing, it either to internal dispositions (enduring traits, motives and attributes) or to external situations in office. Such as, in office environment, these three factors, consistency, distinctiveness and consensus influence whether the staff (criminal behavior leader) attributes colleague's individual criminal behavior to internal or external causes in office. First, consistency factor indicates that: Does the staff usually behavior this criminal behavior (way) in this situation ? Second, distinctiveness factor indicates that: Does the staff behave differently in different situations in office environments? Third, consensus factor indicates that: Do other colleagues behave similarly in this situation in this office environment? Thus, it seems, office environment is one external factor to cause the staff's criminal behavior occurrence in office as well as the staff internal factor, e.g. feeling no people discover or know whose criminal behavior is carrying in office, so whose feeling can motivate who have confidence to attempt to do whose criminal or immoral behavior in office.

How can employers prevent crime and misconduct in whose business from staffs' immoral or criminal behavior in working environment? Nowadays, investing in crime and misconduct prevention tends to be more financially advantages rather than setting losses after staff's individual criminal behavior has occurred. So, corporate security protects the company's business activities, interest groups, data and property from human error, misconduct and criminal intent. To support their efforts, to establish a secure environment, companies need information about criminal practices and methods of safeguarding themselves. However, small and medium sized companies invest all too little in risk-reducing measures. The reasons for this can often be found in limited available resources and a lack of awareness about the types of crime and other threats who may be facing. Otherwise, the largest companies clearly invest the most in measures to reduce potential security risks. However, a notable higher number of crimes and acts of misconduct are directed at large companies.

In global , the majority of companies rely on technical security measures. However, companies should invest in security training in addition to technical solutions, because training in addition to technical solutions, because security fail as a result of intentional or deliberate actions made by personal. Information leaks can also be reduced through training. If the company has not provided any guidance in formation management, then the easiest way to gain access to confidential company information may simply be any contacting one of its employees.

In fact, by global statistic showed that half of the companies had not trained their personnel in how to handle confidential information. A though employee recruiting process, including background checks, assists in developing corporate security. These processes help the company to reduce the security risks related to its personnel and ensure that a staff is suitable for the task who is being hired to perform.

Nowadays, attempted crimes and acts of misconduct are often directed at company records and files. The most common breaches involved attempts at unauthorized entry into the company's data network. In large companies, the number of attempts at unauthorized entry has higher than the average. The risk/ threats related to data security include: attempts of unauthorized entry or hacking into the data network, copying information for one's own use prior to leaving the service of the company, unauthorized disclosing of critical corporate information to a third party, unauthorized snooping into corporate records or files (content), intentional destruction of files, unauthorized entry or hacking into the data network, unauthorized surrendering of confidential corporate documents to a third party and unauthorized altering/ false of corporate records of files (content) etc. stealing company's confidential data criminal behavior. Every company has information that needs to be protected. However, confidential information about a company can be leaked to an external party with deliberate intent. In every fifth company, an employee had copied internal company data prior to moving to another company within the same field of business. The chance of that confidential business information may be sent to competitors and may significantly harm a company's business activities from which staff's individual criminal behavior.

In order to define a crime as it relates to business secrets and to acquire the appropriate legal safeguards, the company must determine which information might be considered as secret, establish instructions for handling confidential. Besides, the risks/threats related to property may also include: theft of tools or equipment, forced entry into an office or production facility, vandalism of an office or production facility, significant loss. For example, many construction companies has experienced unauthorized entries into offices and production facilities. The greatest loss of material is experienced in construction and trade field. In order to reduce loss, companies can utilize a wide variety of technical security systems and security guard services in order to protect property. Moveable property is well marked and protected. Moreover, in order to reduce the risks, companies should need to invest in training and determining the human risk factors. For example, the use of a monitoring system requires that personnel acquaint themselves with the procedures required by the systems. Also, the threats of violence were clearly more common than actual acts of violence, since every third company states that their employees had experienced threats at work. Violent or threatening situations arose in connection with, among others, meetings with drunk or intoxicated customers or in different burglary, seizure or petty larceny situations. The risk of violence is increased when an employee works alone or late at night. To some extent, violence can be reduced through training and technical safety measures. Monitoring equipment also assists often security threats because of their company's activities or field of business. Among the large companies, every eighth stated that key personnel or their families had been threaten . The risks /threats related to personnel may include: an employee has been threaten at work; an employee has committed a crime/ acts of misconduct against your company; another type of work-related crime toward an employee has occurred; key personal or their families have received threats in relation to their work; an employee has been victim of violence at work; an employee has committed a crime/act of misconduct against your clients.

Thus, I recommend that management needs to show the direction. The security culture of a company refers to the behavior and attitude of the company's personnel towards security. A good security culture reduces security risks and supports a company's competitiveness. Risk prevent is most successful in a company where the management is committed to risk management. In four out of five companies surveyed, the management personally participates in security development. A lack of internal co-operation and co-ordination may also form a significant obstacle to corporate security because potential risks should be examined from the different viewpoints of all areas of operation. A quarter of the responding companies reported do not co-operate with each other when dealing with security issues. Thus, I feel employers need to concern how achieve security development to themselves to reduce loss threats. What are the future focal points for security development? They include: data security, key personnel security, personal security, security of production facilities and equipment, prevention against other threats, preparations to deal with terrorism. Because unknown risks can't be controlled. Before it can prepare for risks, the company must understand the risks that are related to their activities and operating environment, risk assessment helps a company to evaluate the internal and external threats, it may be facing. So, a through assessment that is regularly updated helps to guide risk management work.

Why does employer need to prepare psychological medical records or confidential employment check for any employee job application before who decide to employ any new staffs? This method is pre-employment evaluations method to judge or predict whether the employee has criminal record or possible criminal behavior caused before the employer ensures to choose to employ the staff to enter whose firm to work. For example, the employer can require the mental health professional to conduct pre-employment an forensic evaluations frequently receive requests for release of the job applicant's forensic psychological medical records report. When a routine clinical report is prepared to guide treatment, it is clear that the report should be released of there is an appropriate patient-initiated authorization. Although, these records belong to the patient. But, does an applicant for job or subject (examinee) of a fitness for duty evaluation have a right to a copy of a report commissioned by an employer or lawyer?

There are many types of evaluations that can generally be referred to as forensic or employment evaluations, and each has characteristics that may make release of the report to the examinee unwise of problematic. Additionally, laws and regulations that define rules for disclosure of these reports are often unclear or contrdictory. So, why employers need to concern this issue. For example, a police department refers an employee to a fitness for duty evaluation. The officer has been involved in a series of confrontations in which deadly force was deployed, and the department wants to know whether the officer has psychological problems that predispose him be more aggressive thn necessary. So, as a employer, you need to concern whether the department has sent or has not sent the officer any file containing internal investigations reports of the various incidents, including names of witnesses and their statements to concern the job applicant's individual behavior to judge whether the chance of who has possible to perform criminal or immoral behavior will occur during who are working in any working environment from whose personal behavior's history medical record. So, you will have more accurate to judge whether who is an easy criminal or not easy criminal person to make decision whether you ought to choose to employee whom or not.

As provisions of health information portability and accountability act (HIPAA), 1996, states that even test results belong to patients as part of their history medical records. If include copy righted and trade secret information, such as test manuals is released by the patient's request. But professional ethics and HIPAA regulations don't fully consider the complications of release of information issues in employment and forensic evaluations. Also, the mental health professional can't simply conclude that examinees have a right to them file. However, access of individuals to protected health information, the regulations recognize the right of an individual to access a record set except for the following: 1) psychotherapy notes 2) information compiled in reasonable anticipation of, or for use in a civil, criminal or administrative action or proceeding and 3) when a correctional institution or a covered health care provider may deny access to protect the safety, security, custody, or rehabilitation of other inmates, or the safety of the employee at the institution. Access may also be denied if the information was obtained from someone than a health care provider under a promise of confidentiality and the access would be reasonably likely to reveal the source of the information.

The reasons of internal theft threat occurs in
working environment

Why do employees steal? The motivating factors for employee theft are opportunity, rationalization, or need. The removal of any of these factors particularly opportunity will reduce losses. As risk of being caught increases, the probability of theft decreases. When the risk of being caught of low theft may raise. Criminal psychologists indicated that 10% of your employees would not steal from you regardless of the circumstances, 10% will steal at any opportunity and 80% can go either way, waiting to see how serious you are about theft and weighing the risks. Thus, the best defense against internal theft is comprehensive pre-employment screening. A criminal records check and a credit history are a vital part of this process. Because the criminal records check will verify whether an employee has been honest in answering questions about a criminal record. Employers may arrange for a criminal records check by requiring a prospective employee to obtain one as a condition of employment. Also a credit history can reveal whether a person (new staff) is experiencing or has experienced a financial problem. This can help expose a unusual financial need.

How to develop honest behaviors to employees ? Employers must demonstrate to employees that loss prevention is important to them by setting an example. Employers can do this by developing a code of conduct for staff and encouraging communication. To implement proper procedures and policies and ensure compliance to encourage reporting of suspicious circumstances or persons to someone prepared to deal with it, to educate staff on recognition and response to employee theft.

What is burnout? " Staff burnout is defined as a condition of emotional exhaustion, depersonalization and reduced personal accomplishment that can occur among individuals who work with people in some capacity" (Maslach, Jackson & Leiter, 1996, p.4)

How has close relationship between low staff morale and burnout? When economic downturn occurs, the staff size is being reduced, causing longer workdays, fewer opportunities to recharge and relax and greater responsibilities for remaining employees. Ultimately, these changes in the workplace dynamic could cause reductions in staff morale and an increase in burnout in a normally bright and happy workforce. Why does trends/issues of low staff moral and burnout cause? Why does staff burnout behave? Burnout behavior will cause employee attempts to do theft. Who is emotional exhaustion, depersonalization and reduced personal accomplishment. Emotional exhaustion refers to the energy discharge of emotional resources , which is considered the keystone of staff burnout. Staff effects in work environment: higher rates of illness, lower staff moral, increased use of alcohol and drugs, lower creer satisfaction, high staff turnover, reduced quality of service and poor productivity, even more serious criminal internal theft behavior will occur in any workplace.

As unexpected staff burnout is complex problem. Bad emotion factors can cause burnout, include escapism, reflection, long term stressful feeling. So, employers need to concern about how to avid burnout cause. Burnout can cause poor staff morale, such as intrinsic poor motivation, poor organizational commitment and lacking work pride. Why employers need to concern about how to raise staff morale culture because which can notice improved productivity, improved performance and creativity reduced number of days taken for leave, higher attention to detail, safe workplace and n increased quality of work. Otherwise, poor staff moral lack of motivation and interact, decreased working efficiency and could lead to staff's refusal to provide services, even the individual employee who is burn outed who will be influenced to plan to perform criminal theft behaviors to compensate for whose psychology and financial unfair loss from whose employer or colleagues. So, it seems burnout will have chance to cause the employee who is burn outed who choose to do any insider criminal behavior in working environment.

How to predict potential insider threats in working environment

I shall recommend that a behavioral model for predicting potential insider threats in working environment. It is an alarm about employees who pose higher insider threat risks. The insider threat refers to harmful acts that trusted insiders might carry out. For example, something that causes harm to the organization, or an authorized act that benefits the individual. The insider threat is when human behavior depart from established policies, regardless of whether it results from disregard for security policies. The serious types of crimes and threats include terrorism, corruption, bribery etc. as well as the not serious types of crimes and threats include copyright violations, negligent use of classified data, fraud unauthorized ccess to sensitive information and illicit communication with unauthorized recipients in workplace environment. Commonly, it is difficult to predict how the motivation of insiders who commit security fraud. The most of the threats could have been prevented by timely and effective action to address by timely and effective action to address the anger, pain, anxiety, or criminal psychological in cause of risk well in advance of any insider crime.

How can psychosocial behaviors that be predicted increased risk for insider threats? Some criminal psychologist explained insider threat detection, which is based on multiple indicators that not only address work station and network activity logs, but also include preparatory behavior, verbal behavior and personality traits. Instead who recommended consideration of nonclinical instruments that measure personality and behavioral characteristics tests, that not only focus on job suitability and skills, but who don't contain the obvious psychiatric questions, that are easily picked tests indicated any employee selection, but who allow that largely due to the unpredictability of the employees' life and work circumstances in relation to their workplace behavior after being employed. The poor immoral behaviors, such as absenteeism, disciplinary issues and drug alcohol abuse will be caused by an insider risk evaluation when the employee feels whose employer consider whose personal moral behavior considerately. So, it will cause employee's individual negative attitude to be caused if who feels whose employer's dissatisfaction with whose work organization is a powerful predictor of workplace fraud to himself/herself moral behavior in any workplace environment. Thus, it is an substantial relationship between the employee's perception of injustice of the workplace and whose deviant behavior, such as theft, violence.

In the case of an employee trying to gain financially be exploiting a corporation's intellectual property, a desire may be driven by the satisfaction of causing costly damage to the corporation, but it can be also include a motive of financial gain. In either case, the employee may have exhibited stress or some for of dissatisfaction about whose circumstances. These factors, if properly evaluated in a timely manner, could alert an organization about a developing insider crime . Identifying employees who show risk of insider threat has two benefits: preventing an unnecessary cost to the employer, and helping the employee before a bad situation changes worse.

The relationship between workplace monitoring and trust is complex. On the one hand, opponents claim workplace monitoring that an employer's use of monitoring devices, whether convert or overt, threatens both employee privacy and morale. Such as, when the employer feels doubtful to lack of trust whose behavior may contribute to employee job dissatisfaction. Also, some criminal psychologists explain when attitudes are negative about surveillance, employees are less likely to be committed to their work, who will display lower organizational citizenship behaviors. So, it seems employer can not let any individual employee discover that who is doubtful whose attempts to do immoral behavior and to use surveillance to supervise when who is working in any workplace environment daily. Because who will raise whose employees feel unhappy to work in whose workplace environment and to influence who reduce productivity or providing poor customer service performance long term. Hence, employer needs to let whose employees to have more confidence to work in whose workplace environment to avoid staff (leaving) turnover numbers will increase.

How to reduce internal risk and fraud losses in work environment
I shall recommend how to reduce internal risk and fraud losses. Advanced detection techniques, such as behavior profiling, peer analysis, fraud correlation and complex statistical analysis can quickly help identify fraudulent employee activities, mitigating direct financial losses, and non transactional losses, including data theft, regulatory fines and reputational damage. Other methods include: out-of-the box, browser-based investigation capabilities, such as advanced query tools, case and workflow management, and SAR filing combined with integration of various systems, eliminates the manual processes of sifting through the data, automates detection of common employee violations, and supports case-building efforts. Besides identify and discover all content inside your network that represents risk. Effective insider threat management requires an organization to locate and classify its assets and to remain continuously watchful of insider behavior and associated risk. For example, key members of your organization should meet to prioritize critical areas of concern. You could use a simple scoring system, such as 1 to 10, or low, medium and high to assist in your prioritization. Your focus, should center on those assets that receive the highest priority or those that would be most costly to your organizations. This content should include all data and files containing personal or customer information and intellectual property or other sensitive data. Each organization may define these assets and incidents differently as they will vary depending on the industry or focal point of your organization.

What is insider scientific theft? It may include secret documents, company financial data, client's confidential data. Example assets at risk by vertical market include: Banking and credit companies which identifies theft, account skimming, funds, diversion. Financial firms whose mergers and acquisition plans, non-public financial information and private research. Retail organizations whose pricing information, personal information, on credit card holders. Public companies whose earnings information not yet distributed to the market, new product information before release, intellectual property. The government whose national secrets, classified and personal information.

How to reduce insider scientific theft risk? Once identified and prioritized this content should be fingerprinted and inventoried to ensure that it is not sent out via e-mail, instant messaging (IM) or copies to USB or other mobile storage devices. Security risks are not circumvented through simply data-leak prevention, as which are fair detectors of mostly one vector of communications, such as out bound data streams, mostly e-mail. The insider scientific theft, such as typical customer data-loss investigations include that deliberate theft of client lists for profit by employees with access to client data (ID theft); leak of customer data is lost or stolen laptops with client data, However, client data losses are sometimes accidental , e.g. losing a

Laptop containing tens or even more than one thousand customer records, but the data loss that enterprises need to monitor mostly closely are the deliberate acts, such as theft of personal data for resale (ID theft). A laptop can happen to anyone, from a junior salesperson to the CEO. For example, some deliberate client data thefts involve contractors or outsourced service, such as call centers users have little management oversight to the company.

How to predict insider intellectual property theft behavior? Typical intellectual property investigations include that deliberate theft of IP for financial gain, unintentional leak follow up when also open to accidental disclosure, intellectual property, such as CAD files, product plans, proprietary formulas etc. are typically targeted for deliberate theft in a manner that either harms the company for reasons of deliberate press leaks, anonymous sending to competitors etc. or to further the perpetrator's own direct objectives taking IP to a competitor for a new job. Also, company can achieve policies that monitor off-hours activity hundreds of pages printed at 4: 50 AM. Per working day, unusual mobile storage use (gigabyte transfers daily), or suspicions activities with applications (taking a screenshot of a custom CAD design window) are helpful with investigations.

What kind of organizations need to concern intellectual property theft? Hospital, financial institutions are retailers are all highly regulated due to the high volumes of confidential data each organization manages. Banks and financial institutions most protect customer's confidential personally identifiable information. Internally, enterprises need to monitor to corporate governance issues (i.e. employees handbook issues, like harassment that might also put the company at legal risk. Cases involving theft of confidential information include cases in which current or former employees or contractors intentionally exceed or misuse an authorized level of access to networks, systems or data with the intention of stealing confidential information form the organization. Some psychologists had researched to indicate who take insiders were in any organizations. 80% of the insiders who stole confidential information worse and stole over half hold technical positions, 25% were former employees, the other 75% were current employees when who committed whose illicit activity. Interestingly, 45% of the insiders who were current employees at the time of their theft had already accepted positions with another company. Why who do it? Some insiders were financially motivated, for example, stealing information to commit credit card fraud or selling information to their company's competitors. Others were about to start new jobs or form their own companies and felt entitled to the information.

How who did it? More than 75% of the insiders had authorized access when who committed their theft. Only former employee was given authorized access to do some additional work, who used that access to commit whose theft. The rest of the authorized uses were fairly evenly split between privileged and unprivileged users. More than 75% of the insiders used their own usernames and passwords to commit thefts. However, an important factor in dealing with insider threats is understanding the profiles (job, status with company etc.) . Clearly having an idea of user and behavioral profiles can make investigations easier. Thus, an enterprise could have built strong general monitoring policies around its core intellectual property, when deploying more policies around those with constant access to core IP. Additionally the enterprise can work more closely with as human resources department to identify at risk employees and deploy, even more focused policies to those users that specifically look for activities, such as high volume printer output after hours, or large files copies to USB drives or other leading indicators of taking IP out the door to their new job. So, employers could not neglect to concern high technological insider theft behaviors from any organizational key employee's immoral performance in any organizational computer departments.

How to use psychological methods to avoid insider theft loss?

The challenge of fraud directed against a business is increased by the diversify and deceptive nature of those crimes.

Deception is a key element of workplace fraud, and a company may realize too late that it has been victimized. An appropriate response to the threat of potential areas that are at risk, recognizing the fraud related threats, and understanding the potential fraud, organization points both internal and external. The criminal mind is ever alert to seeming new and unique ways to separate a business from its assets. In business crime, it can seem white-collar crime, such as fraud, misconduct and related financial threats anti-fraud professionals agree that fraud and misconduct activities involve dishonesty and deception that can drive value to any business, either directly or indirectly to earn benefit. Fraud involves the intent to defraud, it relies on the person's deception to accomplish their fraudulent activity. Some criminal psychological research showed fraud is not accomplished via honest mistake or error. Also fraud can manifest itself in a wide variety of ways and originate from a number of different sources.

What does motive people to commit fraud? Criminologists have identify three elements, that are often form the rationalization, opportunity and pressure. Opportunity refers to the situation and circumstances that make it possible for fraud to occur. For example, an employee with uncontrolled access to company funds has the opportunity to misappropriate those funds. So effective internal controls can reduce or even eliminate opportunities for fraud. Pressure and/ or incentive helps explain why and when fraud occurs. Fraud occurs when fraud pressures or incentives outweigh and overcome, the pressures and incentives to act honestly. Thus, it can become the motivation to act fraudulently. The cause of seasons include lifestyle issues, living beyond one's means; personal debt, e.g. excessive credit and use gambling results, .e.g. poor operating results, desire to avoid business failure, meet requirements of lenders. So, if a company can recognize when and where excessive pressure/ incentives may to present, it can use that information in fraud prevention and may be have detection efforts and take action to avoid business-related pressure/incentives in order to reduce fraud risk. For example, in effective fraud prevention program can increase pressures and incentives to act honestly by emphasizing a perception of detection, underscored by the company's demonstrated, consistent commitment to taking appropriate and certain action once fraud is discovered. Rationalization means to the need for people to somehow justify their fraudulent actions in their own minds. A person involves in a fraud attempts to psychologically accept whose own actions and emotionally. Rationalization are not generally known to others and therefore difficult to detect. In addition, persons with low moral mind may feel little need to rationalize their behavior. In fact, some employee with to those criminal matters in office, e.g. asset misappropriation, fraudulent financial statements and records and corrupt or prohibited practices. White-collar crime includes the company's financial statements , internal and external, books and records of business may be targets for fraud, Such as manipulated to hide fraud , e.g. to prevent discovery of an asset misappropriation and/or falsified to accomplish a fraud, e.g. to cause unjustified financial rewards, such as executive bonuses based on falsified financial performance data. This occurrence is not employee's stealing behaviors, but if one staff, e.g. accountant who has incorrect or fraudulent mind to do wrong financial data presentation to aim to get himself/herself benefits from whose employer. Then, whose immoral behavior is such as carrying on illegal stealing criminal behavior in office.

Modern high technological theft and insider threat often occurs in office, including concerns around intellectual property (IP) theft by employees or outsiders impersonating employees. The increasing incident of IP theft, data and other assets are caused by company insiders. With the rapid transition of every industry to being driven by software, it's not surprising that the impact of cyber-theft has more potential than even serious damage clearly . Clearly leakage of IP has consequences damaging competitiveness, innovation and potentially leading to massive commercial losses. For example, computer games industry, if its new launch was stolen by an insider computer department employee or programmer, who is already to leave the company. Or being an automotive firm that is just found out that is top secret code associated with a new breakthrough in vehicle engineering, other side of the world, simply because someone managed a valid employee's ID to steal the new vehicle engineering invention to sell to competitors. Other example, organized criminal groups' frequently use the intent to commit fraudulent actions in the banking and financial system and the underground marketplace where cyber-criminals can buy and sell stolen information and identities to earn illegal money.

How to avoid company's secret data loss or theft from insider? Employees who move data to insecure locations in order to ease their work processes create risk by exposing the data to external hackers or bad actors who work within a company at supply chain partner companies or among contractors. Besides, employees leaving are taking sensitive data with them is a problem. This includes not only trade secrets related to the programs with which on close employees were involved. In many quick action incidents, attackers will access data who have rarely on never accessed, execute events that change data and finally move large amounts of removable data to storage devices, personal machines or public cloud storage. So, employers also need to concern computer department any employee individual secret data theft behavior to avoid intelligence asset loss.

In addition of white collar labor crime, non white-collar or blue labor crime also include armed robberies offer a great opportunity for injury or death, current and former employees and their friends are often involved, the most of common times for an armed robbery are during opening and closing periods. So, cash in the restaurant should be kept to a mini8mum and anyone either hourly employee or manager , none of employees will be allowed to be alone in the restaurant and employees should enter and leave utilizing the safe security system to reduce any lose in restaurant any environment. For hospitality industry, it also often occurs stolen matters, credit card stolen behavior is popular in hotels. Because some hotel accept clients to choose to use credit card to pay hotel rent commonly. Another concerning trend, not only attentions to the hospitality industry, when once used to be primarily a guest services issue has now grow into a big financial problem. With the adoption of the new payment card industry security standards, hotel will not being compliance with these security standards risk processing fee surcharges that can amount to thousands of dollars in additional expenses. In order to reduce the occurrence of theft of credit card data, I shall recommend methods, such as precious guest folios with credit card information should be placed in secure offsite storage, 30 days after an event. Never put guest credit card information on internal documents; swiping the credit card will transfer the required data to the property management system , displaying the last four digits of the credit card number is adequate for all routine transactions. One of the main reasons for a chargeback is fraud, it is important to monitor chargebacks and the reason codes, and implement procedures to reduce the number of chargebacks occurring, store all guest credit card data in one secure location. This site be monitored be closed circuit television system and have an electronic lack to provide an audit trail, use fax programs that can only be assessed via secure password protected computer; restrict access to guest data to a limited number of trusted employers will help to reduce employee theft of this information.

So, I feel how to create a positive work environment which is needed. This encourages employees to follow the best interests of the business. Fair employment practice, written job description, clear organizational structure, comprehensive policies and procedures, span lines of communication between management and employees and positive employee recognition will help to reduce the likelihood of internal fraud and theft. For pharmaceutical industry, it also has insider theft occurrence. I recommend to use video surveillance to implement an expanded two-person rule, recording attention to security, and establishing incident databases and experience to supervise staffs behaviors. All situations involving protection against potential insider threats involve some combination of managing the potential insiders and managing the items to be protected which might to thing, that might be stolen, areas of a facility that might be targeted, people who might be stolen, damaged or misused. Most high security organizations perform some form of background check before giving people access to items, areas or information to be protected or information about how these are secured. The thoroughness of such checks varies widely, ranging from a simple criminal background check (or less) to a full investigation, in which the person's career, health to detect notable changes in behavior or circumstances that may bear on their inappropriate behaviors noticed by environments. For example, insiders must undergo new background every few years to maintain their clearance and staff are encouraged to report any changes in their own circumstances. Both initial background screening and ongoing monitoring of employee behavior raise issues of privacy and civil liberties. Also keeping up staff moral and motivation and convincing them to active participants elements of an effective program to protect against insiders. One obvious step is ensuring that staff are adequately paid, so that anger at the organization for undervaluing, they don't add to the motivation contributing factor. At the moments, the organization's ability is offer incentives and disincentives is much demanded and the employee's loyalty to the organization's may be minimal. For example, no one would be allowed if no legal arrangement to enter restricted drug (pharmaceutical) store. It can reduce drug theft chance occurrence in drug store easily.

An insider threat is generally defined as a current or former employee, contractor or other business partner who has on had authorized access to an organization's network system or data and intentionally misused that access to negatively affect the confidentiality, or availability of the organization's information or information systems. Insider threats to include theft, fraud and competitive advantage are often carried out through abusing access rights, theft or materials and mishandling physical devices. Insiders don't always act alone and may not be aware they are aiding a threat actor (i.e. the unintentional insider threat). It is important that organizations understand normal employee baseline behaviors and also ensure employees understand how who may be used as an theft insider. Because prediction to who will be insider, it will reduce loss of risk to any organizations. How to deter the theft insider behavioral threat? Building a baseline understanding of the personalities and behavioral norms of those previously defined as an theft insiders will detecting their immoral easier. However, some general behavioral characteristics of theft insiders at risk of becoming a threat include: introversion, financial need, destructive behavior, passive aggressive, ethical flexibility, reduced loyalty, self image, minimizing their mistakes or faults, inability to assume responsibility for their actions intolerance of criticism, self-perceived value exceeds performance lack of empathy, immoral behavior towards law enforcement, pattern of frustration and disappointment, history of managing crises ineffectively.

These are psychological characteristics of personal insider at risk of becoming a threat to any within organizational businesses' departments. Individuals that exhibit these characteristics may reach a point at which who carry out immoral activity against the organization. One of the best prevention measures is to train employees to recognize and report behavioral indicators exhibited by peers or business partners. Some behavioral indicators of threat activity include: remotely access the network when on vacation, sick time, works odd hours without authorization; notable enthusiasm for overtime weekend or unusual work schedules; unnecessary copies material especially, it it is proprietary or classified; interest in matters outside of the scope of their duties; signs of ability, such as drug or alcohol abuse, financial difficulties, gambling activities, poor mental health behavior. So wen behavioral characteristics, who ought concern how whose personal performance or behavior in office or workplace environment considerately.

Based on above warning signs among employees, such as expected wealth, unusual foreign travel, irregular work hours or unexpected absences. Identifying behavioral indicators may be difficult, particularly if who don't occur for a long period of time and therefore don't set a pattern. Therefore a good understanding of risk characteristics and events that may predict those characteristics is essential . However, individuals cause threats for a variety of reasons; some theories are considered by criminal psychologists such as: general deterrence theory, it indicates that person commits crime if expected benefit outweighs cost of action; social learning theory, it indicates the person commits crime of associates with peers. Theoy of planned behavior indicates the person's intention (attitude subjective norms and perceived behavior control) towards crime key factors in predicting behavior; situational crime prevention theory indicates crime occurs when both motive and opportunity exist. These behaviors and indicators whether detected via technology or human observance techniques are intended to detect the insider. It is equally important though to create productive and healthy work environments to help to reduce the unintentional insider threat. Some countermeasures include training employees to recognize social media threat vectors; training continuously to maintain the proper levels of knowledge of knowledge skills and abilities, conducting training and improve awareness of risk perception and cognitive biases that affect decision making, improving use ability of security tools and software to reduce the likelihood of system induced human error, enhancing awareness of the unintentional insider threat; providing effective security practices , e.g. two factors authentication for access; maintaining staff values and attitudes that co-operate with organizational mission and ethics.

Nowadays, some security technologies can detect/prevent insider attacks, such as: data/file encryption, data access monitoring ; SIEM or other log analysis; data loss prevention, data redaction; enterprise identity and access management, data access control, detection/prevention systems and enterprise digital rights management solution etc. technology insiders detection systems. Besides, some deterrence methods include: deploy data centers, not system, centric security, crowd source security, use positive social engineering, thinking a marketer to build a baseline on volume , frequency and amount based on hourly, weekly and monthly normal patterns, using centralized logging to detect data near insider termination, requiring identification for an assets, e.g. access cards, password, inventory check out, frequent visits to sites may indicate how productivity job and potential habit, announce the use of policies that monitor events like unusual networks traffic spikes, volume at USB/mobile storage use, volume of off hour printing activities and inappropriate use of encryption; implement employee recognition programs that offer public praise to insider threat motivated; provide avenues for employees to vent concerns and frustrations to insider threat motivated; authorize users based on access and conduct periodic audits to detect inappropriately granted access or access that exists from previous job functions and should be removed.

Finally, I feel continual training is always a recommended option. For example, free of charge courses that organizations may want to consider offering to employees, contractors, and others that meet the description of an "insider". Training ought concentrate on teaching how to protect your organizations teaching how to protect your organizations information and systems from unauthorized insider misuse for technology criminal insiders. Otherwise, employers need to provide psychological criminal training to teach how to predict whose staff individual behavior to avoid any staff who do theft behavior before any staff's immoral behavior will be caused in whose working place environment.

To conclude, business crimes are very popular. However, technological theft insiders or non technological theft insiders both are the same important factors to influence any business development for long term successfully. Thus, employers ought need to concern employees' immoral behaviors to avoid high risk loss in office, factory, shop or any workplace environment.

Essentials of organizational behavioral learning

The importance of management skills is essential, if any organizations hope to raise efficiency or improve performance. Organizations need to learn how to balance hard and soft skill, how to manage social and human skills whch reflect the ability to get along with other people are increasingly important attributes at all levels of management.

Managers ought need to spend most time operating between the " hard skills" , such as conducting disciplinary matters or how to allocate of budgets, and "soft skills" , such as counselling, or giving support and advice to a member of staff. Managers also needed to be trained to raise technical competence, related to specific tasks, how to supervise and train subordinate staffs, and with day-to-day subordinate staff, and with day-to-day operations concerned in the actual production of goods and services; social and human skills relates to interpesonal relationship in working with and through other people, and how to judge to achieve effective teamwork and direction, and leadership of staff to achieve co-ordinated effort to particular situation and flexibilty in adopting the most appropriate style of management, raising conceptual ability in order to view he complexities of the operations of the organization as a whole, including environmental influences.

Mc Donald soft skill organizational behavior

It also involves decision-making skills, relates to the overall making of the organization and to its stragegic planning in long time, such as McDonald restaurant has good strategic management to manage its global branches of franchise restaurants in organizational behavioral view successfully. So, it can attract many investors buy its franchises to learn how to do McDonald fast food restsurants . It's investors number is increasing, due to it has good significant organizational behavior as well as its managers know how to apply " soft skills" and " hard skills" to manage them effectively.

So, organizational behavior and organizational performance seems have close relationship. If the organization can build the most effective and efficient organizational behavior, managers know how to manage employee individual behavior, then the performance ought will be improved , even customers won't complaint or feel unsatisfactory easily, they will feel satisfactory to their staffs service performance, such as McDonald fast food restaurant case, global McDonald fast food franchise restaurants eating customers complain bumber is low in general, because instead of their front line service staffs performance and attitude can let them to feel satisfactory,

The most influential soft skill to bring its fast food eating customers feel satisfactory or they are persuaded to choose its sale service to replace other similar fast food restaurants sale service. The reason is because that , when they buy its fast food, or soft drink, they must be arranged to give one number ticket. So, they do not need to spend long time to queue in any McDonald fast food restaurants, they can leave McDonald restaurant to go to other places and they wont' worry that McDonald staffs forget to make their fast food or soft drink when they leave. Because they can give the number ticket to indicate their number to the staff to take their fast food or soft drink any time. For example, if the eating customer's ticket number is 30, and the screen indicates next number future cooking is 10, then he will feel that he can leave McDonald to spend about 15 minutes to come back. Even, if his coming back time is exceed 15 minutes, and the screen indicates number is 40. Although, he is late, but he may ask the staff to take his fast food or soft drink immediately. So, he does not need to worry about that he can take his fast food or soft drink even he is late to come back. So they avoid to queue long time in McDonald, they can come back after half hour, even after one hour. When they come back, they only need to give their number ticket to confirm that the had paid money to buy fast food or soft drink. When the front line staff see that number from their ticket. They will go to kitchen to take their prepared fast food or soft drink to give them immediately. it is one effective time management " soft skill" to avoid eating customers feel angry or bad emotion when they need to queue in long time in any one Mc Donald restaurant. They can choose to leave Mcdonald restaurants any long time. It is one efficient and effective 2 soft skill customer service management skill in any one nowadays McDonald front line . So , it's success depends on its front line staff " don't need eating people to queue long time" in any one McDonald restaurant.

Convenient framework of analysis of organizational behavior

Any organizations ought need have a convenient framework of analysis if they hope to manage their organizational behavior efficiently. I shall explain what a convenient framework of organizational behavior analysis means as below: The top level is what nature and purpose of the organization, then next middle level concerns learning how to manage " behavior of people", " process of management", " organizational context" , next is middle level learning how to adapt any environment influences. The final process to any organizations. They hope to achieve improving organizational performance in success as well as organizational processes as well as how to execution of work to the most success. It is one important service soft skill method to let global McDonald restaurants can continue to attract many eating people to choose to but their fast food or soft drink , instead of reduced price or coupon sale method in global fast food restaurant market. So, its success depends on how to mix of the practical and the soft skill service performance strategy to eating customer long time queue bad emotion theoretical psychological strategy, it must be linked to a single aim, such as Mc Donald has its single aim to front line staffs, is that how to avoid eating people need to stay in McDonald restaurant to queue long time to let them to feel angry and unsatisfactory to its global any McDonald franchise restaurants. So it comfirms that , many its global eating people don't like to queue and to stay in McDonald long time, when the Ms Donald has many people are staying in McDonald in busy time.

Thus, in organizational behavioral view, they will be persuaded to choose to buy MsDonald fast food in perference, because its unique service feature, when other fast food restaurants can not implement this front lines do not need queue method in their fast food restaurants. It implies that effective front line service skill may be one important factor to influence any clients' choices in preference.

How to apply hard skill and soft skill to solve inefficient problem?

The theme of inefficiency will experience to any organizations, if they lack effective organizational behavioral management strategy. It assumed that workers who were not good at one particualr task, would be best at some other tasks in any teams. There is however, no certainty of this in practice. It concerns workers from an engineering view point and as machines , but the one best way of performing a task is not always the best method for every worker. So, the reduction of physical movement to find the one best way is or always beneficial and some " wasteful" movements are essential to the overall rhythm of work.

So, if the organization hopes to achieve effective organizational behavior, the organization needs to concern these soft skill and hard skill issues they may include:

1. High wages from increased output.

2. The removal of physical strain from doing works the wrong way.

3. Development of the workers and the opportunity for them to undertake tasks , they were capable of doing and

4. Elimination of the " boss" and the duty of management to help workers.

For example on factory raising efficient organizational behavior aspect, the factory may implement these soft skill and hard skill both strategies, such as: To assist the stores in better customer service by having the merchandise ready to go on the floor, saving space in the stockroom, and creating customer goodwill, to increase the units per hour produced, to performance the job duties as efficiency and effectively as possible, avoiding bureaucracies organization, it emphasised the importance of administration based on experise (rules of experts) and administration based on discipline (rules of officials). Because one when burea staffs are working in one serious or strict bureaucracies organization, they will feel not happy and unsatisfactory to their manager behavior. So, managers' soft management skill ought often need to revise when need to be changed to be better or improve their performance, such as:

The tasks of the organization are allocated as official duties among the various positions, there is an implied clear -out division of labor and a high level of specialisation, a hierarchical authority applies to the organization of offices and positions, uniformity of decisions and actions is achieved through formally established systems, of rules and regulations. Together work a structure of authority , this enables the coordination of various activities within the organization, an imperaonal orietnation is expected from officials in their dealings with clients and other officials. This is designed to result in rational judgments by officials in the performance of their duties as well as employment by the organization is based on technical qualifications and constitues a lifelong career for the officials, e.g. how to apply specialisation more to the job than to the person undertaking the job.

This makes for continuity because the job usually continues of the present job holder leaves, hierarchy of authority it makes for a sharp distination between administrators and the administered or between management and workers, within the management ranks these are clearly defined levels of authority, system of rules aims to provide for an officials and impersonal operaton, sules are generally stable although some rules may be changed as modified with impersonality means that how allocation and exercise authority should not be complex.

Reference

Maslach, C., Jackson, S.E. & Leite,M.P. (1996). Maslach Burnout inventory manual (3 rd ed.) Palo Alto, CA: Consulting psychologists Press

VII

How society influences human public transport need change

What the psychological need differences between rail and bus passengers

● Reasons we need to improve public bus transport tool service quality

The ways that we need to improve public transport, e.g. bus transport service, we try our best to ask these questions: During periods of stress on the bus, like weather conditions or maintenance failure that slows the bus service system? How to improve mass transit on bus service frequency, when looking at ways to improve public bus service transport , riders want frequency? Interestingly, speed is not as much of an issue, if they are waiting downtown in the rain, or on some suburban backstreet, riders want to know that a bus will arrive soon, preferably in less than 15 minutes. Therefore, the wait becomes part of the transportation cycle. Even, if the bus is lightning fast, in the mind of the rider, the trip begins right when they arrive at the bus station, and start waiting for the bus to pick them up.

`What does efficient bus ticketing system mean? It is big part of how to improve bus transportation efficiency is improving transit ticketing system, because ticketing systems have to be quick and practical to allow for prompt loading and unloading of passengers. So, inefficient ticketing systems also slow down bus frequency, as drivers need to wait for everyone to tap before they can drive away to the next stop.

How to let passengers feel comfortable? Riders want comfortable buses that can seat as many people as possible. Face-to-face seating is not appealing and being knee-to-knee in a confined space creates awkward moments between strangers. However, comfort also extends beyond the buses' seating arrangements. A smooth riding, quiet bus plays a significant role in reducing the overall stress of a public transit experience. Among the consistent feedback from riders of fuel cell electric buses is a surprised delight about how quiet the buses are when in motion.

On reduce greenhouse gases environment prote3ctoin aspect, exhaust spewing buses are on ongoing concern. One of the significant factors that commuters consider when deciding to take public transit is the environment impact of their alternative transport method. And although a diesel bus packed with 40 people may be less environmentally damaging than 40 separate diesel cars, it will still have negative impacts on both local air quality and the overall climate situation , when given the choice, we've found nearly all riders prefer " zero-emission buses" to conventional diesel buses nowadays.

IN fact, we are always thinking of ways to improve public transportation by dev4eloping new clean fuel technologies. Fuel cell electric buses resolve some of the above issues for both transit bus operators, bus performance is continually being proven and improved over millions of miles of operation in environments ranging from mountain villages to desert communities to busy cities. Hence, the first step to creating better public transit networks is becoming aware of the available options. Many communities are taking measures to improve public transport by implementing innovative sustainable transport solutions that have profound impacts on the live ability of their communities.

So, I shall recommend these ways to improve public transport methods to bus service as below:

Firstly, making interchanging easy for public transport has most efficient public transport service improvement aim at linking areas that are outside a city to the city center., doing this is beneficial in two ways. It helps people who should not at the city center , but needed to pass through because the outlying areas are not connected together to keep off and hence reduce congestion at the center. Also, connecting the outlying areas provide a backup for the public transport system in case of a problem which often happen.

Secondly, minimize the number of stops/ stations, stops and stations improve the efficiency of public transport , but there should be a balance between enabling accessibility with more steps or stations and reducing the costs of operation by increasing transit need of ensure trips are covered in time. Therefore, core should be taken to ensure that stops and stations are located on streets to balance accessibility by commuters on one hand and reduces operating cost on the other hand.

Thirdly, lessen traffic congestion by deploying a number measures. Reducing traffic congestion at city streets could be done, implementing a number of strategies, such as providing lanes dedicated specially for the use of public transport, deploying strict regulations , such as queue bypasses or queue jumps. Another means of reducing traffic congestion is by providing feeds and data from public transport systems, freely to commuters to educate and help them avoid areas of traffic congestion and finally, giving priority to public and trams operating efficiency, increasing the travel time of these engineering mechanism whereby a traffic signal turns green at the light of a public transport at an intersection. All of above these improvements may be future public transport bus passengers service improvement need, if any bus companies hope to increase their bus passengers number absolutely.

● What rail passengers really want rail innovation improvement

Public transport systems, such as rail provides benefits including less traffic congestion, less pollution, safe travels, lower expenditures , less effort and better predictability in comparison to road transport. In fact, bus and train riders experience the most negative emotions in comparison with other transport modes, such as private cars , walking and cycling. Hence, technology has the potential to bring about the changes, needed to increase efficiency of rail transport, e.g. cost-effective ways to improve the quality of public transport and increase ridership may involve comfort and convenience improvement, or technology has the potential to provide more up-to-date information and customized service to train passengers and therefore improve the rail journey experience . On the overall, passenger journey , e.g. the importance of automated traveller information systems, and electronic fare payment collection systems can bring rail passengers look for this information in different interfaces from localized displays installed on platforms to smartphone applications.

Moreover, technology can also improve fare collection and management which of made manually can be prone to error, and time consuming , unified cards, smartphones can make it easier for rail passengers to obtain ticket, with the potential to increase the user satisfaction with the rail system. Because rail passengers demand not only pre-trip information for planning their travels, but also information during journeys, such as punctuality, connections and platform allocation. One extensive review indicates that accurate communication, for example, giving effective way finding information, can optimize passengers' experience with public transport.

Also, technology can facilitate the process of finding free seats on trains, which is a current demand from rail passengers and the cause of stress during the boarding process. IN fact, many rail passengers have specific preferences regarding seats and would appreciate having control of where to sit. So, navigation and way finding information can be delivered directly to passengers to inform where they could stand aiming to board less busy carriages, for example, choosing to travel on a less crowded train, or spreading themselves out on the platform before boarding in respond to crowding information, e.g. smartphones are frequently used by passengers of public transport and can make waiting times seem shorter. Furthermore specific system features designed for train passengers have the potential to improve the journey experience of the travelling public.

What ferry passengers service improvement need

● How can ferry service be improved affordable, reliable, convenient, flexible and clean will get drivers out of their cars ad onto environmentally responsible to passenger ferries?

Ferry transportation provides an environmentally friendly commuting alternative to the congested roadways in many of countries , so ferry transport service needs to meet long term air quality goals, it is critical to move beyond traditional technologies to zero-and near zero emissions technology. Clearly putting a transit system in operation that demonstrates emission control technology and the development of zero-emissions, ferries will help achieve air quality goals to our societies, for example., new shipping rout4es are needed to increase in order to satisfy ferry passengers different rapid ferry journey short distance need, when they need to choose one kind of public transport service either bus or rail or ferry transport service among of them.

None ferry accident occurrence, ferry service needs to let passengers to feel it is the safest sea pubic transit, expanded recreational service is also needs, particularly on weekends when bridge , corridor traffic congestion is becoming an increasing problem. Ferry service needs have uniquely provided flexible, vital transportation supports in response to a natural or man-made disaster that shuts down bridges and roads, fuel –cell technology is needed , that will lead to zero-emissions ferries, e.g. on-board emissions monitoring is far less polluting than previously through, e.g. 149 passenger boats are designed to travel 25 knots or less , and 300-350 passenger vessels designed for speeds up to 30-35 knots.

This emissions standard will perform specifications and the cost of this technology is accounted for in the ferry company vessel capital budget ,e.g. vessel design capabilities to accommodate existing and new docking configurations . This maximizes fast ferry passenger loading, including bicycles, carriages and wheelchairs. Hence, future global ferry service needs have these positive influence to our societies: Need for flexibility, desire to help the environment, need for time saving, which includes the importance of reliability, sensitivity to personal travel experience, such as a need for personal space or quiet feeling ferry seat any time, insensitivity to transport cost, e.g. the ferry ticket price is cheaper than rail or bus fares sensitivity to stress.

However, ferry service is different unlike rail, bus because expanded ferry service can be launched quickly at low initial cost and with great flexibility. Unlike buses, ferries are not hindered by traffic congestion on roads and highways or in tunnels. So, ferry service can be safely expanded to bring new service to new places and add more service to existing routes more easily than bus and rail public transport both, e.g. expanded ferry transport service can operate safety and provide with a robust, flexible and effective emergency response capability if the region is hit with a natural or man-made event that disables roads, other transit, bridges , before any.

Hence, ferry companies need to decide to improve their ferry transport service, they need to answer these questions: Is the new shipping route a good transportation investment? Does the new shipping route have fatal environmental negative impact? Does it offer a transit option that can be initiated in a timely and cost-effective manner? Can it provide ferry transport service that is reliable, safe and fully accessible after the ferry recovery would be unreasonably high charge to ferry selection is decided to implement to increase?

Also, ferry safety is needed to consider because it can influence any ferry passenger choice, when the ferry is moving on the sea, when the passenger is sitting on the boat. The ferry safety issue may include: Ensuring that access to all ferry operational areas, including, machinery spaces, pilothouse and gear lockers, remain locked at all times and accessible only to authorized crew, posting night watch security guards at terminals, conducting diligent onboard inspection for unattended passenger bags, briefcases and packages after each run, before the next boat load is allowed to board, creating coded signals and response to report suspicious activity, requiring positive identification before allowing any contractors, vendors or others access to ferries, providing additional security training to crew, developing a security plan to account for potential threats, outlining preventive measures and detailing an action plan in the event of a threat or actual emergency.

Future Human Transport Need Change

How future our transport need change? What factors influence our future transport need change? In general, these factors may influence our transportation need change. They may include fuel cost, the labor market for commercial drivers, demand for frieight , customer loyalty , vehicle capacity, government regulation, geographical events, the public transport tool reputation to passengers as a merchant. However, the factors that influence the development of transport system in an area? They may include as below:

Environment at the local scale existing hydrographical and geomorphological characteristics are string, factors in transport development, particularly in terms of the technical challenges (bridge, gradients,) they present to construct, other factors may include historical, technological, political and economic factors. All of these factors may influence our future transport system how develops. For raiway development influential factors, they may include: Geograohical factors, e.g. the North Indian plain with its level land, high density of population and rich agriculture presents the most favourable conditions for the development of railways in India. However, the presence of large number of rivers makes it necessary to construct bridges which involve heavy expenditure to Indian Government publich transport expenditure.

How transport has changed from past to present?

There has been a remarkable development in modern transportation. The stream engine and then the stream trains have emerged and spread at this time and in abundance until the discovery of natural gas and oil was an evolution of transportation. Thus, the sedams and vehicles began to run in oil, until present battery changes energy vehicle need, even future non-manual driving artificial intelligent driving vehicle need. These new transport technology may influence our future public transportation from gas energy to battery changed energy, even non-manual driving vehicles need to our daily transport need.

So, our future purpose of public transport need is the unique purpose to oversome space, which is shaped by a variety of human and physical constraints, such as distance, time. These both is our future main public transport need main purpose factors, short distance and reducing journey time, they influence that why we need to choose to catch any kinds of public transportation tool to replace purchase private cars to drive transport tool choice. So, future any kinds of public transport tools, they need to consider above both main factors , how to attract passengers to choose to catch themselves public transport tools choice in this competitive public transport tools market.

On the other hand, the economic importance of transportation development can be defined as improving the welfare of a society, through appropriate social, political and economic conditions , such as US Government spent too much money to assist MTR (MAss transport railway firm) to develop underground thrain transport. Its aim to let many passegner can reduce journey time and reduce distance between destinations, it also hopes US citizen passengers can pay cheap transport fare to buy ticket to catch underground transport train for many families their transport expenditure in social transport welfare view.

However, US Government neds to solve those challenges, before it implements to develop rapid underground railway , e.g. lack of knowledge of geographical fwatures, lack of manpower necessary to operate the rapid underground railway construction work, lack of construction materials within the US itself. For Brazil rail network transportation development example, the factors influence the use of rail network for transportion is highly restricted in Brazil. Thus, the development of roadways and waterways is the main modes of transportation that caould be used in Brazil given its topography and drainage benefit to society . So, brazil can develop rail network for transportation development in success.

So, transportation system is important in the development of any nation, because transportation plays important role in rapid economic growth of a nation. Thrapsortation increases the quality and variety of consumer goods, thereby stimulating the demand and development of trade and economy of the nation. Moreover, transport provides various employment opportunities and boosts up the economy of the country.

Also, any transport tools need to improve themselves transport service in order to attract passengers to choose their public transport service more easily. They may attempt to sign up for an autonomous vehicle pilot program, free phone enquiey concerns whether the passegner can catch which bus bumber to go to the destination, hou much bus fare, how long journey time, when the bus will arrive teh bus stops or leave the bus stop etc. bus service questions, before any one passenger prepares to choose to catch bus (free bus go phone call enquiry), free download a public transport tool transit app. even water taxi tranport tool innovation can replace ferry public transport tool, it can let passengers have more fun an enjoyable catching feeling. So, water taxi tranport tool is one kind of future new transport tool change to replace ferry , it can influence ferry passengers to choose water taxi public transport tool to replace ferry. Although, its fare may be more expsnse to compare ferry, but it can reduce jounrey time and distance between both water stations, when ferry can not arrive the other destinations, but water taxi can arrive any one water station destination. It can bring convenient to future any one ferry passengers. So, water taxi may be developed to some countries, e.g. New Zealand , Auckland city, US , Washington and New York cities they had developed water taxi public transport tools to let ferry passengers have one kind new water public transport choice.

However, instead of new transport innovation improvement to water transport service public transport with input from the public on bus transport service aspect, bus frequency improvement, it means when booking at ways to improve, bus frequency from long times to less times, efficient bus ticketing system, a big part of how to improve tranportation efficiency is improving transit ticketing system.

In fact, my future transport system may still include these five types, modes of transport are: railway, roadways, airways, waterways and piplelines. Also, among different includes of transport, railways are the different modes of transport, railways are the cheapest. Trains cover the distance in less time and comparatively, the fare is also less to other modes of transporation. Therefore, railways is the cheapest mode of transportation to compare ferry, water taxi , sea transport, bus, taxi, road system.

On conclusion, transport price is not the main factor to attract passsegners to choose to catch. The importance to have a good public transport system in place. It may be one main factor to help the kind of public transport tool to attract passengers to choose to catch, because a good transport links can widen people's job search area and help them find employment. It can also reduce commuting times and reduce the cost of living, and high skilled workers are more likely to travel across longer distances to work, especially if they are following good job opportunities. So, future any one kind of public transportation tool service provider ought consider how to satisfy working people working time need to shorten journey time to any working places or student learning time need to shorten jounrey times to any schools as well as let they feel comfortable to sit on comfortable chairs or provide free internet service to themselves mobiles , laptops, when they are sitting down or standing up in the kind of public transport . It is the important factor to influence any kind of public transport service in success.

Future Non-Manual driving vehicle How Influences Public Transport Tool Passenger Need

Nowadays, artifical intelligent (non-manual) driving vehicles are invented, it may be accepted to any countries families to feel comfortable to drive on roads, because any people choose to buy any kinds cars, when any people choose to buy kinds of non-manual (artificial intelligent) vehicles, they do not need to use their hands to drive cars, because artificial intelligent (robotic auto control wheels, it means that robots can help human (drivers) to control wheel to drive to avoid any cars crash occurrence on the roads more easily.

If one day, non-manual driving robotic control whoole vehicles are invented in successful, whether it will persuade many different conuntries families choose to buy non-manual (robotic auto control wheel) vehicles, then it will cause bus, tram, train, underground train, road transport need will be influenced to reduce or even if non-manula boats are invented, whether it will cause ferry sea transport needs will b influenced to reduce. Hence, future non-manual driving vehicles or bats invention whether they will influence public transport tool of road and sea transport passengers number reduces. It is one interesting question. I shall attempt to discuss as below:

In fact, non-manual vehicles are very attraction, to excite any person chooses to buy to drive, because people do not need often touch wheels and touch foots button to control cars to move often forever, when robotic can be invented to help human to control car wheel and foot button, any person only needs to sit on his/her car, then the car can move rapidly, because any drivers is lazy, he/she hopes machine can help her/him to drive car on the road safely. So, he/she can read book or listen music or eatch mobile movie to enjoy his/her entertainment when he/she is sitting on his/her car.He/she will feel more comfortable and enjoyable when robotic can help him/her to drive car. So, robotic (non -manual driving vehicle) can encourage people to choose to buy cars because any drivers won't need to drive cars, robotic can help drivers them to drive on the road easily, when global any one family can own one robotic auto control (non-manual driving) car at least, it may influence these owning non-manula diriving vehicle owners do not feel need to pay any fares to buy road public transport tools of bus ticket, train ticket, underground train ticket , tram ticket to go to anywhere. So, it seems that robotic (non-manual driving) vehicles may influence future any road transport passengers number reduces , because traditional catching any kinds of road public transport tool passengers will be influenced to choose to sit themselves auto (non-manual) driving cars to go to offices to work, parents do not need to follow their sone/daughters to sit on themselves non-manual auto driving cars to go to schools, because their sons/daughters can sit on themselves non-manual driving cars to go to schools more easily. In holidays, they can sit on themselves non-manual driving cars to go to cinemas, music halls, breachs, theaters, shopping centers, gardens different entertainment places to enjoy their any leisure safely because robotic can help them to drive their cars on roads safely.

So, it means that robotic auto control driving cars can influence global every family to feel that they do not need to catch any kinds of public transport tools, e.g. bus, train, tram, taxi underground train to go to anywhere because robotic auto driving cars can help any one, he/she does not know how to drive car to go to anywhere safely. So, future any one won't need to learn driving car skill, when he/she likes to buy one auto driving car. So, in passenger public transport need view, non-manual driving cars will influence them to feel any kinds of road public transport tools can help them to go to anywhere conveniently, because themselves non-manual driving vehicles can help them to drive cars to go to anywhere conveniently. They only need to tell robotic that where they want to go, when they sit on their non-manual driving cars, then robotic knows whether where destination, they want to go, their cars will auto move on the road immediately. It is one exciting and enjoyable ourney when the driver does not need to drive his/her car on the road. So, it seems that robotic (non-manual driving) vehicles invention may bring negative influence to any kinds of public transport tools service needs to passengers , when passengers had owned one non-manual driving car at least.

Why and how non-manual driving car owners need

raise public transport quality on travel time and fare
    aspects
    ● How non human driving behavior can be influence by non-manual driving cars

In fact, impact of automated vehicless on travel mode preference, it can bring both trip purposes and distances aim raising need to any kinds of public transport service passegners. Because of technology penetration in the transportation system, the automated vehicle is set to be a future mode of transport, it may bring negative impact to future any kinds of public transport passengers needs, in special on the potential impact of these non-manual driving automated vehicles on travel behaior negative impact to public transport passenger behavior. Automated vehicles will influence future public transportation passengers feel it can bring more short time travel distances and short trip purposes more benefit than any kinds of public transport choices, e.g. bus, taxi, ferry, train, tram, underground tram etc. road and sea public transport tools, e.g. ferry, water taxi. It means that when future any passenger feels above these any one kind of public transport tool needs to spend longer travel time on journey distance and trip to compare future automated vehicles, then they will choose to sit on automated vehicles in preference, due to automated vehicles can help global any one person needs to go to anywhere rapidly.

So, automated vehicles may replace general traditional public transport tools in possible, when they are popular accepted in societies. On the other, instead of shortening journey travel distance time, (travel time) aspect, public transport fare, travel cost will be another influential factor to influence future public transport tool passengers to choose automated vehicles to replace to catch any kinds of public transport tools.

In fact, conventional cars and public transport s are perceivd as being the least attractive alternative in relation to in-vehicle travel time on short and long distance communting trips. So , future automated vehicle drivers (non -human driving) behaviors will be likely changed to prefer this mode for long distance leisure trips rather than short distance commuting trips by automated vehicles.

In fact, advanced technologies have revolutionized many aspects of human life, include the automated vehicle transport system. Also, transport system is one of the essential development aspect to particular , such as non-manual driving automation , vehicle aims to make trips safer, faster , more efficient, automated vehicles passengers and drivers can feel enjoyable to do themselves leisure behavior , e.g. read books, listen, music, listen mobile, watch laptop movies when any one does not need to consider whether their cars are safe to be driven , even any one needs to drive the automated car, because robotic can help them to control how to automatic drive this car on the road safely.

Robotic will bring confidence to let them feel that themselves cars are moving safely on the roads . In recent years, the concept of automated driving has been introduced as on outstanding platform for the next generation of driving systems that is expected to improve safety, traffic flows efficiency, reducing traffic jams occurrence chance, avoiding traffic accidents occurrence chance, e.g. avoid to crash any one person when he/she is walking across road or crach any car is moving on the road easily, capacity, accessibility , and reducing congestion through the application of some technologies , such as vehicle to vehicle and vehicle to infrastructure communication.

So, future automated vechicles can have good driving facility systems to be installed in their cars, in order to raise safety, rapid driving speed level to let any one to feel , when they are sitting in their automated cars, e.g. using cameras, sensors, global positioning system adaptive cruise control, light detection and ranging, and advanced driver assistance system, automated vehicles can steer the vehicle and drive it automatically when passengers delegate control to a computer. Absolutely, ny replacing the driver role with an automated driving system , future one automated vehicle is able to totally free up passengers under automation levels.

So, unless future any kinds of public transport tools may apply automated robotic automated driven system replace the bus driver, taxi driver, train driver, tram driver, underground train driver to raise automated driving system service improvement level to let any one passengers to feel. Otherwise, when automated vehicles are popular to be accepted to buy in any one country in global. Then, global public tansport tool passegners number may be influenced to reduce when global any one family owns at least one automated vehicle at themselves homes .

In other words, automated vehicles can bring thes benefits to let global any one household family feels, future automated vehicles users , they can mostly behave like passengers inside the vehicle, which implies that they will be able to multitask and productive by allocating the travel time to do other activities, e.g. reading, eating, working, drinking, watching movies, listening musics, even sleeping. So, automated vechicles will motivate humans to change non-humanly driven behaviors from conventional humanly driven behavior. This non-humanly driven behavior may be one main factor to influence or encourage future any one kind of public transport passenger won't choose to pay fare to buy ticket to catch any one kind of public transport tool again, because non-manual driven behavior may hel many lazy people do not need to consdierate how to learn to drive cars skills to prepare pass any road test in order to earn the driving licnece to permit to drive cars forever. When automated vehiclesa re popular to be accepted to replace manual-driven cars in societies.

Hence, automated vehicles could potentially change the traditional human driven vehicle market to cause their manual driven cars sale buyers number reduces, when the automated vehicle buyers number increases, also they can chance globa public transport passengers behaviors to reduce to pay fares to catch any kinds of public transport tools when automated vechicles users may sit on themselves automated vehicles to go to anywhere in short time rapidly and safely in any countries.

On conclusion, future global public transport service competition is serious, because instead of global passengers had began to compare whether which kinds of public transport fares are cheaper, more safe, shortening journey time between leaving place and destination, more comfortable feeling, e.g. clean and comfortable chairs , mre free internet service facilities in order to make any one kind of catching public transport tool choice in preference. On the other hand, future automated vehicles number will increase when traditional manual driven car users begin to believe that automated vehicles can bring more safe , more comfortable, more fee- time using, more leisure satisfactory feeling, more than traditional manual driving cars. Then, when global any one household family had made choice to buy at least one automated vehice to replace themselves car(s) at home. When, they are habit to sit in themselves automated vehicles to go to anywhere, however, short or long trip . Consequently, global any one household family won't feel any kinds of public transport tools may bring personal economic saving cost, comfortable, enjoyable, free-time using benefit to compare themselves automated vehicles . It will cause global public transport tools passengers number will reduce , when many different kinds of home automatic vehicles are purchased to replace manual driving cars by global household automated vehicle users. So, in passegner transport tool choice psychological view, automatic vehicles will be possible to replace future public transport service tools. So, any public transport service providers can not neglect how to desing and improve their facilities , charge reasonable transport fare, provide more comfortable, and enjoyable sitting feeling , even applying automatic driving system to replace human drivers in order to attract passegners ' catching need choice more easily.

● Boeing 747 manufacturing fuel cost strategy

For Boeing 747 air plane manufacture example, how it can help airline to avoid travellers number reduces. Boeing 747 air plane manufacture company how achieve air plane manufacturing strategy to reponse airline traveller number market changing. What is fuel conservation strategy to Boeing 747 air plane manufacturing firm? The cost index, (CI) feature of the flight manufacturing computer (FMC) can help airlines significantly reduce operating cost. However, many operators do not take full advantages of this powerful tool. What does CI ratio mean? The CI is the ratio of the time-related cost of an air plane opertation and the cost of fuel. The value of the CI reflects the relative effects of the fuel cost on overall trip cost as compares to time-related direct operating costs.

The equation form, CI= time cost-$/hour / fuel cosst -cents/lb

The numerator of the Ci is often called time refrated direct operating cost (minue the cost of fuel). Items, such as flight crew wages can have an hourly cost associated with them, or they may be a fixed cost and have n variation with flying time engines, anxiliary power units, and air planes can be leased by the hour or owned, and maintenance costs can be accounted for an air planes by the hour, by the calendar or by cycles . As a result, each of these items may have a direct hourly cost or a fixed cost over a calendar period with limited or no correlation to flying time.

What does this air plane fuel, cost strategy advantages to airline companies? In the case of high direct time costs, the airline may direct to time costs, the airline may choose to use a larger CI to minimize time and thus cost . In this case, where most costs are fixed, the CI is potentially very low because the airline is primarily trying to minimize fuel cost. Pilots can easily understand minimizing fuel consumption, but it is more difficult to understand minimizing cost when something other than fuel dominates. So, the cost of the CI ratio. Although, this seems straight toward, issues such among the operating locations, fuel tankering, and fuel hedging can make this calculation complicated. So , this fuel consumption cost, air plan manufacturing strategy can help any airlines to reduce air fuel useful cost and waste fuel.

However, CI can be an extremely useful way to manage operating costs. Because CI is a function of both fuel and non-fuel costs. It is important to use it appropriately to gain the greatest benefit. Appropriate use varies with each airline, and perhaps for each flight.

How low fuel situations can bring less fuel consumed benefit in the more environmentally friendly flight? Fuel conservation strategy can help airlines significantly reduce operating costs. However, many operators do not take full advantage of this powerful tool. Cruise flight is the phase of flight that falls the largest percentages of trip time and trip fuel are consumed typically in this phase of flight, which also impact trip time and fuel significantly can often be avoided through appropriate cruise planning. This fuel conservation strategy includes these characteristics. These objectives which depend on the perspective of the pilot , dispatcher, performance engineer, or operations planner can be groups into five categories , such as:

1. Maximize the distance traveled for a given amount of fuel (i.e. maximum range).
2. Minimize the fuel used for given distance covered (i.e. minimum trip fuel).

3. Minimize total trip time (i.e. minimum time).

4. minimize total operating cost for the trip (i.e. minimum cost, or economy speed).

5. Maintain the flight schedule . The first two objectives are essentially the same because in both cases the airplane will be flown to achieve optimum feel mileage.

In addition to one of the overall strategic objectives for cruise flight, pilots are often forced to deal with shortage term constraints that may require them to temporarily abandon their cruise strategy one or more times during a flight. These situations may include:

Flying a fixed speed that is compatible with other traffic on a specified route segment. Flying aseed calculated to achieve a required time of arrival at a fix. Flying a speed calculated to achieve minimum fuel flow when holding (i.e. maximum endurance). And when directed to maintain a specified speed by a air traffic control. Hence, when the air plane faced with a low fuel situation at destination, many pilits will opt to fly LRC speed, thinking that it will give them , the most miles from their remaining fuel. Also, if fuel prices increase relative to other costs, a corresponding reduction in CI will maintain the most economics operation of the air plane. If however an airline experience rising hourly costs, an increase in CI will retain the most economical operation . For this reason, flight crews typically reserve a recommend CI value from their flight operations department, and it is generally not advisable to deviate from this value unless specific short term constraints demand it.

How it can help air planes to execute for maximum fuel savings efficiently? For example, but times have clearly changed. Jet fuel prices have increased over times from 1990 to 2008 year. At this time, fuel is about 40% oa a tycpical airline's total operating cost. As a results airlines are reviewing all phases of flight to determine how fuel burn savings can be gained in each phase and in totel.

Boeing 777-200 extended range and 747-400 and (long-range, e.g. short range e.g. 717, medium range, e.g. 737-800 with winglate commercail air planes can impact fuel usage. However, flap setting must be appropriate for the situation to ensure air plane safely. Higher flap setting configurations use more fuel than low flags configurations.

The difference is small, but at today's prices the savings can be substantial especially for air planes that fly a light number of cycles each day. Hence, top fuel conservsation strategies for flight crews include: Take only the fuel you need, minimize the use of the nuxiliary power unit, taxi use efficiencly as possible, take off and climb efficiently , fly the air plane with minimum drag, choose routing carefully, strive to mantain optimum attitude, fly the proper cruise speed, descend at the appropriate point, configure in a timely manner.

Fuel conservation is a significant concern of every airline . An airline can choose an approach procedure and flap setting policy that was the least amount of fuel, but it should also consider the trade off involves with using this type of procedure.

Hence, Boeing flight crew can earn benefit, when they fly or air planes, such as to conserve fuel and reduce noise and emissions or to accommodate speed requests by air traffic control. All of these are fuel consumption reducing strategy to airlines.

● How airlines and airports implement successful netwpork strategies

What is airline network strategy ? Network management includes route planning, scheduling optimization, airline business planning and data analysis . How implement airline network strategy, airlines need to evaluate strengths and weaknesses of the current network strategy, identification of additional potential, recommendations for adjustments, network integration, due to merger or cooperation. Fleet and capacity evaluation , analysis of estimated passenger volume over time combined with option aircraft size and frequencies for current and potential future rotes / markets; competition response, modeling of results as an impact of competitor's action and reaction; establishing best practice network managment for new carriers include: route selection, network planning, scheduling, airline business planning includes forecasting of revenues and costs. Finally, any airlines need to establish network planning, such as network optimization and development, traffic and revenue forecasting, market -and -competitor analysis, scenarios for profit-optimized networks include: hub-strategies, evaluation of aliances, cooperation includes: route joint ventures in industry environment.

● Performance measurement system strategy

Any airlines may apply performance measurement methods to design the indicates of performance. Different models and frameworks are excellence models. Any airlines hope to achieve useful performance meaurement strategy. They need to answer these kep questions: Who are the key stakeholders and what they want and need? What strategy airlines have to put into place to satisfy the key stakeholders' want and need? What critical process do airlines need if they want to implement this strategy? What capability do they need to operate and improve this process? What does cost leadership strategy mean? Competitive price is decided for customer . Indoneasia, Malaysia , India and China countries are implementing, it can provide cheaper workforces and the cost of production will be covered.

In aviation service industry, cost strategy , it much relevant to be applied cost carrier, such as Vigin Blus, Ryanair Airways are implementing . However, some airlines combined the low cost carrier and full service ,which is known as low fare limited services.

Innovative marketing strategy is not only how to carry many more passengers, but also how to enable significant reduction in the costs of distribition and marketing. Such a strategy is used as a competitive strategy of low cost tariffs . For example, low cost focus strategy serve tourists or groups with certain destinations, e.g. the flights are carried out by certain airlines.

There are also tourist groups who travel to certain tourist destinations. Passengers only are transported be the tourist destinations, thus departure schedule won't be a basic need, lower price of ticket and flexible departure schedule as well as comfortable cabin are still the standard.

Another improvement of performance method, it is market orientation, it is believed to give psychological and social benefits to the employees , in the forms of greater pride and sense of belonging, as well as greater commitment to the organization.

Another strategy improves to service performance, it is distribution management strategy . Everyone can be brought benefits. It may achieve these benefits: Raising passenger numbers, as some airlines and airports are running at near full capacity. The effects of disruption are only becoming compounded. Social media can help airlines and airports to tackle dissuption management and avoid damaging their reputation with consumers.

So, when discuption is solved. It can help airports reduce discuption cost and damaging their reputation with consumers . Innovation may include: airlines attempt to develop standard procedure for common disruption situations, responding to regulations, such as the delay rule and compensation for cancellations with faster, more proactive decisions, collaborating with air traffic control facilities, airports, themselves views of resources, identify available options.

● What factors influence cost-related management quality ?

Thus, the reduction of costs lies at the core of the low cost airline model, which aims to offer lower fares, elimating some comfort and services that were traditionally quaranteed, e.g. employed to refer to low-cost flight. The use of an airline booking system, the suppression of free-in-flight catering, the use of secondary airports connected through a point-to-point network, and the use of homogeneous fleets are only a part of the innovative choices made by low-cost airlines. However, these are main important factors to influence route structure, type and characteristics of the aircraft cost of labor and management quality . For example, if the airline's pilot, airline passenger service people, cleaners , all salaries can be reduced to employ. Then, the airport or airline's labor cost will be reduced and it can influence it's air ticket price to be also decreased.

When the airline's air tickets price reduces, it will bring competitive low air ticket sale price to win other airline competitors more easily. How air ticket sale attractive prices ? The airline's air plane type and characteristics,, whether they ae comfortable to let passengers catch in their whole trip time. Whether their air planes are new or old model ? Whether their air planes' facilities can satisfy passengers entertainment need, e.g. chair can be bed to let passengers to sleep, television or movie is attractive to watch, music is soft sound etc. psychological entertainment facilities can let the airline passengers feel satisfactory or not.

Final view is management quality, such as whether the airline or airport CEO's management ability performance is either excellent or good or general or poor . They can influence whole airline or airport front -line service staffs' service performance to let passengers or airport visitors feel their services can satisfy their needs when they choose to catch the airline air planes to fly to the country to travel or work, but the country's airport staffs' service performances and airport facilities will influence their revisiting to the country's airport or rebuying the airline's air tickets again.

The final strategy is flying route strategy. I believe that whether the flying route is attractive or not, it can influence passengers to choose the airline preference. Which factors determine choice of flights on the Dhaka-London route? How could the airline be able to cope with the competitive advantages of its major rivals in this flying route? How is the competitive environment for airlines operating in this route? How could the airline sustain its competitive advantage and what can it do to gain more market share in this route?

A successful and attractive flying route design needs to amend and adjust its flying route design strategies and capabilities as the airline firm goes through its flying route design life cycle, when changes in passenger's flying route choice preferences. Hence, any airline needs to know whether what its SWOT (strengths, weaknesses, opportunities, threats) before it decides to implement which flying route(s). Because manay flying routes choicew will be influenced by its current SWOT environment situation. For organization of new flying route to the UK airport from UK , e.g. London ciry airport, the HK airline needs to know whether what its strengths , e.g. customer loyalty, its strengths can provide the most rapid . The most cheapest, the more comfortable flying feeling from HK airport flys to UK London airport or from UK , London city airport flys to HK airport, its UK , London city flying route can provide competitive fare al promotion, extra baggage allowance, airline brand image , whether is famous to UK travellers, providing online seats reservation for any UK , London flights services, airline organization size and airline brand , whether it can get travelling passegners, loyalty or confidence either to fly to UK , London city from UK city airport, or flying to HK city from UK, London city airport, providing regular UK , London flying route schedule, network presence how much UK flying route cost cutting, Uk air planes' aircrafts facilities whether are enough to satisfy HK or UK to catching the airline's air planes flying entertainment needs. Does it one new route development opportunity of direct flights from HK airport to UK , London city airport. HK air port has enough terminals number to let facilities to provide passengers stay in HK airport when UK , London city travellers arrive HK airport? Does HK airport lacks technologica facilities to satisfy new UK , London city airport flying route development , e.g. providing enough spaces to let air fleets stay in HK airport, aircraft manintenance whether is enough? Does HK airport encounter shortages of experienced front line counter service staffs to serve UK , London city travellers in airport? When the seasonal time is holiday travelling time for UK visitors, is UK new flying route rising fuel cost? Does new entrants to develop another UK , London city flying route from HK? Has new UK , London city from HK flying route , these weaknesses , such as lacking enough resource to develop another another new flying route or no direct flight or long hour flight after the HK airline developed the new UK , London city flying route to the HK airline from HK airport. Has new Uk, London city flying route development enountered these threats: strong competiton, high interest and UK foreign currency exchange rates, raising fuel cost, economic recession decline in the UK airline industry, environmental pollution etc. issues influence UK travellers choose to travel to HK desires. So, SWOT analysis must be needed to consider in order to develop any new flying route in order to avoid servious high cost expenditure loss to any airlines.

So, above these tangible , e.g. fuel cost control , route choice, network cooperation choice and intangible, e.g. service performance factors can influence whether the airline's network cooperation strategy, route choice strategy or low cost strategy can succeed or fail. So, airlines or airports can not neglect these factors to be revised in order to achieve any strategies in success more easily.

Economic Environment Influences Airport
service performance

Airline employee positive emotion method
Emotional labor factor

Airline service industry, front line travelling passengers service workers' emotional challenge concerns cabin crew and airline ground service employee whose service quality or performance how to serve travelling passengers in order to reach service level or satisfy their service performance needs to be accepted. So, how to influence airline service labour individual emotional matter which will be one major factor to let travelling passengers how they feel satisfactory to the airline service.

The question concerns how to let airline service cabin crews and air ground service employees build long term good emotion to serve their airline travelling passengers. Because
bad emotional airline service labors will damage the whole airline employers' loyalty as well as reducing travelling passengers number in possible.

Will a lot stresses at work cause bad emotion to airline ground service employees? The hospitality industry comprises of travel and tourism and the major segments include lodgings and cuisines (hotels, restaurants), transport(airlines, rentals, cruise and railway companies), travel and tour operators. All of these related travelling industries' employees , they are emotional labor, whose service performance or service attitude will influence future potential travelling passengers' airline choices to the airline operating servicer again. Any airline service employees in these service sector industries, have to interact with their travelling clients, be its customers on a regular emotion reflecting basis. So, they must be patient to listen any travelling passengers' enquires in order to help them to solve any problems considerably.

Emotional labor is managing one's feelings to generate a publicly accepted facial and bodily display of emotion. Emotional labor is an expression of emotion for a wage. Jobs involve face to face or voice to voice interactions with clients (travelling passengers), jobs demanding the employee to produce and alter an emotional state in other person, and jobs allowing the employer to implement certain amount of control over the emotional activities of the employees, produce or create emotional labor among the employees.

Thus, long time bad emotional airline front labors number increasing, it will influence the airline whole service member performance to be its airline passengers. However, many airline organizations have their owning set of norms or policies that determine these feeling rules. These are specially seen in customer service industries. IN long term, these strict policies will let airline front service staffs feel stress or pressure, because they won't feel to be punished in possible, e.g. without salary continue increasing, dismissal (lose jobs), changing to another position to do more simple or boring job duties, if they are discovered that their working service performances are not satisfied to their airline employers in any time.

So, strict airline organizational policies will be one strict or pressure emotional regulation to any airline front service staffs. This emotional regulation refers to a person's capability to accept and understand his or her experience of emotions to get involved in healthy strategies in managing emotions which are uncomfortable whenever required, when they need to contact their airline passengers every day. In fact, it has possible that they will accept unreasonable complaint from their airline passengers, even they perform very good or they have help their airline passengers to solve any enquiries when they feel any needs, they stay in airports any time. So, it has close relationship among airline front service staffs' emotions and the airline's policy as well as their service attitude. Thus, good airline policy will build good airline service staffs' emotions and good service attitude or service behaviour to serve their airline passengers every day in possible.

Any airline organizations can not neglect to consider how to build (keep) good airline front labor emotion issue. Because they are any airlines' representatives, if they can build good
images to let the airline the airline passengers to feel. Then, it will influence many airline passengers to choose to buy the airline tickets to replace other airlines because they like its front airline front staffs' services. SO, any airline organizations need to consider front service staffs' health status and definite psychological or mental diseases more than physical diseases, because many airline front service staffs only need to serve their airline passengers and they do not need to move any heavy things in airports in general. They need to spend more time to contract their passengers more than any things. When their passengers give their passports or/and any related travelling documents, e.g. air tickets to them to check in to find whether they can allow to enter airport restrict areas, and if they give their luggage to them, they also need to help them to measure its size and weight heavy to decide whether they need to pay extra fee and their luggage are permitted either to keep to them together to enter the air planes to fly or separate air planes to fly to destination. So, they need to make accurate judgement need to avoid any error occurrence. They do not allow to do any wrong judgement or error in order to be complain by their airline passengers often. Hence, any airline organizations need have good method to help their airline front service staffs to avoid to do any wrong judgements in order to influence any flights delay or customers' complaints , due to their personal wrong

judgement to their passengers cause in possible.

Thus, any airline organizations require to enquire themselves these questions: Is there any influence of emotional labor (surface acting and deep acting) on the general mental health or psychological disease of airline employees? Is these any difference in the experience of emotional labor across demographics (age/gender/mental status/work experience of airline employees influence their service performance? Because above any one factors , such as every airline front service staff individual age, airline service experience, marital status of these factors will influence their emotions to be good or bad to serve their airline passengers every day. Hence , any airline organizations need to investigate every airline front service employee individual background in order to arrange the most suitable policy to train their front line or ground airline service staffs' skill in order to let them to feel less stress or pressure
or they can feel happy to enjoy to serve their airline passengers.

On conclusion, reducing airline front or ground service staffs' psychological stress or mental pressure issue which will be the most effective or the best solution to assist them to raise confidence to serve their airline passengers in airports in long time. I believe that it is the most rapid psychological solution method to assist any one airline front or ground service staff to raise service level in short time.

Airports service environment factor

The environment of airports service environment for the airline services, which will also influence travelling passengers' travelling destinations and travelling frequent times choices. The airport price factor includes income growth, aviation technology and local economic / geographical features of the country's domestic or overseas airports both. IN fact, airports, airports are indeed two sides businesses, it has commercial relationship between both airlines and passengers. So, airports' pricing will influence passengers' travelling demands to the airlines in the country. Any countries' airport(s) need(s) to respond how to help themselves country airlines how to increase passengers number and airlines choices in order to achieve attracting traffic on frequent air planes flying aim. Because the country's travelling passengers number increases , it will influence the country's airport(s) ' income increases indirectly, instead of the countries' any airlines themselves incomes.

Hence, any country's airport(s) will be one good platform to let travelling passengers to stay in the country's airport(s). It means that id the country's airport(s) can build good service image and reasonable products sale price and comfortable shopping environment to attract any countries' passengers feel comfortable and worth to stay in themselves countries' airport(s), when they need to transfer air planes to stay in the country's airport, e.g. one hour to five hours short time, even overnight long time staying. However, if they
feel the country's airport(s) are(is) more comfortable and clean to stay, less noise, as well as they have enough chairs to let them to sit or sleep and large area to let them to work in the airport ground floor.

Moreover, the country's airport(s) can have enough restaurants , bookshops, any electronic or other kinds product shop[s, even cinema etc. shopping or entertainment services to satisfy
the passengers whose eating needs, entertainment needs, shopping needs in the airport. Then, I believe that the country's airport(s) can help itself airlines to attract many passengers
to choose to increase travelling times to the country frequently. For example, when the country's airport passengers feel that the airport restaurant food concessionaires will probably provide enjoy positive external gains from having more flights at the airports, additional or better eating facilities are unlikely to provide external benefits to the airlines by stimulating many more passengers with local origins or destinations to use the airport. I believe these airport restaurants can influence the choices of transit passengers whether which country will be their transfer air plane's short journey staying airport destination to fly to their final destinations. Although, transit passengers usually stay to the transfer air plane airport in short time, but they hope that these any one transit staying airport can have any restaurants to provide good taste food to them to eat when they feel hungry, if the transfer air plane country's airport can provide enough restaurants and they can have different food taste choice and reasonable price. Then, the airport's restaurants may attract many short time transit passengers to choose to eat their food, even many passengers will like to choose the country's airline to buy tickets to stay short time to wait to
transfer another air plane to fly to their final destination to replace another country's airport to stay short time.

Hence, it seems that any countries' airports' entertainment, eating and shopping service environment will influence any countries transit passengers whether they ought either choose to stay short time this country's airport in prefer or another country's airport to stay short time in prefer in order to decide to buy the country's airline air ticket for transfer airplane to another destination. Hence, any airports service environment will influence any countries passengers how to make transit airport destination short time staying choice.

However, I also suggest that an airport will place a lower revenue -over cost burden on that side of the travelling market that benefits the other the most. Assuming one passenger
can earn benefit enjoyed by airlines from an extra- passenger using the airport, the airlines will be willing to pay up to this amount to increase passenger enjoyed benefit feeling.

The airport can extract rent from the airlines up to above their allocated costs for providing the airport short time staying platform (transfer air plane short time staying airport) for eating, entertainment, shopping need service of increasing their destination arriving passengers or transfer another air plane passengers number base. This involves transferring the external benefits derived by airlines from additional passengers using the transfer airport to the another destination airport.

On the another view, from a airport location choice perspective, locating or expanding an airport near a city center can reduce or at least contain passenger access costs . But, because land is
like to be more expensive, the airside costs to airlines are serious higher and if the various other external costs of aviation are included. Hence, countryside or the airport is built far away from city center in the country. This location is one reasonable location choice, because it can reduce noise to influence people who are living when air planes are often flying or landing on the airport and the rent cost to the airport's any business renters will be influenced to reduce. Then, their food , product or entertainment service prices charge to the airport consumers will also be reduced. Thus, any airports ought nor neglect their building location choices in any countries because they will influence airport business renters sale prices.

Lean maintenance repair and manual
error factor

Any airlines must need air plans to catch passengers to fly to travel. So, any air plans will need often to fly. Every flight will need long time to fly, e.g. short trip needs to fly less than five hours, even long trip needs to fly more than five hours, even ten hours. If many passengers choose the country to travel, the air plan needs to fly
frequently to catch every flight passengers to go to the travelling destination frequently. So, any airlines air plans often need to check whether they have any engine machines has broken, need to be repaired in possible in order to let passengers feel the airline air plans are safe. If the airline's any air plans have occurred any accidents when they are flying, even the accidents cause any one passengers hurt, even death. Then, these flying accidents will let passengers feel life risk to choose this airline's any air plans to catch to fly. IN special, long time trip(s) flight(s). So, lean maintenance and engine check is needed to consider for any one airplane to any airline in order to improve efficiencies and minimize costs, maintenance, repair,
and overhaul services in the aviation industry sector, even avoiding any flying accident occurrence or reducing serious flying accidents occurrence chance to bring any one passenger
hurt, even death when they are catching any one of the airline air plans to travel. Thus, any one of airline safety is one important successful factor to any airlines.

Instead of passenger safety aspect, the flying logistics safety factor is also important. The central tenet of the lean to a flying process can mainfest in a variety of ways , as over stalled
and underused inventory and misallocated labour, time transportation and logistics. From a customer's perspective, value-added activities are necessary and customers are willing to pay for activities(Bamber, 2000, Glass, 2016). For example, improvements caused by lean introduction in aviation industry in order to avoid misallocated labour time, increasing number of old broken tools, and obsolute jigs and fixtures. Aviation MRO services have been reported by the MIT Lean Aerospace Initiative (2005) to result in:

(1) Set up time: 17 to 85 percent improvement.

(2) Lead time: 16 to 50 percent improvement.

(3) Labour hours: 10 to 71 percent improvement.

(4) Cost: 11 to 50 percent improvement.

(5) Productivity: 27 to 100 percent improvement.

(6) Cycle time: 20 to 97 percent improvement.

(7) Airline airplane manufacturing factory floor space: 25 to 81 percent improvement.

(8) Travel distance (people and products): 42 to 95 percent improvement.

(9) Airplanes engine inventory or work in progress: 31 to 98 percent improvement.

(10) Scape, rework , deflects or inspection: 20 to 80 percent improvement.

Hence, any airlines' airplanes need to be achieve any one of above improvement at least percent level in order to keep airplane's accident occurrence chance to the least level.

Moreover, airplanes' pilot employees their flying experiences or flight numbers factor is also important to influence airplane safe flying issue. Because if the pilot has less flying

expereince or he is not proficient pilot, or his flight number is less. This pilot's individual flying factor will also influence the airplan's safety when he is driving the airplane.

So, any airlines need to consider how to train any one of pilot to be one proficient pilot, because id less experienced pilot , he/she is not proficient to drive any one airplane to fly. Then, the flying accident occurrence chance will also raise. It is one critical successful factor to influence passengers' confidence to choose the airline's airplanes to catch, instead of maintenance repair and checking engines factor.

On conclusion, raising travelling passengers' safe confidences factor will be one critical successful factor to influence any airlines' services level, because flying safety issue

must be one important matter to be considered to any passengers when they decide to choose the airline's airplane to catch to fly to any destinations. If one airline can not guarantee any flying accidents won't occur, to cause any passengers hurt or death. Then, any passengers won't have confidence to feel its others services level can satisfy their basic flying enjoyment

needs. Due to passengers' life cost must be no worth calculation more than other service cost. When they choose to catch the airlines' any one airplane to fly to the another destination form the

country's airport. Hence, the influence of human factor in airport maintenance factor will influence any airlines' services feeling level to their passengers because human factor is one of the safety barrier which is used in order to prevent accidents or incidents of aircraft.

Therefore, the question is to which extent the error caused by human factor is included into the share of errors that are made during aircraft maintenance, such as flying

accidents, incidents, injuries, death, damages related to aircraft operation and maintenance. More airlines' detailed analyses have led to the knowledge that it is necessary to study the

interrelation of repair people, machines, airline factory maintenance and manufacturing working environment, and the air planes production processes. Human is the key factor production

process and in the process of operation of technical means since gives new value to the object of any one airplane manufacturing process.

As a factor, the human is not perfect and introduces unintentional error in the system. It is important to develop a system of ever identification and to work constantly on error

prevention. The works and activities on aircraft maintenance can produce hidden and active errors on the aircraft. Hidden errors are a type of errors that are seemingly invisible during aircraft

flying. Active errors are errors that occur immediately and result in immediate aircraft damage or injury , even death to any travelling passengers.

Hence, non human or without human factors will be less number to compare human factors to cause any flying incidents or accidents occurrence easily, e.g. damaging engine, old engine (no renew engine), fire, crash etc. different kinds of causes. However, the main causes of human errors to cause any flying accidents may include: lack of

communication between the pilot(s)
and airport airplane landing staffs, complacency (assessment of work according to previous working experience), lacking of flying knowledge to the pilot, distraction, lack of
team work, fatigue, lack of materials and technological support), pressure on the work performer, lack of assertiveness (lack of self-confidence or technical approach to work),stress (working under pressure), lack of awareness etc. different human factors. Any one of above human factors will influence any flying accidents cause.

Moreover, instead of human factor, the flying working environment which refers to the space and place for work as well as the conditions of work factor will also influence human
error occurrence increasing chance, e.g. time pressure, equipment and tools enough number supplies, night shift, all of any one work environment factor will also influence human error
occurrence increasing chance in any flight flying. However, the factors that lead to cause of maintenance error may be caused from wrong information system supplies of equipment , aircraft
manufacturer, wrong working equipment and tools, wrong design of aircraft equipment and parts, incorrect working task arrangement, lacking technical education to the aircraft maintenance
workers, employee's bad personality, poor aircraft factory manufacturing working environment, poor airline company organization structure, working management and control and poor
communication etc. different manual or non manual factors.

Hence, all of above any one non manual factors will also raise manual error factor to cause any flying accidents occurrence chances. However, if any airlines hope to satisfy their passengers' flying service level. They must consider non manual and manual both factors for aircraft lean maintenance repair service aspect.

Influence of airside and off airport to airport geographical choice factor

What does airport airside means ? It includes a system of three components: runways, taxiways and agron-gate areas, on which aircraft and aircraft support vehicles operate. It brings this questions: Why can airport airside operation influence passengers feeling to the country's airport and airline services? How does it influence airport ground service staffs' service performance?

In fact, this airside airport physical area choice has direct relationship between aircraft and apron gate areas of the terminal processing of passenger and cargo. They are major factors to influence operations on runway component. It means that airport ground service staffs' service efficiency, used for the passengers and air fright catching any airplanes processing.

Hence, in a geographical sense, landside and airside capacity on how designing and building og geographical area can bring indirect influence to passengers. They need to enter or indirect influence the airport , in special, many flights are staying on the airport runway as well as many passengers need to leave from the airplanes or enter to the airplanes in the same time on the airport boundary. Hence, if the airport has good airside design , then many passengers will feel convenient to leave or enter the airport from the airside areas.

Airports are perhaps truly intermodel terminals in the transportatoin system. They provide an intersafe among air highway, rail and even water way travel. They are an important part of the medium and long distance intercity transportation system in our future transportation tools. Hence, it has enough reasons to support airside geographical airside and off airport factors can influence an airport and its airline flying service providers on its capacity as well as how it's capacity can influence passengers' satisfactory level when they arrive the country's airport. Hence, airport's congestion growth problem that is needed to consider to any airports because when one airport 's congestion is growing.

It will influence passengers service satisfactory level to be fallen down in possible, e.g. capacity is increased by the addition of a new access road, such as additions provide a major increase.Thus, the stair step growth, it will cause congestion growth because if the airport had used many areas for stair step growth and passengers will have less space to let them to walk on the ground and their airport congestion feeling will also increase when passengers are staying to leave the airport or waiting for check in or check out or waiting to transfer another airplane in the country's airport.The major airside factors to influence travelling passengers whose airport service feeling may include as below:

Availability of enough land for expansion for runways, availability of aids to navigation and air traffic control techniques that could result in reduction of separation between aircraft , noise, aircraft mix, load factor, exclusive use and use of gates , enough airside and outside facilities, availability of airspace, whether aircraft large size is enough capacity and where is location of gates, staffing, equipment freight, environmental protection regulation, and community attitudes toward airside operation.

Thus, whether the airport has enough facilities to satisfy passengers staying in its airport service need, it will have indirect influence further passengers increasing or decreasing number problem. For example, if the airport terminal functions are spread over a large geographic area, access and facilities have to be expanded to accommodate the spread-out configuration of the terminal or if terminal facilities are grouped together, the access facilities can be congregated into a smaller geographical area.

The capacity of the landside is a function of the terminal design , which has a major influence on the relative to between airside and landside capacity. Also, these off airport factors can also influence landside capacity, they may include: off airport parking, off airport terminals, urban development pattern, multiple jurisdiction, financial resources etc. issues. The sub factors of the off-airport access functions , they can influence passengers' services feeling to the airport. They may include: user and vehicle characteristics, e.g. occupants per vehicle, separate and preferential guide way subsystems, roadway traffic management, access link to major transportation , transportation connections. All of these airside and off-airport facilities will influence passengers' servicing feeling when they arrive any countries' airports. Hence, any countries' airports ought not neglect any one of these minor airside facilities of inside airports to outside airports both.

The another geographical choice airport building issue, it is also one critical factor for how the development of airport cities. It will influence passengers' service feeling to any country airport. The questions may include: Why may any country need to develop an airport city? Can it bring economic benefit and attract many passengers to choose to travel the country? Can the airport city reform to raise airport service performance or service level? Airports have become new dynamic centers of economic activity, incorporating several commercial and entertainment services inside passenger terminals, when developing a hotels and accommodations , office complexes, conference and exhibition centers or leisure facilities choices for leisure passengers and business passengers both.

Airport-centered development may occur at different spatial scales (from the micro scale of the passenger terminal to the regional or metropolitan scale), thus assuming different shapes and mainfestations. Different concepts to address these developments can be found in the " airport city", airport corridor, and aerotopolis (Guller, M. & Guller, M, 2003).

I shall explain how airport city concept can help to raise passenger service performance feeling in airports and airlines as below:

In general, airport passengers hope airports ought provide these different kinds service and achievement the lowest satisfactory service quality or performance level to let them to feel, such as air transport needs have complex airport -neighborhood interactions (in what concerns an eventual development towards the concept of airport city) requires the identification of thes takeholders involved and an awareness of the relationships between them. Any airport's main task needs to provide traveling, air transport, shipping, entertainment services to the dual market of airlines and travelers. As such, its primary interaction consists of the supply and demand relationship with the users stakeholder group (passengers and airlines), which results in broad terms in the airports aeronautical revenues. Furthermore, non-aeronautical (commercial) revenues also result from the interactions between airport and users, namely from agents such as cargo and passengers oriented organizations who pay rents or concession feeling to the airport authority, depending on the commercial arrangements binding these agents.

Thus, one successful airport city, it ought provide good neighborhood transport service to travelling passengers, e.g. bus, taxi, ferry etc. public transportation service. It aims to avail any airport passengers can catch any one of these public transportation tools to arrive airport or leave the airport easily. It also needs to provide hotel, conference service for business visitors as well as retail shops, cinemas for shopping visitors or entertainment visitors when they are staying in the country's airport(s). Also, it ought provide facilities to any cargo -oriented organizations to deliver any cargo in short time rapidly. So, one airport's any neighborhood facilities have relationship to influence any passengers and airport organizations' service performance feeling between different user agents including: service provision (e.g. between passengers and businesses), business transactions, supply and demand (e.g. between public transport providers and passengers and passengers or visitors) and employer-employee relationships (businesses and workforce , such as airport airline ground service workers). Because if they feel that they can work in one comfortable airport working environment, they will feel happy and enjoyable to serve their passengers more everyday. It means that any airports' facilities will have indirect relationship to influence airport ground service workers' psychology to feel either enjoyable or hate to work in the airport environment often.

On conclusion, airports ought need to consider themselves airside and off airport facilities whether they have enough supplies and innovate their facilities to be better , even perfect in order to satisfy any airport visitors, travelers, user organizations and airport ground service employees to enjoy to work and use their services if they hope their service level or performance is satisfied to their service needs for long term.

Influencing air connectivity to service quality factor

Can air connectivity growth decreases travel costs for attracting travelling passengers, consumers and businesses and facilities global productive growth? This seems to be particularly an issue when airport capacity is scare or when new airports are added to an existing airport system. What is air connectivity ?
Why does air connectivity raise passengers services? How to measure air connective service?

When direct and indirect connectivity relate to the airport connectivity available to local travelling passengers, any airports ought need to raise extra
airline services to raise service quality , e.g. cheaper air ticket price, in-flight service extra service provision, e.g. comfortable and clean and quiet air port waiting environment
service provision and feeling. However, passengers will generally prefer direct, non-stop connections over indirect air connectivity service.

Air connectivity service can assist airlines to raise competitive effort an offer and they provide access to the many destinations with too little demand for a direct flight, such as minimum connecting time differs in quality , due to in-flight time differences, the inconvenience and risk of missing a connection and transfer time for direct or indirect flights. Hence, any airlines can reduce passengers indirect or direct flight in-flight time to wait airplanes arrive to catch when they arrive any airports. This air in flight waiting time shorten service will attract many passengers to choose the airline to catch airplanes if its inflight waiting time to airport passengers is lesser than other airlines' in-flight waiting time in any airports. It can raise airline service quality, due to the airline has many passengers feel in-flight waiting time is shorten than other airlines often.

In fact, airport connectivity is one good concept method to raise passengers' satisfactory service level. One of the important factors for the connectivity of airports may include: The size and economic strength of the local catchment area how drives outbound demand, size and economic activities as well as tourism attractiveness are an important cariable factor in explaining inbound demand (including the propensity to flying demand), landside accessibility drives the size of the catchment area that airlines can serve from a particular airport within a certain landside travel time, apart from the socio-economic variables factor, also cultural , political and the historical ties play a role in explaining demand the origin-destination level factor. All of the research on the factors that explain air level, demand at the origin-destination or airport level is widespread, including gravity modelling (e.g. a bed at al., 2001) and regressions on aggregate
airport demand (Dobruszkes, 2011). All of any one factors may be airport connectivity service to influence passengers' service feeling level in airports and airlines both service quality.

ON airport visit costs aspect, airlines also need to consider airport visit costs in their route development strategy. Visit costs may also influence passenger choice behavior when
airlines pass on higher/lower charges to the passenger through air fares. Although, airport visit costs generally represent a limited share of an airline's total operational costs, this share can be more significant for short haul flights

as well as fair airlines. All of any one these airport charges and passenger fees variable may influence passengers airlines choice. They may include:

Fees variable, landing charge, parking charge for their vehicles or aircraft, passenger luggage charge, security charge, boarding bridge charge, noise charge, emission charge, airport development service increasing charge, check -in charge, terminal charge, cargo charge. So, if any one of these charges influence the airline ticket price rises, it will influence passengers' air ticket purchase choice to the airline in possible.

On airport service levels aspect, for keeping and attracting passengers, airlines and airports need to compete with services that improve the passengers experience. Such service factors concern for immigration and luggage, but also relate to the terminals, waiting transfer another air plane time, shopping facilities, toilets, atmosphere and space cleaniness, friendliness of staff and availability of delicated lounges. Together they determine the image of an airport and its perceived value by passengers and airlines.

On airline routes development aspect, it can also influence passengers choices to the airline, e.g. Australia airline had developed long route to England destination. Any Australia passengers can fly to England route directly. They do not need to transfer another air plane to go to England. Although, flying time is above 12 hours long time, but it can bring available to passengers. They do not need to spend time to wait another air plane to transfer to go England in Australia any airports. THus, airline route development strategy airline planners require detailed, accurate information to make new route decisions, but airlines usually do not have the resources to fully evaluate every new route market. So, they need a sound well articulated business case, can convince airlines to introduce new air services, as well as airport / destinations can influence the airline planning process.

For example, Interviewer indicates that new routes are a huge investment and risk to an airline in airline economic view point, if the airline had not gathered any data to evaluate whether the new route is worth to develop and predict passengers' new route choice behavior. It assumed 75% lead factor will influence any new route development in success. It indicates these different aircraft type and seats per flight, annual passenger requirements data for these aircrafts: Boeing 747 aircraft needs to satisfy 400 at least seats per flight and annual passenger requirement need 219, 000, aircraft airbus A340 aircraft needs 280 at least seats per flight and annual passenger requirements need 153,300 , Boesing 767 to 300 aircraft needs 220 at least seats per flight and annual passenger requirements need 120, 450 . Boeing 737 to 700 aircraft needs 76,650 and regional Jet aircraft needs 100 at least seats per flight and annual passenger requirements need 54,750.

Hence, any airlines need have route priorities strategy before they decide which new flight route(s) will be developed , in order to achieve airlines add service in order of expected profitability, different airlines have pursued different strategies, destinations can move up the priority board with: solid research and analysis (always) and incentives (sometimes).However, any airline questions for new routes may include as below:

What is the current, actual market for a potential route?

How much can my airline stimulate the flight flying market?

How will the competition react?

How much market share will achieve?

How will be the connectivity contribution?

Will the new route be a financial success?

Hence, any airlines need to reduce uncertainty and risk, before they decide to develop any new route market.

The air service development process may include as below:

Step one: market assessment, required a quantify the time size of the existing air travel market

step two: strategy, deficiency analysis and detailed route analysis

step three: business case analysis, packaging and presenting the information to airlines

step fourth: evaluate and negotiate airline incentives

It is the final steps an appropriate incentive, in certain circumstances, helps airlines commit to new air service to satisfy any new route passengers' more satisfactory flying needs.

Similarly, the strategy steps follow: benchmark air services, identify deficiencies, identify new route opportunities, identify potential air service providers, assess viability of potential air services and prioritize route opportunities and target carriers.

Any airlines may find any information concerns new route business cases to decide their countries flying new routes choice , such as: catchment area profile: demographics, economy, tourist etc. information, airport profile : traffic and facilities information market profile; market sizes , top city pairs, traffic leakage etc. information, suggested service : frequency , schedule, airport routing information, route analysis: market share, load factor, stimulation potential, self-diversion etc. information, any airlines' past flying routes strategic considerations etc. information in order to predict and evaluate whether how many further passenger number is flying that they accept to choose the new flying routes travelling needs.

Hence, how to design to impact either the supply or demand for any new flight routes that is only important because of the country has less number of passengers accept to choose the new flying route to fly. Then, the new flying route does not needed to be design to supply to the country's travelling passengers because their acceptance to this new flying route ends are very less. However, the demand level is low new flying route needs to satisfy these three qualifying services criteria, such as: Are new routes only? Increase on existing routes? Does it work service rent incentives? Will the new flying route be satisfied to air service to the airline passengers and airport waiting passengers, e.g. strategically important? Marginally (unprofitable) self-sustaining in the short term? New flying routes only? Increase an existing routes? Service rent incentives?

How can airports afford aggressive airline incentive / fee discounts and still fund route development marketing in a difficult economy? I recommend that the solution method may include new flying route design and developing and maximizing non-aeronautical revenue streams both, such as retail and duty free, food and beverage, parking , loyalty and premium programs and land development to airport building. Marketing funding strategy may be an ineffective incentive for travelling destinations. However, it may not differentiate a market, as route marketing incentives are used by over 80% of communities in the U.S. marketing incentives can be: Unilateral airport pays 100% or cooperative airlines matches some portion, funding amounts are often tied on the capacity of inbound seats to be available on the new flight (flying) route. By calculating the economic impact of new visitors (spend at the destination), a destination can calculate the return on investment in cooperative new flight (flying) route market.

On conclusion, air connectivity is one important factor to influence any country's travelling passengers to the airline's service quality or service level in order to achieve new flying (flight) route design , reducing inflight transfer another airplane waiting time in airport, or marketing development in success. So, any airlines can not neglect this air connectivity will influence their passengers' service quality. Hence, air connectivity factor is also very important to influence any travelling passengers' service satisfactory level.

How to measure and rise airline
service quality

How are airline performing ? Nowadays, the rise of the low cost airlines' competition is serious, due to airlines hope to rise themselves attractions to influence passengers to choose to use their travelling services. So, different airlines have spend long time to build their unique person-to-person passenger services, which passengers use of different airlines, e.g. digital electronic air tickets purchase method. Any airlines hope to make each journey personalized to the individual will gain market share and improve its service quality to be more unique in order to reach the efforts of airlines to build high levels of customer service appears to have been generally noticed by passengers, when they choose to buy the airline's digital electronic ticket or paper air ticket to use its flying service.

Hence, improvement their digital e-ticket purchase experience and communications factor, for example, if any passengers can enter the airline's air ticket purchase website to buy electronic ticket to pre-book seats in the short time rapidly as well as there are enough seats number to supply to them to pre-book. So, they do not need to worry about without any seats to supply to them to catch the airline's flight to fly to anywhere in any time available conveniently. So, it seems that there is plenty of space for airlines to grow and improve their digital experience and communication method to let any passengers to feel, if the airline hopes to let its passengers to feel that it has unique service to compare others airlines.

The aviation industry plays a major role in the aspect of work and leisure to passengers around the global. So, nowadays passengers' demands to any airlines' service quality had been raised. Hence, any airline service industry messengers are under pressure to prove their services are customers oriented service improvement of performance that guarantees competitive advantages to the global travelling marketplace. So, it also implies that any airlines' services performance will be influenced to cause many passengers feel more poor and let passengers dissatisfy the airline's service performance. The, the airline will possible lose many passengers, due to passengers have many airlines choices, they can find any airlines to replace which any one airline to buy air ticket from internet at home immediately.

However, airlines' comfortable seats arrangement service provision feeling factor is still important in preferable to compare other factors, because passengers must need to sit any seats in any air planes. So, whether the air plane can provide new comfortable seats to let passengers to feel this factor is still the most important factor to influence any passengers to choose to the airline's air plane to catch. For example, service comfortability is how passengers observed the quality of service offered them by the airline's cleanliness, quiet zone, shops, restaurants and business pavilion in functioning like staffs, information desk, and in flight announcement are included as tangible features by the passengers (Geraldine et a.,2013). All of these factors are needed often to measure whether their service performances are satisfactory to themselves passengers service needs.

Moreover, the other factors may include service affordability , it can be regarded as given passenger the opportunity to select from inclusive air ticket prices made available to the different group of passengers by the airlines, as a gesture of goodwill , to establish and reinforce customer loyalty and repeat purchases essential for the airline continuity as well as service reliability. it is the probability that airline will carry out its expected function satisfactory as stated in the flight schedule. Hence, there is a strong link between different airlines' service quality variables, airline image and repeat patronage from the passengers.

Service quality is a measure of how well the service level delivered matches passengers expectations to measure service quality based on input from focus groups. It consists of five factors (tangibles, reliability, responsiveness, assurance and empathy). All of these factors will be identifies that how the airline service quality can be satisfactory to its passengers ' psychological and emotion enjoyable service needs.

Any one of these any five service factors will be important to influence the airline's passengers service feeling level to the airline. It means that the passenger will have more chance to choose the airline's service again (repeating purchase its air ticket). Hence, any airlines can not neglect any one of service feeling to its passengers. It needs often to enquire questionnaires to evaluate whether its these five aspects of service quality , if it discovered any of these five aspects of service level is poor, e.g. 5 scale is the best service performance level, then it can attempt to find its error whether which aspects, it needs to very need to reach the 5 scale , the best service performance level when many passengers feel, e.g. enquiring 100 passengers who give 5 scale to reliability service aspect, before reliability service aspect has less than 50% passengers from 100 passengers who feel the airlines concerns this reliable service level aspect questions to be the best. It is one kind of measurement service quality method to any airlines.

Other service performance evaluation factor is satisfaction in the job to every airline front service or ground service staffs to the airline. Job satisfaction describes how content an employee is with his or her job. It is how the employee responses to a job. It can be considered as a part of life satisfaction to one organization, when the employee is working in the organization. Hence, if one airline front service as ground service staff who can feel more job satisfaction to compare his/her prior airline employer. Then, he/she won't be easy to change his/her present airline employer.

However, some factors can influence job satisfaction are pay and benefit, fair performance appraisal, career and promotional opportunities, proper reward and recognition, work-family life balance, the job itself, proper working conditions, leadership chance, autonomy in work.

Job satisfaction can also involve complex number of variables, circumstances, opinions and behavioral tendencies and a variety of work related outcomes, such as commitment, involvement, motivation, satisfaction, attendance. Hence, any airlines also need to concern how let their employees feel job satisfaction issue in order to avoid their leaving turnover number increases, due to job satisfaction and dissatisfaction depend on the expectations what the job supplies for an employee not the nature of the job.

Finally, instead of concerning employees job satisfaction issue, any airlines also need to concern passengers satisfaction issue because it will have any passengers will choose the airline, if it can bring more service satisfaction to let them to feel , then they will become repeat passengers to the airline.

What kinds of factors passengers were looking for and what were the reasons of choosing a specific airline? When one airline often is complained from its passengers. It will have more mistakes to let them to feel or dissatisfy its service. Hence the airlines needs to find which are its mistakes and improve in order to satisfy its passengers' expectations, e.g. finding what are the mistakes to the airlines' serious concern regarding passenger complaints and complaint satisfaction in order to make the airline more likely to meet its passengers' expectation in case of a problem. Hence, any airlines need to concern how to improve its employees' satisfactory service as well as its passengers' satisfactory service both issues as well as how to measure their service quality whether is enough to achieve general service acceptable performance to its passengers.

Reference

A bed, S. Y. A.O. Ba-Fail and S.M. Jasimuddin (2001), " An economatic analysis of international air travel demand in Saudi Arabia". Journal of air transport managmement, vol. 7, pp.143-148.

Bamber, L., & Dale, B.G. Lean production : a study of application in a traditoinal manufacturing environment. Production planning & control, 11 (3), 291-298, 2000.

Dobruszkes, F.M. Lennert and G. Van Hamme (2011). " An analysis of the determinants of air traffic volume for European metropolitan area". Journal of transport geographyy, vol. 19/4/pp.755-762.

Gealdine, O., & David , U.C. (2013). effects of airline service quality on airline image and passengers' loyalty: Findings from Arill Air Nigeria passengers, Journal of hospitality and management tourism, 4(2), 19-28. doi: http://dx.doi: 10.5897/HMT 2013, 0089.

Glass, R., Seifermann, S., & Metternich, J. The spread of lean production in the assembly, Process and maching industry. Procedia CIRP, 55, 278-283, 2016.

Guller, M. & Guller, M. (2003) From Airport to airport city. Editional Gustavo , Gili, Barcel on a.Intervistas Consulting Inc.

Massachusetts Institute Of Technology (MIT), Lean Aerospace Initiative, Available: www.lean.mit.edu, 2005.

Bibliography

Backman, K., Backman, S., Uysal, M. And Sunshine, K. (1995). Event Tourism : An Examination Of Motivations And Activities. Festival Management And Event Tourism, 3(1), 15-24.

Fishbein, M., & Ajzen, Z. (1975). Belief, Attitude, Intention And Behaviour: An Introduction To Theory And Research, Boston: Addison Wesley.

Hsu, C.H.C., Cai , L.A., Li, M(2010). Expectation, Motivation And Attitude: A Tourist Behavioral Model. Journal Of Travel Research, 49(3), 282-296. http://dx.doi, org/10.1177/004728750 9349266.

ICT Information And Communication Technology Switzerland, 2005. ICT Fakten (ICT facts). Available from http://www.ictswitzerland.ch/de/ict%2fakten/factsfigures.asp(retrieved Dec.12, 2005) in German.

Lind, (2001): Befolkningen, Familjen, Livscykeln- Och Ekonomisk Tillvaxt. Institutet For Tillvaxtpo-litiska studier/ Vinnova/Nutek.

Lohmann, Martin (2001): The 31 st. Reiseanalyse-RA 2001. Tourism: vol. 49, no.1/2001;pp.65-67, Zagreb.

United Nations Population Division (2001). World Population Prospects: The 2000 year Revision, New York.

Weber E.U., & W, P.Bottom (1989). "Axiomatic

Measures Of Perceived Risk: Some Tests And extensions." journal of behavioral decision making, 2 (2): 113-31.

Artificial Intelligent In Road Transportation Strategy

● How artificial intelligent vehicle may interact intelligent transportation tools

Can artificial intelligence (AI) and machine learning (ML) be used in the search for new " consumption" behavioral type variables that affect consumer individual or transportation service organization individual different transportation tools choices, such as road or sea or sky transportation tools? Can artificial intelligent vehicle may interact intelligent transportation tools market development?

Consumers usually have bargaining and on risk choice when they are already shopping, such as who need to accept to use any (AI) new technological products to replace human traditional behaviors, such as intelligent non-manual driving transportation market, e.g. cars are needed to be driven by human drivers on road, but it has bargaining and on risky choice, when non-manual (AI) vehicle buyers who need to depend on non-manual artificial intelligent (ML) system assists them to drive their cars on the roads.

So, any non-manual driving auto car buyers must need to believe (AI) non-manual driving vehicles (ML) systems can make accurate driving judgement to reduce or avoid any traffic accident occurrences more than human drivers' driving judgement when the (ML) systems are driving their cars on the roads. Then the intelligent vehicle manufacturers will have possible to sell their non-manual driving vehicles success.

This is the first reason or idea influences consumer individual choice to buy any kinds of (AI) non-manual driving vehicles, when consumers believe (ML) systems are more safe and make more accurate judgement to compare human or computer systems, when they are sitting in one non-manual auto driving vehicle on the road.

The another second reason or idea is that some common limits on driving consumer prediction might be understood as the kinds of errors made by poor implementation of machine learning.

Supposing driving consumers believe (AI) machine learning ability is worse to compare to human learning ability. It will also influence driving consumers do not accept to use any (AI) non-manual auto driving vehicles to replace every driver is essential on driving by himself/herself on the road. The third idea or reason is that it is important to influence driving customers believe how (AI) non-manual auto driving technology is used in them can both overcome and exploit human driving skill and safe limits and raise more auto driving safe judgement to compare human driving safe judgement.

However, how to predict any kinds of (AI) non-manual driving vehicles future consumption effort, due to different kinds of (AI) non-manual driving transportation vehicles which have different unique functions and designs to be used by different kinds of road transportation or driving demand of consumers. For example, lorry drivers need non-manual intelligent system can help them to drive fast, but safe to assist them to transport cargo to arrive destinations from their factories or offices. Otherwise, private car driver expects whose (AI) non-manual driving vehicle can auto drive to send to whom to arrive destination in safe way and non-too fast and non-too slow speed in order to avoid accident occurrences.

So, a different road intelligent consumer demand is to define whose individual driving behavior and driving habit and driving attitude and driving judgement and driving speed demand to decide how to design whose intelligent vehicle to satisfy those driving demand more generally, as simply being open-minded about what variables are likely to influence every consumer economic choice, when who decide either to buy any kinds of (AI) products or not to buy any kinds of (AI) products to replace the different demand of consumers their different (AI) useful demand.

Hence, for these three (AI) products group of stakeholders, such as home (AI) consumer group, firm (AI) consumer group and government (AI) consumer group . These consumer groups may consider whether different kinds of (AI) products can give what is special beneficial interest to them to use. These variables can be measurable properties of choices to influence them to choose to buy any (AI) kinds of (AI) products to use, e.g. psychophysiological, biological, social influences, consumer's wealth, moods and personality, (AI) product price etc. variable factors which will influence them to decide to attempt to buy any kinds of (AI) products to use.

If behavioral economics is as open-mindedness about what variables might predict. Then , (AI) machine learning system is a way to do behavioral economics because it can make use of a wide set of variables and select- which ones predict.

In behavioral economic view point, when general consumer overall demand to the product is much than the other similar (AI) non auto driving vehicle products, such as any kinds of (AI) non-manual auto driving vehicles and any kinds of manual driving vehicles case, then any kinds of (AI) non-manual auto driving vehicles will be more attractive to cause many manual driving vehicle buyers choose to buy (AI) non-manual auto driving vehicles. Hence, it seems if any kinds of (AI) non-manual auto driving vehicle products can make more attractive variable efforts to influence overall driving consumers to feel that they have more needs to drive non-manual auto vehicles to compare more than driving manual driving vehicle.

What is the main variable effort to intelligent vehicles to attract driving consumers to choose to accept to drive them ? However, I believe that (AI) machine learning system is a main factor to raise overall driving consumers' acceptances to drive it to replace manual driving vehicle. If it can persuade or prove (AI) machine learning system ability and judgement effort is more accurate than human or computer learning effort or judgement effort, then it is possible that any kinds of (AI) non-manual driving vehicle products will be accepted to drive on the road in popular.

Machine learning system is able to find prediction value in details of how the bargaining occurs. This discovery is the beginning of the next step for driving consumer individual driving behaviors or driving habits. It raises questions that include: What variables predict to influence driving consumers to change whose driving habits or driving attitudes? How can driving consumer individual emotion, face-to-face talking with whose friends when they are sitting in the non-manual driving vehicle to influence whom driving habit or driving attitude to be changed ? Do driving consumers consciously understand why those habit driving attitudes variables are important when they are sitting in one intelligent vehicle? Can (AI) driving machine learning methods capture the effects of motivated cognition to influence driving consumers decide to buy any kinds of (AI) non-manual auto vehicle products more attractively. So, it seems (AI) driving machine learning method is a main variable factor to influence driving consumers to feel who have more confidence to drive them more than any other kinds of similar manual driving vehicles on the road.

Consequently, (AI) driving machine learning system will be one important psychological method to influence driving consumers to choose to buy (AI) auto driving vehicle products to replace manual driving vehicles. The reason is because human and driving machine learning system both which will have limited variable factors to influence general different countries (AI) driving consumers' need desire to be raised.

● Why can (AI) driving machine learning system main factor influence driving consumer individual desires ? Driving consumer expectations are hard to measure or predict driving attitudes and driving behaviors in (AI) non-manual driving vehicles market. Artificial intelligence is another kind of computer science development to apply intelligent vehicle market. Why do driving consumers feel need to buy any kinds of (AI) auto driving vehicles to drive to replace manual driving vehicles on the roads? What are (AI) auto driving features different to manual driving features?

(AI) is the recreation of cognitive functions in computers; it enables machines to perform tasks like humans and perhaps even better than human. In the real world, scientists develop the technological singularity, in which a superintelligence emerges with unfold human consequences.

Professionals in many industries are intensely interested in the specifics of what (AI) can do today, and how can it helps. They are considering the impact of applied (AI), in which computers are used to address a particular problem, extracting and utilizing patterns found in large volumes of data. Of all (AI)'s subfields, machine learning is attracting the most attention. I shall explain why (AI) machine learning system is the main factor to lead consumers feel need to buy any (AI) products to use. Such as below:

For smartphone, fraud detection to medical diagnosis etc. applied (AI) technological products examples. (AI) machine learning systems can help any one of these products to do any exceed general computer learning systems which (AI) learning systems can do any skills to supply (AI) users to use to compare computer learning systems can not do any skills to supply compute users to use. It seems that (AI) machine learning system is the unique feature to attract consumer consideration in technological product market.

An term for different types of learning, and can be accomplished using different techniques. This has led to a perception that all marketing teams should have (AI) to bring a unified personalized customer experience, when consumers choose to buy any (AI) products to feel what are the different or unique characteristics to compare general computer products. Such as (AI) product has this unique machine learning characteristics, we can predict (AI) and machine learning is connected to influence consumers to feel needs.

Furthermore, over the same time period, and in contrast to predictions for roles in many industries. (AI) won't take the place of marketers and merchandisers themselves although it is already a new value to analytical and strategic marketing skills to persuade consumers to buy any (AI) products. It means different kinds of (AI) products will have different machine learning effort and unique characteristics to attract consumers to choose to buy them to use. Such as, when intelligent vehicles need have unique road driving or sea transportation or flying machine learning system when they are applied on these three kinds of transportation tool aspects. They need have good response safety driving and immediate response learning systems to avoid any boats or air planes or vehicles to crash to them to reduce accident occurrences immediately on any one of either road or sky or sea journey environment.

What is the reason why (AI) driving machine learning system can influence good at making sense to driving consumer desire? Only humans (drivers) , preferably experienced, well informed humans can understand their driving customer needs and decide how to design or reengineer any (AI) intelligent vehicle product functions. (AI) intelligent vehicle can give these professionals the means to do this better to compare manual driving immediate response control function when any vehicles are driving or they will stop immediately to close / near to them in order to reduce crash occurrence on the road, and then maximize relevance through real-time customization of the non-manual auto vehicle driving user experience.

For example, as ever, senior decision makers need to be informed, decisive and results-oriented or risk losing out. Harvard Business Review indicated : Over the next decade, (AI) won't replace managers, but managers who use (AI) will replace those who don't. Such as intelligent vehicle won't replace drivers, but drivers who use intelligent vehicles will replace those who can not control how to drive their vehicles in the most safe way. So, (AI) driving machine learning system will have possible to do any drivers' (human's) driving judgement, driving analytical mind and driving effort to be more accurate than manual driving skills. Such as how to control to drive the intelligent vehicle in the most safe way. It is general manual driving skill can not achieve to drive in the safe way.

For another (AI) digital commerce example, (AI) and machine learning are the most exciting developments in marketing and merchandising to be applied to digital commerce, such as making better decisions through trend and cluster analysis, deploying product and content in mutually reinforcing combinations, increasing customer engagement and satisfaction in real time.

Hence, the key attraction in digital commerce circles is that machine learning is designed to be self-optimizing. Optimizing for revenue example will surface are increasingly profitably selection of products (within the brand parameters selected).

When to apply (AI) capabilities and what value (AI) is delivering for customer and company like. Unlike any technology before it, (AI) is analytical and predictive capabilities offers the prospect for each and every individual. It can maximize real time and engagement. Effective tailored (AI) technology, such as digital experience cloud technology is available now. And once integrated, (AI) starts learning and delivering incremental value from day one. So (AI) could transform the digital experience to any business organizations.

Hence, (AI) driving machine learning system can be applied to road driving skill aspect. When intelligent vehicles are invented to own the most safe driving judgement skill and they can know when either they may auto drive fast speed, when they are feeling to know when there are not many vehicles are moving close/near to them or when they need auto drive slow speed, when they are feeling to know when there are many vehicles are moving close/ near to them. Then driving consumers will have more confidence to choose to buy any kinds of intelligent vehicles to replace manual driving vehicles to drive on the roads.

● Non-manual driving transportation tool market development

If Non-manual driving vehicle manufacturers expect their (AI) automatic vehicles can attract drivers to buy. I feel them to need to consider how (AI) driving machine learning system can achieve these requirements in order to satisfy manual driving vehicle drivers' requirement to change their traditional driving habit to choose non-manual driving needs. It means (AI) driving machine learning systems can help them to drive vehicles to replace manual driving vehicles on the road. This is the main factor to influence car buyers choose to buy intelligence driving vehicles replace to manual driving vehicles. I believe (AI) non-manual driving vehicle machine learning systems, need to be designed as below:

(1) Improving driving safety by preventing accidents from happening.

Every year, drivers are facing a large number of casualties, due to traffic accidents. The amount of killed and injured road traffic related accidents is increasing every year. The real cost of an accident can go well beyond the limits of immediate material destruction, and is impossible to evaluate.

Hence, researchers and car manufacturers are looking for solutions in order to reduce the amount of accidents. They already developed a considerable set of technologies in order to decrease the amount of casualties. Most of them (like airbags, seat-belts, anti-lock systems, shock absorbing car bodies) are efficient in decreasing the impact of an accident, and in protecting the passengers of the cars. The technologies already saved a lot of lives, but they are rarely able to avoid accidents because they do not anticipate them. Moreover, if they are protecting in many cases, the passengers of the car, they do not prevent most traffic participants, like pedestrians on bicyclists from getting injured. it causes (AI) non-manual automatic car manufacturers need to consider how to design machine learning safety system is to prevent accident from happening instead of just reducing their impact.

This can only be possible using intelligent systems that can observe the driving environment, reason and decide if there is a danger, determine how to avoid it and act if necessary

(2) Reducing energy consumption by optimizing the driving.

Nowadays, global air pollution is serious. (AI) non-manual driving car manufacturers need to concern how to design (AI) machine learning system can reduce degree of air pollution to be the most minimum level to compare to traditional manual driving vehicles.

The reduction of energy consumption if certainly one of the main challenges. Transportation is one of the major factors in fossil energy consumption, and it is also responsible for a large amount of $CO2$ pollution. It is difficult to ask individuals to voluntarily limit the use of their vehicle of they do not have a strong incentive to do so. Specially in regions where vehicles are needed to drive to go to work every day. It stands to reason that if it is difficult to decrease the amount of vehicles, part of the solution is to make them more energy efficient.

Hence, non-manual driving car manufacturers need to design how to improve engines, which are more optimized and need less fuel to operate, and hybrid and electric cars have been developed and are continuously being improved. But we can go beyond these solutions that do not take into account the environment in which a vehicle is driving. A growing number of scientific contributions presented intelligent systems used in order to improve energy efficiency and reduce fuel consumption, based on the optimization of the way (AI) non-manual driving (AI) vehicles are performing. Such as recharge batteries and electric engine will be predicted the popular fuel in order to limit fuel consumption to future (AI) non-manual driving vehicles. They can reduce air pollution, consume less fuel for (AI) non-manual driving vehicles.

(3) Improving comfort by anticipating (AI) non- manual driving vehicle drivers.

Finally, another application for intelligent vehicle is the improvement of driving comfort. Car industry is very competitive market. Many potentials (AI) intelligent vehicle customers need to enjoy to sit more comfortable intelligent vehicles, who will be attracted by (AI) comfortable systems improving when driving, so part of the research in intelligent systems from cars focuses on how to improve the driving experience, i.e. make it easier and more enjoyable, more comfortable to compare to traditional manual driving vehicles.

As an example, lane keeping assistant systems are technologies that actively keep the vehicle in the lane in highways of the driven drifts out of it. Automatic speed regulation keeps the car at a certain speed without requiring to touch the gas pedal. This can be really interesting for, e.g. (AI) non-manual driving truck drivers that spend a lot of time on highways. But these technologies have a limitation in the case of automatic speed regulation, this technology can not copy of a vehicle ahead drives slower than the desired speed, or if another vehicle cuts into the lane.

This case requires the driver to have a constant focus on the road. In order to achieve more comfort, it is better of the system can adapt to changes in its dynamic environment: let the (AI) intelligent vehicle adapt to the speed of the man-manual vehicle, or autonomously change lane when requires. Again, this requires knowledge about the environment, detection capabilities, reasoning and action planning. Intelligent systems can be used in order to create more attractive and more comfortable and more safe, less energy consumption and less fuel expenditure by intelligent vehicles.

● Underground train transportation needs to know passenger behaviour reasons
Understanding individual passenger behaviour is essential for the design MTR transportation, because who can choose to catch bus, taxi, tram, train ferry etc. different kinds of public transportation tools. Individual traveler who decides to catch which kinds of public transportation tools, it depends on whether the public transportation tool can provide real time travel information, liking link travel time schedule. So, MTR underground train needs to understand where it has terminal to give convenience to the local living areas of time travelers to choose to catch MTR easily. Although, MTR ticket fare is one factor to influence any passengers choice. But, those other factors can also influence them to choice. e.g. MTR any terminal location of convenience, short time travelling, none crowding in busy (peak) time, MTR platform waiting arrival time, none sudden MTR engineering machines broken accident events occurrence frequently etc. different factors, any one of these factors which can influence passengers who choose to catch MTR or other kinds of transportation tools.

Why route choice can influence passenger behavioural choice ? Usually, the busy time passengers will regard the route choice as a coordination problem to influence them to choose to catch which kinds of transportation tools. The route choice is as an opportunity costs to influence any busy time passengers to decide to choose to catch which kind of transportation tool which is the best right choice in the right time among of them. In the short time, for example, it seems any busy time passengers will choose to catch bus to substitute MTR underground train transportation tool, due to who feels the bus can arrive any destinations to compare other kinds of transportation tools in the most short time. However even if the MTR can either charge cheaper ticket fare to sell full day or charge discount ticket fare to sell in the busy (peak) time to compare to bus fare. It is possible that the busy time passengers will still choose to catch bus, if between the bus terminal and the another bus terminal that distance is the shorter time route to spend time to arrive destination to compare between the MTR terminal to the another MTR terminal arrival time . Also, although the busy time passengers will feel to enounter traffic jam to influence sitting or waiting bus time to be longer time in possible and who also feel MTR can avoid traffic jam problem. However, usually any busy (peak) time passengers will feel the chance of traffic jam occurrence will be less. So, the short bus route choice is more potential factor to influence the busy (peak) time passengers still to choose bus to catch.
However, if anyone wants to investigate results of day-to-day route choice which can be transferred to more realistic environment. It is necessary to explore individual behaviour in an interactive experimental set up to ensure busy (peak) time passenger transportation behavioural choice. For example, a passenger has a choice between a main road (M) and a side road (S) for travelling from (A) to (B). (M) is faster if (M) and (S) are chose by the same number of passengers. So, this method can be researched whether MTR terminal station is located at the main road (M) or the side road (S) where is more suitable to accept to passengers generally.
Why trip time reliability and crowding factors can influence MTR passenger choice? Other problem is MTR busy (peak) time's crowding in public transportation occurrence of MTR underground train transportation tool is becoming a growth to concern as MTR demand growth at a busy (peak) time. To capture the MTR passengers benefits with reduced crowding from improved MTR public transport service and image. It is necessary a identify the relevant dimensions of crowding that are meaningful measures of what crowding means to MTR passengers. Two main influences on MTR model choice that are growing in relevance are trip time reliability and crowding. It represents a benefit-cost framework. In fact, MTR passengers can be willing to pay more expensive ticket fare, it MTR can avoid crowding and short and the accurate arrival trip time between terminals is reliable to occur. How to measure of MTR crowding, e.g. weighting the gap between the busy time, the standard (i.e. objective) and the perceived (i.e. subjective) metrics. We are not in a position to definitely map the two dimensions, which is a crucial requirement

for translating objective improvements into equivalent subjective gains that then can be applied, willingness to pay estimates MTR ticket fares to obtain the additional MTR passenger benefits of MTR public transportation investment to any terminal stations. Because MTR crowding has a negative impact on passengers in terms of psychological on emotional distress. MTR passengers are willing to stand for up to 20 minutes of the service is fast and reliable. However crowding outweighed these benefits from a MTR passenger's perpective, experienced crowding leads a increased dissatisfaction. e.g. stress and less privacy during who needs to stand up in MTR. Due to there are no enough places to supply to them to stand up in MTR. If the MTR trip time was longer time between the passenger's terminals, who will feel more dissatisfaction and it will cause who feels whether who ought need to choose to catch other transportation tools to substitute MTR next time. e.g. bus, train, tram, ferry, taxi etc. So, from an operator's perspective, the MTR service frequency or MTR size is significantly influenced by the level of ridership, which sends a signal to respond if the monitored crowding level exceeds the benchmark standard in the busy time. e.g. in the morning time or at the night time, the students or employment people who need to go to schools or offices (working places). The locations of different places between MTR terminals and crowding are regarded as a key service attribute for MTR pubic transportation along with other factors, such as travelling time and reliability, e.g. service quality, none engineering machines are broken to cause MTR stops suddenly.

Given the increasing importance of crowding on both the disutility to existing MTR public transportation users and the influence to it. MTR passenger can choose to use either the MTR public public transportation or other public transportation. It is timely to review the MTR current measures of crowding defined by transportation authorities. MTR operators ought evaluate whether they apporpriately reflect MTR each traveler experiences and perceptions of crowding in busy (peak) time. I suggest that MTR needs to buy other underground trains to supply to the busy (peak) time passengers to let them have enough seats to sit down, so who do not need to stand up in any MTR underground trains when they catch MTR underground trains in busy time. It aims to let who are willingness to pay the estimation of reasonable ticket fares to compare the other kinds of transportation tools in the busy (peak) time.

What is the crowding difference between train and MTR underground train? In fact, crowding won't be happened to brother these transportation tools easily in the busy time and non busy time both. e.g. bus, taxi, train, tram, ferry. Because passengers can not choose to stand up in these transportation tools easily, due to these transportation tools have no enough areas (spaces) to let them to stand up easily . So, the crowding will be avoided to occur in these tranportation tools usually. Otherwise, MTR will have many passengers who can choose to stand up because MTR design of length is very long and it has enough areas (places) to let passengers to choose to stand up, even there have none any seats are provided to let them to sit down. So, MTR passengers will feel more dissatisfaction and crowding easily, especial in any peak (busy) time every day.

Comparing to bus, much more diverse crowding measures are defined in the passenger rail industry. For passenger, different specifications for measuring crowding are found across countries and even within a country. For example, rail crowding measures in the UK, the passengers in excess of capacity is crowding measure that applies to all London and South east operators weekday train services at a London terminus during the morning peak from 0700 to 09: 59 , and those departing during the afternoon peak from 16:00 to 18:59 (office of rail regulation 2011 year). The overall PIXC figure is considered the planned standard class capacity of each train service as well as the actual number of standard class passengers on the service at the critical point. i.e. the location on a trains of standard class passengers that surpass the planned capacity as the difference between the number of actual passengers and the capacity of the train divided by the number of passenger is within the capacity . So, it seems train and MTR underground public transportaton tools had been encountering the crowding problems in peak time, the difference in train passengers need to wait next train or more train arrival is who doesn't plan to enter the train, when who discovers the current train has no seats to provide to them to sit down in whose trip. Otherwise, MTR passengers can choose either to stand up within the large areas (places) if who discovered there are no any seats to provide to them to sit down or who can wait the next MTR arrival in order to who can sit down. It seems MTR transportation tool crowding environment includes in waiting platform and inside of the MTR underground train. Otherwise, train transportation tool crowding environment only includes the waiting platform and the passengers will not have crowding feeling inside of the train, due to none of passengers choose to stand up inside any trains because any train inside has no enough places to let them to stand up.

How MTR can attract many passengers. On the commuter departure time choice of any reference point researching hand, the departure time decisions of communters are of fundamental importance of peak period MTR traffic congestion. However, whether on the demand side, MTR underground train congestion relief measures, such as MTR ticket fare to every terminal station needs to be charged cheaper fare or discount fare in the peak (busy) time every day. To aim to attract many passengers to choose to catch MTR Underground train public transportation tools, substitute to choose other public transportation tools in the peak time.

Over the past decades, there have been very active research efforts in the departure time problem, both in econometric modeling and dynamic user equilibrium fields. Although, these works provide valuable insights into dynamic commuter decision making, they do not identify the commuters' response to gains and losses related to whole actual arrival time to reference points who may have relative. The appliability of the reference point hypothesis of prospect theory to the commuter's departure time decision making to obtain a better understanding of how departure time choice in MTR platform during their waiting underground train arrival time. However, every MTR underground train actual arrival time and deviation variables related to reference points (gains and losses) are the key factors in the departure time choice model. How the MTR underground train of every commuter's daily departure time decision can be modelled when the reference point hypothesis of prospect theory. The MTR underground train's schedule delay is defined as the difference between the preferred arrival time (PAT) and the actual arrival time (AT) for a given MTR commuter. In a daily MTR commute, a commuter in the indifference band actual arrival time is an essential feature of MTR schedule study. Two reference points are the earliest acceptable arrival time and the work starting time for a given MTR platform waiting passengers. In psychological view point, prospect theory proposes that the displeasure of a loss is perceived or greater than the pleasure of a gain of the same attitude and therefore, the value function is stronger for losses than gains.

To conclude, it seems that if MTR waiting passengers need not spend long time to wait underground train arrival in platform and it can provide seats to let them to sit down in the busy (peak) crowding time. It will make them to feel pleasure, even the MTR ticket fare is not fair and reasonable to charge higher fare to compare other kinds of public transportation tools fares. So the peak waiting time factor can influence the passengers to choose other kind of transportation tools to catch easily. Moreover, MTR's two reference points are the earliest role. Similarly a loss is observed when the MTR platform waiting commuter experiences or actual arrival time which is beyond that the MTR schedule time. Due to that a MTR waiting commuter is as an early side arrival of whose actual arrival time is earlier than whose preferred arrival time.

Reference

Bailey, L., Mokhtarian, P.L. Little, A. (2008). The broader Connection Between Public Transportation, Energy Conservation And Greenhouse Gas Reduction, Report Prepared As Part Of TCRP Project J-11/Tasks Transit Cooperative Research Program, Transportation Research Board Submitted To American Public Transportation Association in http://www.apta.com/research/into/online/land_use.cfmi, accessed 17 April 2008.

The UK Standing Advisory Committee On Trunk Road Assessment (SACTRA) (1999). Transport And The Economy (Report To UK DETR). Retrieved From: http://webarchive.nationalarchives.gov.uk/20050301192906 ; http://dft.gov.uk/stellent/groups/dft-econappr/documents/pdf/dft_econappr_pdf_022512.pdf

Wikipedia Contributors (2008). Arterial Roads In Wikipedia, The Free Encycloupeda, http://en.wikipedia.org/w/index.php?title=Arterial_road&oldid=212832640(accessed May30,2008).

● How to let passengers feel impact of undergrouund train transport to their working time efficiency

Any countries must need road, sea and air transport to assist businessmen to transport products in local or overseas. If the country's road , sea or air transport system service quality is poor. It will influence any products transport time, speed, inefficient transport to anywhere.

How to raise the country's transport system in order to improve efficiencies to let any businessmen can deliver their products to anywhere easily,e.g. warehouses, client homes, supermarkets destination in the most short time to avoid delay occurrence to let clients feel unsatisfactory or complaint their perform their delivery services poorly. I shall discuss the factors how to improve any countrues' transport systems to achieve the most efficient way as below:

Any countries' transport systems will create economic value, e.g. demonstrate value for money, economic worth, viable commercial worth, financial affordable worth, achieveable worth. Any countries' transport systems can bring welfare value by economics. It has direct relationship to take the form of measured economic activity, i.e. GDP. The form of measured economic activity can impact on any countries' economic economic geography, locally , regionally and nationally's local GDP impacts. The welfare impacts may include: leisure time savings, e.g. the local people drive cars or catch any public transportation tools to go to any geogrpahical location's shopping centers, big gardens, swimming pools, cinemas etc. places to carry on any kinds of leisure activities.

Environmental impacts may include avoiding noise, air pollution on road transportation aspect , when the main road is only on on focus on the main city,

but the city lacks other roads to let any drivers can choose them to drive, instead of the main road in the city. Then, when many cars are driven on the busy transport

time, e.g. morning working time or night busy time between 6:00 and 9:00 AM, between 6:00 and 9:00 PM. When either many working people need to catch public transport or drive themselves cars to go to offices to work or they need to catch pubic transport tools or drive themselves cars to home. Then, the only one main road problem will need them to stay themselves cars on roads, due to traffic jam or traffic accidence occurrence problem causes when many cars are driven on the road in the busy transport time. It will influence they can not go to offices or homes easily daily, even in the busy transport time, their cars' gas need to be used much to cause air pollution and traffic noise is easily caused easily in the busy transport time on the road. When the city has only one main road for drivers in the busy transport time. So, poor road transport system can bring poor impact on economic welfare benefits arising from proved labour supply from commuting, time savings, including exchequer benefits. Consequently, the county's GDP will be fallen down, due to labour market effects which do not add to welfare value.

Whether can poor transport system impact indirectly on GDP or not on local, regional , or national economic geography impacts? Does transport lead to greater economic activity i.e. higher GDP? DO they lead to change in economic activity location? Does transport impact the existence of business location and new economic activity opportunities? The measurement on every country's transport how impacts on economic change, facilitating geographic division of labour and specialization. It can be analyzed on these general aspects:

Costs and speed of travel time (Economic value of travel time savings) . Travel time savings to users from improved transport is a key of economic value, but it has only less influence,journey time reliability is more important to business frieght as well as business travellers, network connectivity enhancements as well as business travellers, network connectivity enhancement can help people and goods travel more quickly (i.e. linked to jounrey time and journey time reliability, as well as opening new destinations and new journeys, comfort and quality service provision is relevant to public transport, e.g. detering jounreys at particular times or by certain modes (e.g. overcrowding), impact on productivity at work for commuters, safety and security , due to loss of output from workers, transport accidents occur easily. All of these issues will impact any countries' standard of living to local people (geography) , even GDP income.

Why does the direct and indirect effects of transportation have a positive impact on the economic growth and development of a country? Does it influence acccess to goods, services and

employment opportunities in any regions? Underdeveloped countries must need to consider how transport system influences their economic growth. For example, the costs of transportation and production are reduced through timely delivery and enhancing the economies of scale in the production process, when the road is often traffic joam, gas cost, time waste , air pollution cost, noise has many roads, but if one lorry drivers needs drive more than one day to day to deliver goods to another city's warehouse every day. It will bring psychological pressure in terrible, when they need long time to drive on the road. They can not sleep easily because road accident will occur easily when they need to spend long time to drive lorries on the road.

So, how to solve the long driving time on road transport problem will be one issue concerns human life welfare benefit aspect, instead of economic benefit aspect. The transport system welfare worth needs to include human life worth. It is a valuable insight into the causality (ot lack of causality) between transport and economic growth and will serve to compare to any countries' national level and local geographical location level both.

In special, underdeveloped countries' public transport time whether it is long or short factor, it will influence workers their going to offices to work time. If they often need spend long time to catch buses, due to traffic jam,then it will influence their efficiences to be reduced, productive number is influenced to reduce also, because traffic jam causes they often go to offices too lately.It can influence workers' bad emotion to work every day. So, traffic jam will bring negative relationship between low efficiency and bad emotion to the workers, because they need to spend long time to wait, public transportation tools and traffic jam also influence their working emotion. Consequently, service and working performance will be influenced to poor, because long time traffic jam problem causes their bad emotion to work. It is one critical factor in the path of more widely spread economic growth and urbanization for traffic jam problem to underdeveloped countries.

However, transport system can also influence developed countries' economy. How does it influence on environmental impacts aspect from mature stage. Its business activities must raise, dramastic expansion during this period, such as underdeveloped country, US, UK. In order to acheive long term sustainable development , new demands are being placed on transport sector, such as underground mass transit rail transport , ferry, local air frieght transport, train , e.g. Japan, Fance, US high speed prior rail. Because their developed countries , business and entertainment activities needs increase, it influences high time efficient and rapid speed public transportation tools needs are also needed in societies. These new technological public transport tools invention will impact on climate, noise, human health, land use and damage to ozene layer, acidification aspects, instead of economic beneficial aspect.

For long -term sustainable development to be achieved, the various activities within developed and underdeveloped societies must be adapted to what can be tolerated by humans and by the natural environment. Transport is an activity which affects humans and the natural environment for both the development of society as a whole as well as for the mobility for the individual. For Swedish underdeveloped country example, air pollution in Swedish urban areas has beed reduced, but in many places concentrations of certain substances deiving from transport activities are still at unacceptable levels and much more has to be done. Carbon dioxide emissions and noise are examples of environmental problems demanding further efforts. Measures to limit the exploitation of valuable natural and cultural environments to protect biological diviersity are also needed. So, if Swedish still hopes to develop its tourism industry to attract many travellers to choose to travel itself country. It needs to solve environmental problems from different modes of transport are of different dimensions, such as improving its air transport to avoid cause different problems and rail transport differs in turn from road transport.

The transport problem to Swedish may include poor technological communication information to its public and purchasers of transportation and communication services as to the environmental effects of different solutions is significant in creating the demand for environmentally sound public transport service concepts. It is therefore important that such lacking high technological communication and information system is presented in as completem accurate and clear way as a method for non-monetary comparison of the environmental public transport service system aspect.

In real, it's public tranport service system is needed to be improved and upgraded in order to let travellers feel Swedish's any rail, underground train, ferry, bus , taxi etc. different public transport travelling service can provide excellent performance to serve their travelling passengers, when they need to catch any kinds of public transport tools to go to travel. They can feel convenient and comfortable to attract them to visit Swedish to travel again. Then, its tourism industry GDP income will be raised, if Swedish government can innovate any new kinds of purchase ticket equipment to install in and public transport stations to let travelling passengers feel that they do not need to spend long time to queue to buy tickets to catch ferry, train, underground mass transit rail on stations conveniently. Because long time purchase ticket queue waiting will cause travellers feel its public service performance dissatisfaction and they will complain , even they won't choose to catch the kind of public transport, even the travellers won't choose to travel Swedish again, if they feel Swedish is one developed country, but it neglects to take care about travellers' catching public transport travelling service needs.

It is one poor or bad feeing to let travellers choose to Swedish again. Hence, Swedish needs to improve its public transport service performance in order to achieve to raise their comfortable and satisfactory catching public transport tools needs to let travellers to feel. They may include efficient land use for transportation tools, comprising issues concerning natural and cultural environment, natural resources, biological diversity and aesthetics, noise reducing, public transportation energy consumption and time consumption reducing, raising public transport service facilities performance functions and other issues concerning the model. For example, Swedish government can facilitate the public transport price conparison and journey time spending comparison information gathering enquiring machines public transportation selection method of public transportation services to let every travellers can evaluate different modes of public transport when they are staying in ferry, bus, train, underground mass transit rail, taxi stations.

A travelling family can seek its sustainable transport selection system for passenger transport tool. When they touch the enquiry machine, they can compare busm ferry, train, underground train, taxi price and journey spending time from their transportation stations to another destinations. Then, travelling passengers can compare these public transport tools ticket prices, journey spending time immediately when they touch the public transport enquiring machines in stations any time. Then, they can make the most righ choice to decide whether they ought catch which kind of public transport tool to arrive the another journey destination. It is one every attractive high technological enquiry method to help any travelling passegners to choose which kind of public transport tool, it can be the most cheap transport tool at the moment in any public transport stations. So , for developed countries innovative its public transport service performance will need future passengers' journey needs daily. Hence, they can not neglect how to improve public transport service needs to satisfy passengers to feel satisfaction, if Sweden government hopes its tourism industry can raise GDP income in long time.

● How underground train MTR can let passengers to feel catching time reducing

It has close relationship between globalization and global tranport development. How globalisation impacts on the environment via changes taking place in the transport sectors. In fact, it is not clear how the relative price changes that result from openness will affect the environental composition of economic activity. For example, some countries will produce more environmentally intensive goods, others will produce fewer. On the other hand, liberalisation will raise incomes, perhaps increasing the willingness to pay for environmental improvement. These potential income effects increased outweigh the negative scale effects with increased economic activities. When combined with the positive effects with technology transfer, the net effect on local pollutants could be positive . Hence, we need to find methods to solve the problem of raising transport economic activities and serious environmental pollution creating as the same time occurrence.

Globalisation helps to facilitate greater division of labor, and to exploit its comparative advantage more completely. In longer term, globalization also stimilates technology an dlabour transfers, and allows the dynamism that accompanies economic activities to stimulate the development of new transport technologies and short time transport processes that lead to global welfare improvement.

On shipping transport industry aspect, shipping will increase ocean pollution, when international shipping activities are increasing. Trade and shipping encourages energy use in shipping is coupled with the movement of waterborne commerce. The estimates depending on the transport goods number of at-sea or in port days much increase globally every day. The energy demand of international shipping fuel sale number and domestically assigned fuel sales number also increases for global fuel usage. Estimates of ocean going ships now consume about 2% to 3% and perhaps even as much as 4% of world fossil fuels.Hence, when global shipping energy fuel usage number increases, because global shipping trading activities number increases. It will bring the environmental pollution to ocean level increases. On air transport industry aspect, their travellers' catching air plans travelling needs and businesses' goods transport air delivery service needs are increasing from the requirements for high quality , fast and reliable international transport. Moreover, the networks that airline companies operate have changed often to hub-and spoke networks, many new often low -cost companies have entered the air freight market, any long time air journey is needed, e.g.

Australia airline expands its one new air journey flies to UK, it needs two days flying time. It means that every flight to UK from Australia , it needs to use more fuel to fly. Then , air pollution will increase also.

On road transport industry aspect, global road transport cost and transit times, traffic jam occurrence chances also increase because when the road building number is increasing globally. So, it will cause traffic jam and long journey time spending , even fuel usage spending number is also increased. Then, accident occurrence chance is raised. Hence, global business or entertainment transport activities number increasing , it will bring much negative impact on environmental pollution, traffic jams number increases, long journey spending time increases, fuel usage number increases. Although , frequent transport activities may bring GDP income.

On transport service industy aspect, but is also brings negative influence to standard of living. It means that when transport fuel demand increases, transport activities number increases, GDP income on relative any transport activities needs industy , e.g. logistic demand needs, when lorry drivers need to drive lorries to deliver goods from one warehouse to another warehouse or supermarket or office etc. different business places on the road driving activities increase. But, it also bring air pollution , traffic noise and traffic jam etc. transport problems to road and natural environment and raises worse standard of living , bad emotion to working people or learning emotion to students , due to frequent traffic jam causes , low efficiency and productivity to workers, even student individual learning time can be reduced if they need to spend long time to wait bus, ferry, rail, underground train to go to schools , due to frequent long time traffic jam occurs on the roads to influence they can not go to schools on time often when they are catching buses to go to schools absolutely in busy transport time.

Thus, although any countries need to consider how to design their transport system, e.g. how to e.g. how to choose the right locations to build roads to let many cars can be driven available easily when the morning and evening (office and school transport busy time, e.g. 6:00 to 9:00 AM morning, 6:00 to 9:00 PM in the evening transport time usually because these two transport periods are usually , there are many students and working people need to catch any public transportation or drive cars tools to go back homes. So, enough roads number and long and not narrow road area must be needed to design in order to let enough cars be driven on the roads in the transport busy times to the countries have many big cities or have high population , such as UK, US, China, India, Hong Kong. They have many people , but drivers and cars numbers both are increasing. So, efficient road design and road number are also needed to increase in order to let drivers can transport goods to deliver, students and working people can catch any public transport tools to arrive any destinations on reads in the short time rapidly in order to avoid to spend long time transportation time and late to arrive any destinations in possible occurrence. So, any sudden traffic jam is not hoped to be caused by easy traffic accidents occurrence any time.

Hence, global efficient road transport system is needed, when global transport activities are increased, because any road logistic transport activities are increasing, they will also influence the students and working people when they also need to catch any public transport tools or drive themselves cars to go to working places or schools on the roads at the same busy transport time between 6:00 to 9:00 AM morning busy transport time and between 6:00 to 9:00 PM evening busy transport time. Because these both times will be have many students, working people , they need either go to offices or schools or go to homes. Hence, if the country had many lorry drivers need to drive their lorries to deliver goods on the roads in the transport busy morning or evening time in the same driving time on the roads. It will increase the risk to cause frequent traffic jam or traffic accident occurrence easily in possible in the country. So, any countries' governments can not neglect how to design roads and choose anywhere are the roads suitable locations to be built as well as anywhere land useful number to build road location choices in order to solve geographical traffic jams occurrence chance.

Hence, globalization of transport activities may bring geographical GDP growth, but it also bring traffic jams and traffic accidents occurrences, hearing impairment due to traffic noise, air pollution, traffic crashed, bad working emotions to workers and bad learning emotions to students, due to spending long transport time when traffic jam or traffic accidence occurs more easily.

However, transportation is an important tool if a country's progress. Rapid economic growth and increasing level of urbanization enhances a person's living standard have, it leads to a greater travel demands. Hence, governments ought not neglect have to design its roads , measure every road's length or width whether it has how many cars need to drive in morning or evening transport busy time for students, working people and delivery goods drivers of public transportation tools or private transportation tools easy driving needs in order to avoid frequent traffic jams or traffic accidents occurrences in possible.

Moreover, any governments also need to solve these issues, if they hope to develop their transport system successfully. These issues include : What mode of transportation to cost-effective in meeting a region's transportation needs to the country? How should a state department of transportation prioritize its highway delivers to maximize economic growth? What is the trade-off between additional growth in urban area and the cost of expanding transportation systems to accommodate greater growth? What effect does the expansion of transportation systems have on the need to invest in other types of transport modes? For example , the transport expansion may include the construction of additional highway segments, rail lines, runways, or additional sea, air, rail or bus terminal capacity using traditional technology; highway may include the additional of lanes to an interstate highway system; the conversion of an existing two-lane road to a four lane limited access highway, replacement or widening of bridges, and the extension of an existing road. Airport examples, include runway lengthening, apron expansion, and additional terminal gates.

On the other hand, enhancement to new transport technologies may bring efficiency of the existing highway system, examples may include intelligent highway systems, congestion pricing, intermodal freight facilities, geographic positioning systems, and instrument landing systems to mention of a few major transport innovations. So, transport policy makers need to understand the effects of these new transport mode innovations on economic development or GDP growth on transport activities growth transportation services and a more efficient use of limited land supplying scarce resources , air quality ,and noise pollution, traffic jams, long spending transport time to students, working people, entertaining people, even deliver goods lorry drivers their every day essential driving activities or catching public transportation tools needs problems. For example, the concept of intelligent highway systems needs increase trend. In simply , vehicles are being linked to each other and to traffic control devices to improve the efficiency of the total highway system. Similar types of innovations in intelligent traffic management are increasing needs for air, sea, and rail systems. The question is that whether intelligent highway systems can attribute of highways on economic development, raising on productivity of reducing highway congestion or improving pavement condition.

In fact, many developed countries' transportation system is mature. The nation has gone beyond the frontier of building, the interstate highway system and connecting most cities (markets). Tweaking the system with additional lanes and the new intelligent highway systems are useful in China, US, UK, because they have many cities. SO, road efficient traffic congestion control is needed when many students, working people, delivery goods transport people need to drive cars or catch cars on every city's roads in the transport busy time between 6:00 to 9:00 AM morning transport busy time as well as between 6:00 to 9:00 PM evening transport busy time.

However, transportation investment must be needed, if the country hoped to have good economic productivity, efficient transport service can bring good effects on the flows goods and people on roads every day when they use the country's transport system. So, any countries need to collect data, they can not be lack of enough transport information in any time that links anywhere locations of any drivers to the locations of the transport system that provide them with services in any time, e.g. every day morning and evening transport busy time, radio can report the real transport time of any roads traffic jam or traffic accident message to let drivers to listen to know whether anywhere roads are occurring traffic accidents or traffic jams or when the road traffic accident or traffic jam is solved to let the drivers can know whether when the roads can be opened to drive again. So, real time road transport message information is needed to report by radio, in order to let any drivers to know whether they ought choose to drive themselves cars on the road when they need to choose anywhere road to drive to the destination if they can know when the road has traffic accident or traffic jam occurs. They won't drive their cars on the road in the moment immediately.

On conclusion, globalization can being frequent transport economic activities. So, road , air, sea, transport service users' transport service needs are also increased. Every country ought not neglect how to innovate their transport service in order to satisfy their transport needs to achieve economic growth, efficient and short transport time spending, productivities increase, reducing air pollution, traffic noise , raisins standard of living on transport influence aspect to satisfy working people, students, entertaining people, delivery goods transport users' efficient road transport time behavioral spending aspect.

VIII

How human behavior influences social changes

Human Behavioral network job brings social economic benefits

What does human network job mean ? Why may human network job be popular? Why human network job behavior may influence economy ?

Nowadays internet is popular to use. We can apply internet to find data , search any new things, even earn money. Why does internet

may become huma network job source. For example, e-publish may be one kind of new human network job. Any authors may apply internet

channel to help them to sell electronic or paper books from e-publisher web store. They may apply facebook, you tub etc. any online

channel to promote themselves new books to let new readers to know whether when they may buy themselves favourable new topic books to read

from electronic publisher web store.

Thus, future electronic publisher industry may help any authors to build internet network platform to help them to sell and promote

ot advertise their any one new electronic or paper book topic to let global any one reader to choose to buy their any new topic books from electronic publisher web store easily and conveniently. However, it implies that electronic network platform author may be one kind of future new human network job in our societies.

How electronic network platform author job may bring economy benefit in macro economy view? A person can have few friends, contacts and still be very influential if these few

friends and contacts are themselves highly influential, e.g. one author must not need to know any one reader in global society. When they like to choose any electronic books from electronic internet network platform. They may become the author's any one topic book buyer, when they feel the author's any one topic book is fun and attract they make decision to buth the strange author whose the topic book from electronic book publisher's platform web store conveniently in short time. Although, they are strangers, they do not know themselves , but the reader can understand what it way that made Google from writing platofrm to create new creative mind and typing network job method to replace traditional hand writing book method for global authors. It will be one kind of new human network writing job.

Hence, global any one reader can apply an innovative search engine , such as google.com to find whether whom author personal new topic books are value to read from internet.

Then, the electroniuc publisher's web store may be new book store platform sale network to help the author to sell

many electronic or paper books from electronic network platform
in short time. So, internet may be future new network plaform to help global any one author to create network writing job absolutely. Furthermore, internet may be popular social media
to help any one author to build goold relationship between his/her readers. It is one kind of new network, human network job. New authors do not need to buy many paper books to prepare to put in any one book shop warehouse. Their every book can print on demand to reduce out of book stock in any one book shop. They may choose to sell either electronic books or paper books both from any one book publisher web store. So, electronic network platform may be one kind of good writing channel to help human authors to create income and it can also help authors to bring new creative mind and new topic fun content books to let readers to know and buy to read from electronic publisher network platform.

Why does human behavior may be one kind of new human network job to bring global economic advantages. ALthough, it may be free income or without inocme, but the person does the network behavior, his/her behavior may be bring advantages to influence many other people's health. For this case, when a worker in a coffee shop in an airport gets a vaccination aganinst the flu, it does not only helps him or her stay healthy, but also helps the many travellers who might otherwise have been inflected if that workers caught the flu. So, the externality , the result implies the vaccination of even a part of a community conveys benefits to the whole community. For example, governments pay special attention to the vaccinations of school children, teachers, health mothers, and the elderly, categories of people particularly susceptible not only to catching, but also to transmitting a disease.

It is not accidental that governments are heavily involved with vaccination . When there are externalities, free market, fail to persuade individual incentives with society's
their the worker's decision of whether to get a vaccine ends up attracting whether other people get sick. The workers might not fully take all these other people's potential suffering into account when making her or his vaccination decision.

As Stanford University does many suggestions, understand this and tries to help them make the right decisions and so providers free flu vaccines for its staff and students.
Small pockets of unvaccinated individuals can allow a disease to gain a spread more widely well-being. For example, parent weighing the costs and benefits of a vaccine for their child is not always thinking of the consequences of that vaccination to other people. THese are markets in which subsidizing or regulating behavior can make everyone better off. Because the reason for requiring that a child be vaccinated before enrolling in school is not just to protect that child, because each child's vaccination affects others via potential contagions.

Robots take our jobs behavioral and economy influences

Robot job behavior brings economy influences

If one day robots can replace human to do simple, even complex jobs. They will bring what influences to our global societial economy.The popular economic refrain declares that the
global middle class is dying and robots will soon take our jobs, e.g. shopping center customer service jobs, library service jobs, cinema ticket sale jobs, restaurant kitchen cooker jobs,
even, bus drivers, taxi drivers etc. public transport driving jobs, accountant, doctors etc. professional jobs. Whether it is beautiful or petty matter if our future societies have many human jobs can be replaced to do from robots. Businessman must may reduce to employ employees and reduce to pay salary or wage, when robots can be replaced to do their employees tasks. But, societies must bring unemployement rate rises , due to societies will have many people loss jobs when their employers choose to buy robots to serve their clients or do any office tasks or customer service or cleaning etc. tasks.

In micro economy view, employers may save money in long term, but in macro economy view, it will cause unemployment ratio rises , even crime rate rises when there are many people lose
jobs in societies. These models of doom, though, fail to account for the hundreds of businesses riding the waves of change in their industries when robots may be invented to replace human to do many simple , even complex tasks in our future societies.

WE may image that one small factory needs to manufacture fishes canes to sell to supermarket, the small , cheaper stuff and higher margin parts of the fishes manufacture industry. Before, this factory needs to employe many human factory workers need to help every fresh customer makeing the perfect fishing gear, designed for performance, durability, and cost in order to achieve to manufacture every fish cane in whole fished processing manufacturing stages. Every worker needs to spend about 15 to twenty minutes to finish every fish cane , till to delivery to any supermarket to sell. If this fish canes manufacturing factory can apply manufacturing robots to help them to finish any one working tasks , every robot can only spend five minutes to finish whole fresh fish cane manufacturing process. Thus, every robot can

help this factory save 10 to 15 minutes time to finsh every fish cane manufacturing process. IN fact, time is money, because when every robot can help this factory to reduce 10 to 15 minutes time to compare human worker. Then, this factory can finish about 20 fish canes in one hour if it can use robot to help it to manufacture fish canes. Otherwise, if this factory still use human workers to help it to manufacture fish canes, then it can finsh about 3 to 4 fish canes in one hour. SO, the manufacturing efficiency ensures that robots must help this fish manufacturing factory to raise fish canes number more than human workers. So, in robotic behavioral economy view, manufacturing robots must help this fish canes manufacturing factory to raise fish canes manufacturing number and deliver increasing number to supermarkets to prepare to sell every day. Robots can help this fish canes manufacturing factory bring manufacturing time saving, rising manufacturing efficiency, improving performance and reducing wages expenditure long time advantages in micro economy view. However, manufacturing robots can also bring disadvanages to society, e.g. increasing unemployment ratio, increasing crime rate,

this factory workers will lose jobs and income, they need earn social welfare from government and increasing government finance pressure in short time, even long time in macro economic view.

Stanford University graduate program in economics, Scott lecturer explained that "in demand and supply economic theory for robots supply and demand case, robots supply number increasing may influence human workers demand number decrease. It sometimes calls " the efficient frontier".

No specific human beings were mentioned in any of economics classes. As robots supply and demand in market case, They (robots) may be purely theoretical "agents" who reached to the most reasonable sale prices in order to persuade any one businessman buyer to make manufacturing robot buying decision whether robots can help him / her to bring how much saving time , saving money, saving cost, improving performance, efficiency economic benefit before he/she plans to reduce workers number when he/she decides to apply robots to replace human workers in his/her factory or office or any service department, e.g. cinema ticket sale service, shopping center customer service, shopping center cleaning , supermarket customer service etc. service or sale tasks. When robots can replace human to do any one of these tasks in any organizations. So, robots may be human worker agents who reached to prices the way robots would react to a software

command. There was nothing that explained why some people thrived and others did n't or why truly brilliant, hardworking people could fail when much lazier folks succeeded." Having been admitted to the Stanford University graduate program in economics, Scott lecturer hoped to get his answers there.

How robots influence our future social changing? Using the right technology can be a boon to your business in this economy. For internet example, it is easier than ever to find well-matched customers all around the world, to stay in contact with them, and to more quickly design the products they want. If you focus solely on being cutting -edge, though you risk letting the technology

take over what should be very robust relationships with your customers , employees, and colleagues. IN nowaddays society, technoligical advances and cutomation, personal

relationships in business are more crucial than ever. I mean that robots can not replace human to serve clients to let them to feel more comfortable and passion more easily. For shoe shop case example, if the shoe shop apply one robot to serve its clients to replace human shoe salesperson to serve its shoe customers. Robots ensure that they can not persuade every shoe potential buyer to make shoe buying decision more easily when robots need to contact every shoe potential buyer. The reason is simple, because robots can not touch any one shoe buyer individual emotion very easier.

If the shoe buyer needs the robots to help him/her to choose any right shoe styles when he/she can not feel himself / herself can make the most right shoe style choice decision. The robots can not replace human shoe salesperson to make shoe style choice judgement more easily. They must need longer time to analyze whether which shoe style may be the most suitable to the shoe buyer. Otherwise, human shoe salesperson may attempt to make the most right shoe style choice decision to help any one shoe buyer to chooce the most right style shoe because he/she owns shoe style sale experience, shoe style knowledge, the most important reason is that they can feel every shoe customer individual emotion to touch whether he/she will feel comfortable or happy when they attempt to help every shoe customer to seek the most right shoe style in every shoe customer whole shoe searching processing. Othwerwise, serving robots are only one machine, they can not touch or feel every shoe customer individual emotion whether he/she feel comfortable or unhappy or happy when they need to contact them in whole shoe searching processing. Hence, I believe that some tasks robots can

not repalce human staff to do very easily. Otherwise, robots may bring disadvanatges to let any one businessman to loss his/her customers, due to robots can not touch every customer

emotion to compare human staff in service tasks more easily. Robots serving customer behaviors may cause money lose and customers number lose to the shop in micro economic view.

Intellectual human economic behaviors

What does intellectual human economic behaviors mean ? I believe that when we choose or decide to do intellectual behaviors, then our societies will be influenced to bring economic growth in consequence.I shall attempt to indicate pollution case to explain how and why eithet our intellectual or foolish behaviors may bring economic growth or recession in consequence as below:

On one hand, for air pollution social case aspect example, if we only consider to buy cars to drive for working aimr or holiday leisure aim. Then, our societies air will be polluted. Our health will be influenced to bad. Our car driving behaviors may cause global environment air pollution serously. In long tiem, global air pollution will bring our bodies health to be bad. Although, ourselves car driving behaviors may bring our driving travelling leisure enjoyment and comfortable feeling in short time, also we so not need to pay public transport fare often, but we need to compensate ourselves health economic intangible loss due to air pollution , when cars number increases, dirty air will cause ouselves health to become bad.

In the result, we will need to pay more medical expenditure when we are old age, due to ourselves bodies will become bad, due to we breathe global dirty air every day, due to ourselves cars pollute air in long time, e.g. 10 to 20 years, even 30 more without limited air pollution environment. So, driving cars behavior may be one kind of human foolish behavior and our foolish behavior may bring ourselves future long time medical expenditure absolutely.

One the other hand, water pollution social aspect, if we often keep much rubblish to pollute sea, oil exploration porcessing pollute ocean , ships gas pollute ocaen, then fishes will eat polluted food and drive dirty water, due to global ocean is polluted.

In fact, because human only to conside how to buy boats to carry on leisure enjoyment activities, or catch cruises to travel on the sea. Also, oil manufacturers only consider researching anywhere to find new oil exploration places to manufacture oil product, when their oil exploration processes pollute ocarn . Consequently, global fishes drink polluted warer or eat polluted food. They will have poison. SO, human will have high chance to eat poison polluted fishes, due to fishes are poison or are polluted.

So, human is doing foolish activities, we only hope to find oil exploration places to pollute ocean or we only spend money to buy ticket to catch ships to travel anywhere in global ocean. All of these human foolish behaviors will bring pollution to global ocean. On consequently, we will need to compensate to eat polluted or dirty or poision fishes, ourselves bodies health will be bad. In long time, we need have high chance to pay medical expenditure when we are old. So, pollution case may be one good example to explain how and why human foolish behavior may influence ourselves future need to compensate serious medical loss.

All of these human foolish behavior will bring pollution to global ocean. On consequently, we will need to compensate to eat polluted or dirty or poison fished , ourselves bodies health will be bad. In long time, we will have high chance to pay medical expenditure, when we are old. So, pollution case may be one good example to explain how and why human ourselves intellectual or foolish behaviors may influence future long time economic loss or economic growth or recession in micro and micro economic view.

On another water pollution aspect hand, if we often keep rubbish to sea, oil exploration processing pollutes ocean and ships' gas pollute ocean, then fishes will eat polluted food and drink dirty water, due to fishes will eat polluted food and drink dirty sea water because the global ocean is polluted seriously.

In fact, because human only consider how to buy boats to carry on any leisure water activities, or catches cruises to travel on the sea. Also, oil manufacturers only consider any where to find oil exploratin places to manufacture oil products from ocean, when their pol exploration processes can plooute ocean. Consequently, global fishes drink polluted water or eat direty food. They will have poison. So, human will have high chance to eat poison fishes.

Otherwise, such as pollutin case, it can infuence inflation or deflation. Consequently, the reason indicates supply and demand theory. If air pollution is serious, then we will consider health issue, global cars demand number may be influenced to reduce, when global cars number demand will reduce, global car prices and supply number will need to change to fall down in order to attract or persuade global car consumers choose to make car purchase decision.

Hence, global car manufacture number and car price will be influenced to reduce, due to global air pollution issue. Consequently, deflation will occur because when the country citizen usually does not spend much extra saving money to buy car expensive goods. Money value will be low. Otherwise, if global cair pollution is not serious, human considers to buy cars to enjoy driving leisure lives. So, global car demand is influenced to increase , also global car price will also influenced to increase.

Consequently, gobal human will choose to buy cars to drive. Due to we accept to spend extra saving to buy expensive car goods. Car sale price and supply may be influenced to rise up. Money value is influenced to reduce. Inflation may be influenced, due to global car consumers number increases, we would not have extra money to spend easily. Car expensive goods expenditure influences our spending habit to avoid to make car purchase decision more easily. So, human intellectual or foolish activities may bring inflation or deflation consequency in possible indirectly in macro economic view.

On conclusion, above pollution case explain that how and why human intellectual or foolish economic behaviors may bring inflation or deflation consequency as wll as economic growth or recession consequency as well as any goods demand and supply increasing or decreasing consequency. It implies that human behavior may have indirect relationship to influence any goods demand and supply number to either increase or decrease result as well as any goods price will be influenced to increase or decrease in micro and macro economic view.

The relationship between social change and human behavior

Why does economic changes may influence human individual behavioral change? I shall attempt to indicate shopping behavior and staying at home behavior to explain their case and effect relationsip as below:

Human behavior can be influenced by economic change or economic change can be influenced by human behavior? Why does recession may influence consumers reduce shopping desire? In social recession suitation, it is possible that many people lose jobs suddenly, due to businessmen lose many customers. They need to make decision to reduce employees number in order to continue to keep businesses. Consequently, many firms (organizations) their employees may lose jobs. When they have much time, due to lose jobs, they will feel to avoid to spend too much time and money to go to shopping often. Many losing jobs people, they will often stay at homes.

So, they will reduce time to go to shopping, then non essential products won't their preferable choice purchase products. Hence, recession will change many losing jobs people their shopping or consumption desires to avoid to buy non essential products often . Usually when economic boom, many people have jobs to do because consumers number must increase when many people have jobs to do. Then, many people can accept to spend money to buy non essential products often. Many people feel spend time to go to shopping can satisfy their purchase of any kinds of new products useful psychology or desire. So, recession is one good example to explain it can influence many people do not like often to leave homes to go to shopping easily. Many people like to stay at homes, becaue they feel worry about spending too much shopping time when they leave homes. Their staying home time is one good negative shopping behavior example. So, economic change may influence human individual behavior changes , they have direct cause and efect relationship in behavioral economic view.

May human behavior influence economic change? Is it possible that human behavior may bring the country social economic change in macro economic or micro behavioral economic view ? I shall indicate publishing industry example. Do you feel that if there are many students feel learning is very important when they read many books or many of students feel interesting to read or they have reading new books in habit, then it is possible that the country will have many students like to spend time to go to any book shops to choose the books, they feel that they can help they learn new knowledge. Then the country will increase students number, they often spend time to visit any one book shop every week. Their visiting book shops behavior which may become their habits. So, the country will increase students number, they often spend time to visit book shops. Also, it implies that visiting book shops behaviors may be their behavioral habits.

So, when the country has many students often spend time to visit book shops , their visiting book shops behaviors may help any one book shop to raise books sale chance. So, the country's student individual often visiting book shop behaviors, their habitual visiting book shops behaviors must may assist help any one book shop to increase books sale number absolutely.

Consequently, any one book shop , its books sale bumber must be influenced to increase to increase because the country will have many students like or feel need visit book shops habit in order to choose any suitable books to buy to read at home in order to raise themselves learning effort. When the country has many bok shops often have many students visit their book shops, then their books sale number may be influenced to increase. It explain why student individual visiting book shop behavior may help any one book shop sale number increases also.

How human productive behavior may influence economic development

May any country which citizen behavior assist themselves country development? It is one cause and effect economic question. I mean that if the country itself citicen can not concentrate mind or energy to choose to do one kind of industry in order to let themselves country can bring the most benefit, then whether the counry itself economy can bring the most serious economic benefit. I shall attempt to indicate these countries themselves indistry choice to explain whether these countries themselves citizen productive behavior may help themselves countries to achieve the largest economic benefits. I shall indicate as below:

New Zealand farmer individual wine productive behavior

For New Zealand country example, this country concerns itself effort is foucs on farming agricultural aspect. So, this country has many farmers concentrate on farming agricultural aspect. May New Zealanders choose to spend time to produce different kinds of wines, e.g. wine or red grape wine is for the people are eating meat, or they are eating dinner.

When these New Zealanders their behaviors choose to do farming or agriculture to grow and produce different kinds of taste of white or red grape wine drinking products job. Themselves grape agriculture behavior will influence these New Zealanders themselves, they can learn how to improve different kinds of grape wine drinking products in order to achieve every kinds of white or read grape wines taste improving aim during their white or red grape producing process.

Why can New Zealander every individual white or read grape wine producers improve their white or read grape wine taste more easily? In behavioral economic view, it can explain that why any one New Zealander white or read grape wine producer can be encouraged or excited or persuaded to concentrate nervous and energy and effort to learn how to improve their white or red grape wine products easily.

In fact, New Zealand is one agricultural food export country. It has good natural environment resource , e.g. land, seed to provide any one farmer to produce themselves any kinds of agricultrual food products, e.g. fruit, or wine food products. Because New Zealanders know themselves country has enough natural resource . So, in common, many New Zealanders choose to attempt to do farming agricultural jobs in order to export themselves any kinds of fruit or meat or wine products to overseas or sell to domestic in order to earn profit.

So, when these New Zealand farmers number has been increasing every year. This country farmers will feel themsleves competition between this New Zealand farmers themselves are serious due to they may feel New Zealanders choose to do agriculture businesses in order to export themselves different kinds of farming food to overseas or sell to local to earn profit.

Hence, when many New Zealand farmers feel that farmers number has been increasing every year. They will feel themselves competition is serious. They must need to spend much time and nervous and effort to research what method is the best how to produce the best taste of white or red grape wine products in order to let local or overseas wine buyers to choose to buy his/her producing white or read grpae products to drink.

Hence, in competition psychological view, may influence many New Zealand white or reaad wine producers had been beginning to change their learning behavior on researching what method is the best in order to produce the best quality of taste red or white wine products to sell in order to attract overseas or local white or read grape wine drinkers to choose to buy his/her wine products. Their behavior will focus on learning how to raising or improving white or read grape wine taste method more than only focus on producing a large number white or red grape wine products. They believe wine quality is more important to compare wine producing number. So, New Zealand wine producers themselves wine producers behaviors have been changing on concentrating on researching wine quality method aspect more then wine producing number aspect in behavioral economic view.

America high technological productive behavior

For America example, US is one high technological country, it owns many high technological knowledge talent inventors, e.g. computer science inventors. Hence, US must attract many diferent countries owning high technological computer inventors choose to go to US to develop their computer science profession career. Also, it seems that when many computer science inventors or professions choose to go to US to develop themselves computer science new career. In behavioral economic view, due to their leaving themselves countries choice, which may bring influence themselve country job behaviors need to be changed. They must need to adapt US new live. Because they will forgive their past computer science job. These computer science professionals need to spend time to adapt US new lives. They " past computer science job behaviors" will need to be changed to their new US any computer employer's new computer science job model.

Because their traditional computer science jobs needed to be forgot in their themselves countries. They will feel their old computer science job knowledge and behavior needed to change in order to let their US any one new of computer company employer feels satisfactory to accept their new working behavior in any one US computer organization.

So, on the other hand, many US computer company employer will feel that they must need time to accept any one new overseas computer science professions their working behaviors, their working attitude daily, because these foreign comouter science professional, their past computer working behaviors and working attitude must be different to US domestic computer science professions.

In behavioral economic view, these overseas computer science professions, their working behaviors and attitude must be needed to change in order to adapt any one US new computer company itself domestic or local computer science professional stafs themselves daily working behaviors and attitude because these overseas and local computer science professionals must need to team work together.

In behavioral economic view, it is only one way that foreign computer science professionals must need to change themselves past country traditiona daily working behaviors and attitude in order to cooperate with these US local computer science professionals in teams more easily.

Consequently, if these foreign compute science professionals can change their past working behaviors and attitude to let any one US local computer science professional feels to cooperate with them easily in short time. Then, the US computer company itself whole computer professional teams themselves efficiencies will be influenced to raised or improved by the changing past working attitude and working behaviors of these foreign computer science professionals. So, in behavioral economic view, only if US any one computer company hopes itself computer teams themselves efficiency can be raised or improved when it decides to employ foreign computer science professionals and US domestic computer science professionals. They need to work in teams together. They must need to let these foreign computer science professionals to know how to change their working behaviors and attitude to let their domestic computer science professionals feel easy to work together. Then, the US computer company itself whole team efficiency must be rasied or improved easily in short time.

● China share market investing behavior

For China share market example, economic development depends on financial market. Because if many Chinese have interest to invest to carry on shares buying and selling activities in orde to learn how to earn shares interest and share profit when the China shareholder can make decision to sell himself/herself shares in the the high price, then he/she can earn money when he/she can sell the China company's shares in the high sale share price position.

If China has many Chinese like to spend time to carry on investing shares activities. Themselves shares buying and selling behaviors will influence China has many companies can increase fund from many Chinese shareholders in order to have enough money to expand or develop themselves businesses in China in long term.

Consequently, when China can have many Chinese like to attempt to carry on buying and selling shares investing behaviors in China share market. Themselves buying and selling shares behaviors can help many Chinese companies have effort to increase enough money or capital in order to continue to do their businesses in long term absolutely. So, it explains why when many Chinese become shareholders , they can assist China will have many companies continue to develop their businesses if many Chinese like to carry on shares buying and selling investing behaviors in long time in China financial investment market nowadays in behavioral economic view.

Why has any individual country have many people invest share behavior which can influence the country's macro consumption desire?

I shall apply shares market buying and selling investment behavior to explaiin why shares investment behavior which may impact the country's overal consumption desire as below:

In behavioral economic view, I assume that when the coutry has many people have interest to attempt to carry on shares buying and selling investment behavior, then their frequent shares buying and selling behaviors which may bring negactive consumption desire or shopping desire of these shares investors their consumer behavior.

The reason is simple, when the country has many share buyers number suddenly been increasing rapidly. Consequently, these large group share investors must need to spend much time to research any kinds of company shares variations, whether when their share prices will rise up of fall down in order to achieve buying the company's shares in the lowest price and selling the company's shares in the highest price level in order to earn profit.

Basic on this reason, they must need to spend much extra time to research share prices changing behavior every day, e.g. one working person will wait to leave his/her job, after he/she can spend time to gather data to research the day's share price changing behavior after dinner. So, the working person's right time may be his/her share price market research behavior. Before he/she may spend his/her night time to go to shopping after dinner, but nowadays, he/she will fogive to do his/her shopping behavior before dinner or after dinner at hight sometime. He/she will make decision to spend much night time to turn on computer to click on share market website to research his/her share purchase choice to investigate whether his/her share price whether it rises up or falls down at the moment in order to make his/her share buying or selling decision at ever night time.

I mean the when the country has many people are share investors, their shares investment behavioral spenging time which will influence many shops lose customers at might often because the country will have many people feel need to spend night time to turn on computer or watch television to investigate share price variation. So, the country will have many people / share investors choose to stay at home in order to carry on share price variation investigation behavior, they need to listen share market update news from radios or watch the share market update news from computer or TV at home every night. Consequenly, they must reduce times to leave themselves homes at night. So, their shopping behavior also will be reduced. Because these share investors feel need to spend time to investigate share price variation news at homes which can bring economic benefits (high opportunity benefits) when they choose to forgive to leave homes to go to shopping times (opportunity cost) every night.

On conclusion, it seems that when the country has many people are share investors, then their share price investigating behavior may bring negative shopping emotion at night. Consequently, the country's any one shop may lose many customers from this share investor consumer group in behavioral economic view. Hence, when the country's share investors number had been increasing rapidly, it will influence any shops lose many customers from this share investing customer group at night frequenly in short time, even long time in behavioral economic view, because their shopping desires or shopping emotion will be brought negative feeling when they make decisions to spend much time to listen radios or watch TV or computers share price update nes at night. Hence, share market will bring negative impact to influence consumer shopping desire or negative shopping emotion in behavioral economic view.

Can technology influence human shopping behavioral change?

Nowadays, technological development has reached mature stage, whether technological mature stage may bring positive or negative shopping emotion influence to global consumers. I shall aplly internet inventin or ecommerce shopping channel tool to explain whether internet technology can bring postive or negative inf/uence to global consumer behavior in behavioral economic view.

Internet is a good technological tool, it brings e-commerce business chance. In fact, commonly, global has have many businessmen choose to use internet channel to carry on their products transactions between global online-buyers and their electronic websites. So, global many shoppers had begun to feel online shopping is more convenient to compare visiting shops shopping. Their shopping behaviors have been changed from internet technological tool. Global has many shoppers choose to buy any products from any overseas or local businessmen their web stores. They only need to spend time to find any businessmen their webstores to choose the most suitable products to pay visa to buy from their webstores. at homes. So, in general, global had have may shoppers had changed their shopping behaviors from visiting shops to visiting webstores at homes often.

So, it seems that internet technological tool had influenced global many shops disappear, but internet webstores will be replaced their actual shops on streets. Some of businessmen either they choose webstores to replace shops or choose websotes and shops both or still keep shops only. Hence, internet tool influences global businessmen have three kinds of products sale channels to let globa local and overseas consumers to choose how to buy their products. However, in fact, many of global shoppers, youngers and olders had begun to accept to buy any products from webstores. They feel to spend time to leave homes to visit shops , their shopping behaviors will be wasted time to not essential part to their daily lives. Hence, since internet technological invention, it had changed many consumers their traditional visiting shops shopping habit to change to buying products from webstores channel.

However, on the one hand, internet creates webstores ecommerce shopping channel to let global many consumers do not need to leave homes to go to shopping. It brings negative visiting shops shopping emotion to global general consumers nowadays. But on the other hand, it also brings positive visiting internet webstores shopping emotion to global general consumer nowadays. So, it seems that global many consumers feel that they often do not need to spend much time to go out shopping. Many global consumers feel convenient and enjoy to choose any products to buy from different internet webstores, when the online buyer chooses the most suitable product, he she only needs to pay visa card to buy the product from the online seller's webstore conveniently at home.

Hence, online shopping can bring economic benefit to online buyers, e.g. avoiding walking time or spending transport fare to visit the shop to go to shopping, shortening or reducing shopping time to do another important matter.

On conclusion, global many consumers began feel online shopping can bring more economic benefits on shortening shopping time, avoiding transport fare spending aspect. So, online shopping will be popular shopping behavior for future long time. It may encourage global many shoppers can make rapid shopping decision in short time in order to carry on any products buying transaction to global any one online shopper in short time easily in behavioral economic view. So, global many businessmen had begun to build themselves one attraction webstore in order to persuade different countries consumers to choose to click themselves webstores from internet channel to buy any kinds of products in short time easily.

So, internet technology had changed consumers traditional shopping behaviors to build positive online shopping emotion as well as raise online sellers' any products sale chance easily in behavioral economic view.

Why and how human behavior may influence the country's economic growth or recession?

When one country has many people choose to do the same matter for one period, whether their behavior may influence the country's pvera; economic growth or recession . I shall attempt to indicate cases toexplain their relationship as below:

For flowing rubblish behavioral case example, do you feel that when the country has many people often flow rubblish on the streets, instead of their flowing rubblish behavior may bring streets dirty? But, their flowing rubblish behavior may explain that this country has people may have enough money to buy food to ear, or enough cloths to wear, enough bottles of water to drink, even they may have enough money to buy new television, radio, refrigeraters , washing machines, desktops or laptops electronic home products from old to new to use in order to satisfy their living needs. So, when they flow old electronic home products, their flowing old home electronic products behaviors may seem that they have enough money to buy other new home electronic products to replace old home electronic products to use at homes.

However, it seems thaat this country ought have many people have jobs to do. So, many of them, they can easy to make purchase decison to flow any old home electronic products and buy any new home electronic products to use . Because this country has many people have jobs to do. So, they can often not use old home electonic products to become rubblishs to flow on streets after they had bought any kinds of new home electronic homes.

In fact, it also implies that this country's economy grows rapidly. So, many businesses can glow up rapdly. When they expanded their businesses, they must need to increase employees number in order to let they help themselves to raise productivity or serve their clients absolutely. So, when the country has many businesses can grow up, it seems that its economy must be better or it is improved to compare past. Due to many different kinds of home electronic products had been often bought to use by this country people in this period. So, this country's any streets can be observed that expensive electronic home products were flowed on streets anywhere. then, this country will have many electronic home products sellers can sell their home electronic products very easily. When this country has many people can find any kinds of jobs to do easily. So, due to unemploymen rate had been decreasing.

In behavioral economic view, as this many electronic home products rubblish country case, we can observe this country may have many people have jobs to do. So, consumption number has been increased long time. So, cheap food, or expensive home electronic products may be rubblish on any streets. This country's people , their flowing rubblish behaviors may be explained that many of people have enough jobs to do, so they have ability to buy any good taste food to eat or buy any kinds of expensive electronic home products to use. So, this country's economy may be improved for this long period. So, in behavioral economic view, when this country can have many electronic home products rubblishs are flowed on anywherer in streets frequently. It seems that this country will have many people have jobs to do, so it causes they often change old home electronic products or replaced them easily, when they have enough income to spend to buy any kinds of new home electronic products to use at homes easily. Moreover, their flowing old electronic home products behaviors also indicate that this country has many people their salaries may be increased in possible from their emplyers. When this country can have many different kinds of home electornic products are sold. It means that this country's electronic home products needs or demand had been increasing, due to many people have jobs to do and income increases to excite their living of needs also improve. Consequently, this country may seem have better economic improvement. We can observe from this country's electronic home products rubblish increasing income in theis period.

On conclusion, this country ought experience economic growth at this period. So, " flowing expensive electronic home rubblish increasing number " may seem that this country's economic growth is rapidly in this period, due to many people have jobs to do as well as salaries increase in this period.

Technology how impacts human behavior changing?

Technology how influences human behavior to bring changing? For example, online share purchase and sale transaction from smart phone brings share investor can do share buying or selling transation in any where and any time conveniently, non manual driving auto vehicle, bring car owner feels comfortable and spends free time to do other matter, e.g. reading, listening mucis in himself or herself car freely. electrical energy vehicle can help car owner to reduce air polluton and it can brings the drivers do not feel drive long time in any journeys in order to avoid air pollution for environmental protection responsible car drivers in our societies. Thus, they will drive long time in any journeys when they can drive electronic energy cars to replace oil energy cars.

However, online technology can also bring consumers can choose to stay at homes to buy any things from seller individual online webstore conveniently. Such as online technology can bring shoppers do not need to spend much time to visit shops to buy any things. They can choose any kinds of products from any online sellers individual online webstores conveniently at homes. Online technology excite busy consumers can make purchase decision easily as well as it can help online sellers sell any kinds of products from internet easily.

In behavioral economic view, technology can change human behavior to be improved, it can let human feels comfortable, more free time ro use, rapid making any decisions, such as apply smart phones to make share purchase or sale transaction decision, online shopping decision, even travelling any where decision in short time, when the traveller finds the most cheap hotel accommodation room price and air ticket price frm any travel agent online tourism webstore, then the potential travel customer can follow the online hotel accommodation price and air ticket price data to make decision when to buy the air ticket from the airline travel agent or make decision when to prebook which hotel accommodation room to go to the country to travel from online travel agent tourism webstores. So, technology can encourage global any country travelers to make anywhere to trvel rapidly. If the traveler can find the country's general hotel rooms and airline tickets prices had been decreasing more sightly. The traveler may make travel decision to choose the country to travel in short time, then he/she can prebook the country;s any hotel room and airline ticket to pay by visa fraom the country's any hotel and airline travel agent webstores., before one week, even one month or more easily. Hence, online technology can also encourage traveler individual frequent travel times to be increased, due to global travelers can find any hotel rooms and airline tickets prices from internet conveniently at homes. They do not need to spend time to visit any airline travel agent to enquire travel choice country's hotel rooms prices and airline ticket prices. They can compare global travel of countries choices ' all hotels rooms and airline agents air tickets prices to make prebook airline seat and hotel room decision before one week, one month even six months early.

On conclusion, online technology can encourage global travelers can make travelling any where and when traveling time desicions easily. It can excite tourism industry develops in long time. Also, such as electricity cars invention can encourage environment protection car owners do car purchase decision easily, because they can choose to drive electronic energy cars to replace oil energy cars in order to avoid air pollution occurs easily. So, electronic cars can increase electronic car purchasrs number, due to many of environmental protection attitude of car owners can choose to drive electricity cars to bring air cleans, even non -manual driving cars can encourage lazy driving and free time driving car owners to choose to buy non-manual (artificial intelligent) cars to drive , because they can spend much free time to read, listen music or do any matters in themselves cars, they do not need to drive cars, robotic (AI) auto driving machine is such one non-manual driver to help them to drive themselves cars confidently. So, non-manual driving cars can attract lazy and enjoying free time driving car owners to choose to buy to replace traditional manual cars to drive easily. Moreover, online share transaction can help any share investors to make share buying and selling decision in short time easily. When they can apply smart phones technological tool to carry on share buying and selling activities easily. They can observe any share rising or falling price suitation from smart phones in any where any any time easily. So, smart phone technology can help global any shareholders to make share purchase and sale transaction easily. So, technology can encourage human makes decision in short time rapidly.